Living Music

CONVERSATIONS WITH
PANDIT DINKAR KAIKINI

PRIYA PURUSHOTHAMAN

DESIGNED BY
RAVI Y ADIVAREKAR

Popular Prakashan
www.popularprakashan.com

POPULAR PRAKASHAN PVT. LTD.
301, Mahalaxmi Chambers
22, Bhulabhai Desai Road
Mumbai 400026

(4379)
ISBN 978-81-7991-631-5

Cover credits : Ravi Y Adivarekar, photograph property of the Kaikini Family Archives
Photographs credits : Kavi Arya, Nikhil Bhatia, Rajani Kapse, Priya Purushothaman, Sita Saran Singh, Niyati Upadhya
Design & Typesetting : Ravi Y Adivarekar

Printed by : Alert Packaging House, Lower Parel, Mumbai 400013

Published by:
Ramdas Bhatkal for
Popular Prakashan Pvt. Ltd.
301, Mahalaxmi Chambers
22, Bhulabhai Desai Road
Mumbai 400026

"Since our concern was speech, and speech impelled us
To purify the dialect of the tribe
And urge the mind to aftersight and foresight,
Let me disclose the gifts reserved for age
To set a crown upon your lifetime's effort."

T.S. Eliot

CONTENTS

CONTENTS

Panditji teaching Sri Dhruba Ghosh and Samarth Nagarkar at his home in Mumbai

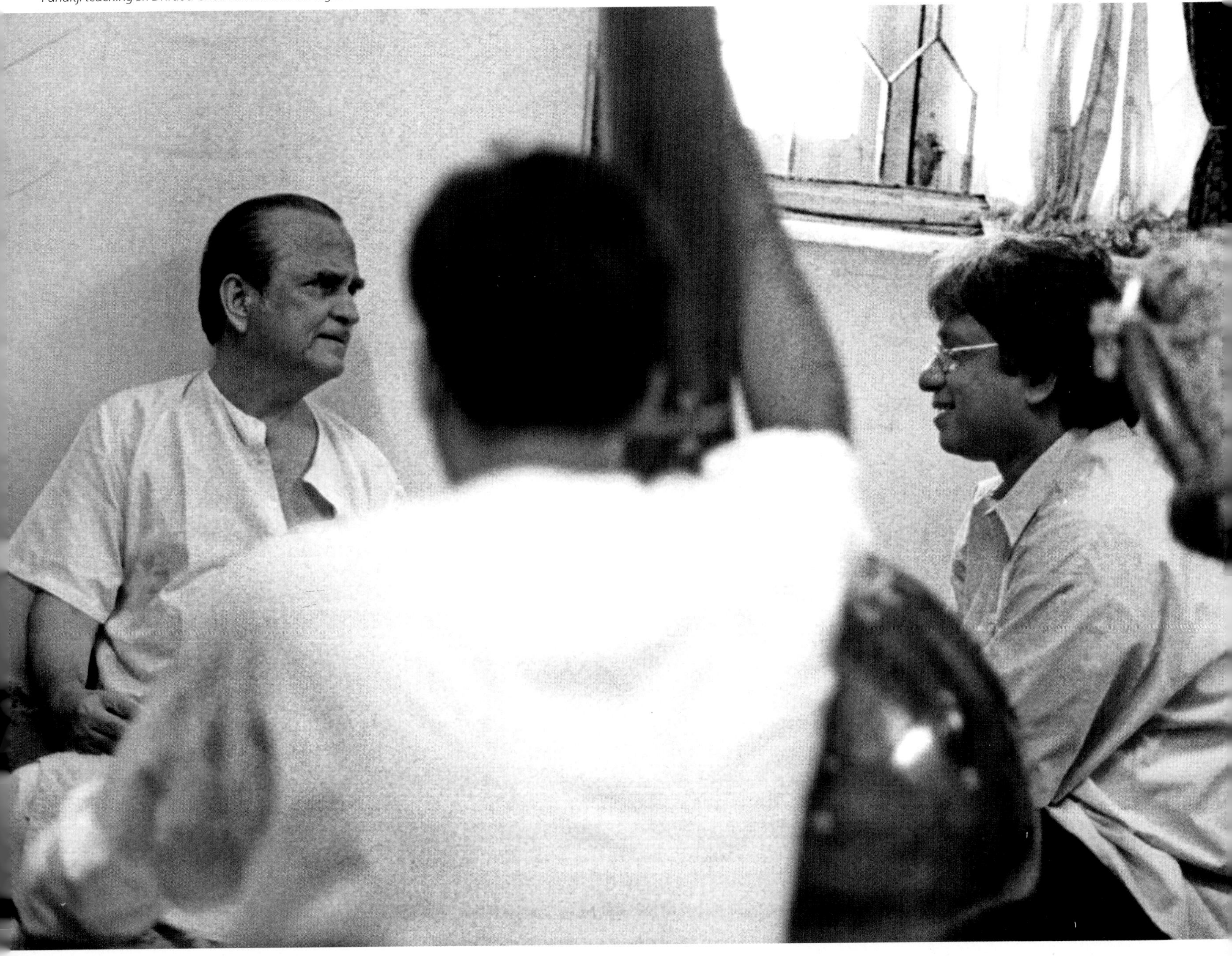

FOREWORD

There are some personalities in the world of music who command our respect, whose work inspires us, and who have put us undeniably in their debt. Pandit Dinkar Kaikini is one of these gifted personalities, comparable to sages of times long past. I am very glad to be writing this foreword for a book about him.

He was a tapasvin - a fiercely meditative thinker - who achieved an elegant balance between theory and aesthetics through deep reflection. He maintained trust and respect for the aesthetic values that were implicit in the style of every gharānā, and never succumbed to the impulse of unduly espousing the cause of one gharānā over others. As a disciple of Annasaheb Ratanjankar, he had of course acquired extensive knowledge as well as thorough tālīm as a performer. And fortune favoured him by gifting him with the same kind of felicity as a composer that Ratanjankar had.

Numerous bandiś-es of the highest quality flowed out of his imagination. This was indeed a golden confluence of many factors: A solid foundation of influences imbibed from the study of countless traditional bandiś-es; his own unrelenting study of rāgā and tālā; an intimacy with the literary idiom of languages necessary for work as a composer (acquired from his long stay in the North); and above all, the divine gift of an insatiable creative urge with which he was blessed.

There can be no doubt that these factors are at the root of the uniform excellence of his bandiś-es, in which we find a superb amalgam of purity of rāganga, a harmonious blend of laya and tālā, and lyrics with an elegant poetic sensibility. His natural temperament was contemplative, leading him to develop a perspective of immense breadth, versatility of approach and innovation. His compositions in every genre - be it Rāgadārī khayāl, ṭhumrī, or Bhaktīsangīt - were of the highest artistic level. His musical thought never found expression through fragmented displays of learning, pedantic theory, or exhibition of virtuosity in technique. An intuitively attained balance between knowledge, theory and technique enabled him to not only scale the highest peaks of musical and aesthetic creativity, but also to maintain that level, once achieved. Thus, the name Kaikini has become synonymous with excellence. His ability to discover a new dawn on the horizon of musical ideas without abandoning traditional values and principles is a distinctive feature of his musicianship, which compels our respect and admiration.

On the other hand, even as he was composing peerless bandiś-es, Kaikiniji's maturity enabled him to prevent himself from becoming infatuated with his own craft. He fully recognised the necessity of giving the concrete intent expressed in a bandiś an abstract aesthetic utterance in its performance, and fully discharged the artistic obligation that was implicit in that recognition. His presentation was in complete harmony with the principle he espoused: namely, the bandiś is the concrete form of music, while the musicianship that the artiste applies to its interpretation is its abstract counterpart. His performances would invariably reveal deep understanding of a rāgā's structure, subtleties of intonation, and sophistication of thought, in addition to a proportioned and disciplined presentation. And even in the act of creating such a complete performance he would be able to involve himself fully in enjoying the music being created. Thus he could carry his audience with him, towards a meditative experience of inner satisfaction that transcended the universe of feeling.

Kaikiniji was generously gifted with a contemplative point of view, which he used to employ with great effect in explaining many delicate points about the art of performance. I will never forget his felicitous explanations, which would resolve many artistic issues that confront a performer.

I used to love listening to his thoughts about such matters. His views were not only informative for me, but they also guided me towards the discovery of my own artistic perspective.

What is music? Why should we engage in it? How should we perform it? Of what use is it? How does it affect our lives? His answers to such questions were so apt and comprehensive that one would feel certain that anyone who followed that path would feel fulfilled.

I would have to say that in making this invaluable stream of musical thought available to a wider public, the author has done us a great service.

Tālyogī Pandit Suresh Talwalkar
With editorial help from **Sri Umesh Moghe**
Translated by **Sri Ramesh Gangolli**

**Original Marathi text is included in the Appendix*

PREFACE

I have no doubt that destiny led me to the doorstep of Anand Ashram. I cannot find any other way to explain how a girl from suburban America, barely acquainted with the art and culture of Hindustānī music, could find herself in the welcoming home of one of its greatest masters, Pandit Dinkar Kaikini.

After graduating from college, I had taken a year off to study Hindustānī vocal music, a style I had merely dipped my feet into the previous summer. This brief encounter made me feel as though I was a painter who had just discovered an entirely new palette of colours - suddenly seeing dimensionality in the subtle difference of shades, and inspired to paint afresh on a new canvas.

In retrospect, I am surprised by the naïve courage I mustered to embark upon such a journey. Although I had studied Carnatic music for almost ten years, I was an ignoramus when it came to the Hindustānī tradition. I had heard a few incredibly compelling recordings and simply thought to myself, "I'd love to know more about this." Little did I know about the demands of the Hindustānī style - the intellectual rigour it required, the physical stamina it called for, the lifestyle it implied, the relationships that it was built upon, the spirituality it nurtured, the purity and creativity it elicited, and the honest human emotion that was at its core. These were all lessons to be absorbed through my musical journey and the precious conversations with a soul whose entire life was singularly devoted to this art form.

To many, Panditji is known as a stalwart performer and exponent of the Agra Gharānā, emerging from the illustrious lineage of Pandit V.N. Bhatkhande, father of modern day Hindustānī music. But I would soon learn that his musicianship was also characterised by a versatility that went beyond performance; he was equally consummate as a composer, philosopher and pedagogue. For these reasons, and for the benefit of others who may not have the access to such knowledge, I felt compelled to have his thoughts documented for posterity.

When I arrived at Anand Ashram, I was curious and completely oblivious to the alternate world that existed behind those doors. As soon as I entered, I was engulfed by a thick enigmatic aura possessing a deeply meditative quality. It was mystifying that this tranquil abode could exist in downtown Mumbai, completely impervious to the chaos of urban India.

One of the first things that fascinated me about Anand Ashram was the co-existence of stillness and intensity. I was initially anxious in the presence of Panditji; even if he was doing his daily rounds of walking or reading the newspaper, it was clear that his mind was buzzing with musical activity. Soon, I realised that this frame of mind was his permanent state of existence, and could not be disturbed by me, or the numerous visitors who came to the house everyday. It is the power of this total and constant immersion in musical thought, or cintan (pronounced "chintan"), which permeated the home to give it that enchanted quality.

As countless students would drop by, for a lesson and sometimes just to chat, I watched with amazement at how this home meant something larger than music itself. Panditji's wife, Smt Shashikala Kaikini, was called Amma by all of her students, all of Panditji's students, and of course, her own children. I knew then that I was in a place where the definition of family defied convention - where biological family and musical family morphed into one.

Only with time could I see how naturally this open-heartedness had evolved. After all, at the tender age of eleven, Panditji had created a new family of his own, willingly leaving his own parents and siblings to start a life with his guru and gurubhais (fellow students). They were his family while he was studying, and the shared pursuit of knowledge, passion for music, and devotion to their guru, would make their bonds thicker than blood. These relationships were not just a by-product of musical study - they were an essential component of the process, shaping the end result.

These were the sanskār-s that enveloped Panditji's childhood. I grappled with an English definition of this word - values, culture, heritage - but something significant seemed to be lost in translation. I listened as he related the stories of his post-student life - his experiences as an All India Radio Producer and as the Principal of Bharatiya Vidya Bhavan - and saw how these too were filled with the sanskār-s inculcated from his early days. And I realised the indefinable and cumulative nature of sanskār-s - how it is the resulting outlook of a lifetime of rich experiences that shapes who we are, and thereby, the music we produce.

Panditji's formative experiences also captured the spirit of a time period, a Golden Age of Hindustānī music, during which the pursuit of this art form was so vastly different from what it has become. It was a time when students heard most great music in a live and intimate mehfil, when artistes visited their cities. Panditji was privy to the music of many legendary masters by giving them vocal support when they performed at his college. It was a time when the radio was the primary medium of propagation and the only documentation of the music being produced. It was a time when a śiṣya would completely surrender to the guru to show him the way. It was a time when India proudly grasped its cultural and artistic heritage, to maintain its identity despite colonial rule. For me Panditji was a window through which I could vicariously experience the charm and vitality of this colourful era of musical grandeur and political and historical transformation.

When I find myself revelling in a past I have never known, I am reminded of Panditji's advice: "You must live in the present, not in the past's glory." The present is full of sound bytes, the word "byte" indicating its tiny size. Fast information is followed by fast results, all requiring short attention spans. Music is meant for downloading and listening on an iPod when a free moment opens up in a busy day. Where does Hindustānī Rāgsangīt fit into this? For how much longer will audiences have the ability to listen to a three-hour concert? Is it already dwindling? And is change equivalent to artistic compromise or musical survival of the fittest? Panditji himself espoused a very progressive standpoint on change - it will happen, and when it does, it happens with reason. What awaits my generation?

What does remain constant amidst all the flux, is the truth of personal experience. Panditji began our conversation by stating simply, "All that I have learned is from my experience. When you share your experience it has an impact, because that is the truth. When a realised soul speaks, it penetrates your soul." Although I intellectually understood his words, I have to confess that the power of his words dawned on me on a different day. I had a lesson with Panditji on rāg Todi. He sang an introductory phrase using only three or four notes, in which he was able to convey the absolute tāsīr, or spirit, of the entire rāg. He proceeded to take the bandiś "Garavā mein san lāgī," a composition for which Faiyaz Khan Saheb's rendition was very famous. As he elaborated, there was an intensity in each utterance, word, syllable, note, and pause; each was overflowing with his admiration for Khan Saheb. Overcome with emotion, he took a moment to look at the picture of Khan Saheb that was next to his tānpūrā to do pranām and remember the man who inspired his musical journey. It was then that I sensed the power of his experience, and how a musician can ultimately relate his experience only through his music. This transformative power of music is an essence that has been passed down through many generations of legends. It is forever embedded within the grains of their personalities, always inspiring the following generations to continue to tell the stories they have inherited and those that they will create.

INTRODUCTION

This book is a humble attempt to share the multifaceted experiences and thoughts of Pandit Dinkar Kaikini. Its main purpose is to document the numerous musical concepts, tools, and philosophies that Panditji had coined over his entire life, a great resource for students, performers, and music lovers alike. It is interspersed with biographical details of his life, though it is by no means a biography nor was it ever intended to be. I felt it necessary to include many memories that he shared with me to give the most complete picture of his persona and his music.

With the encouragement and blessings of my Guru (and daughter of Panditji), Smt Aditi Upadhya, I commenced this undertaking. I made several trips to Mumbai to spend extended periods of time at Pandtiji's home, Anand Ashram, where his wife, Smt Shashikala Kaikini, and the rest of the Kaikini family so warmly welcomed me as though I were a member of the family.

Often over tea and namkīn, while he sat in his pensive chair, Panditji spoke to me about his own theories on sound, svar, laya, rāg, sādhanā, creativity, composition - to name a few. As he said, all that he learned in his life was experiential, and after honestly and acutely reflecting on this colossal collection of experiences, he drew conclusions of his own. In all of his thought, there were consistently three cornerstones that held everything as one: beauty, observation, and awareness. With intense observation and a conscious awareness, Panditji studied the world and brought beauty to his music. This is how he lived, performed, and taught music. All of his ideas are infused with these concepts.

Panditji shared his knowledge in the same way that Anand Ashram functions - with open-heartedness and generosity. He invited dialogue and inquisitiveness on the part of students. As his son Rajesh told me, "Anyone could just enter the house and ask my father about music and he would just open the door to the treasure." I too was guilty of doing this, to my great satisfaction. In this fashion, I sat with him and asked him question after question, and often his answers unravelled more and more questions for which I sought answers.

The first section of the book, Prārambh, deals with beginnings. 'Sound of Music' questions the foundations that we assume. What is sound? What is music? How does a practitioner of music, rather than a physicist or philosopher, define these? How can we understand these in the context of Hindustānī music? Panditji traced the intricate path spun by the web of sound, illuminating all the branches and their constant inter-connectedness. 'Early Sanskār' is a glimpse of the life of young Dinkar and his unusual childhood, initially spent in a determined search for music followed by a total immersion in the field. It was a childhood full of resilience and precociousness developed out of necessity for survival. Most of all, it was living and breathing music.

The second section, Nirmitī, explores creation. In 'Creativity,' Panditji expounds on the philosophy of imagination. What does it mean to create? How do we develop music? In Hindustānī music, particularly, the artiste is the composer, conductor, and performer all at once. How do we approach all of these responsibilities in a highly abstract style while maintaining aesthetic quality? In 'Blossoming Musician,' we follow Panditji's career into his peak years of performance, his tenure at All India Radio, and his segue into family life.

Section Three, Vidyā Dān, details knowledge passed on by Panditji in various forms. 'Sādhanā,' outlines Panditji's advice for serious students of vocal music. What should be the mindset of a disciple? What is effective riyāz (practice), and how can it be achieved? Panditji outlines a specific regimen for aspiring performers, starting from the micro-level of the svar and expanding to the planning of an engaging concert. 'On Education,' follows Panditji as the Principal of Bharatiya Vidya Bhavan, Mumbai, and in the role of guru. What is the responsibility of music institutions?

What is the psychology of teaching, and how can this abstract knowledge be imparted? This chapter also relates the experiences of Panditji's leading disciples.

All of the information presented in this book refers directly to the exchange between Panditji and me. When information has come from another source, a direct quotation and acknowledgement has been made.

The quintessence of our conversations is presented to the reader in what follows as a bouquet of Panditji's ideas - verily an offering to 'disclose the gifts reserved for age' and 'to set a crown upon a lifetime's effort.'

A Note on Diacritical Marks

I have used the International Alphabet for Sanskrit Transliteration for all Hindi words used throughout this book in order to maintain accurate and consistent spelling.
For words that are proper nouns, or Hindi words that have been assimilated in the English language, this does not apply. For the rest, I have, to the best of my ability used diacritical marks. Please consult the chart in the Appendix if you have any doubts about the symbols.

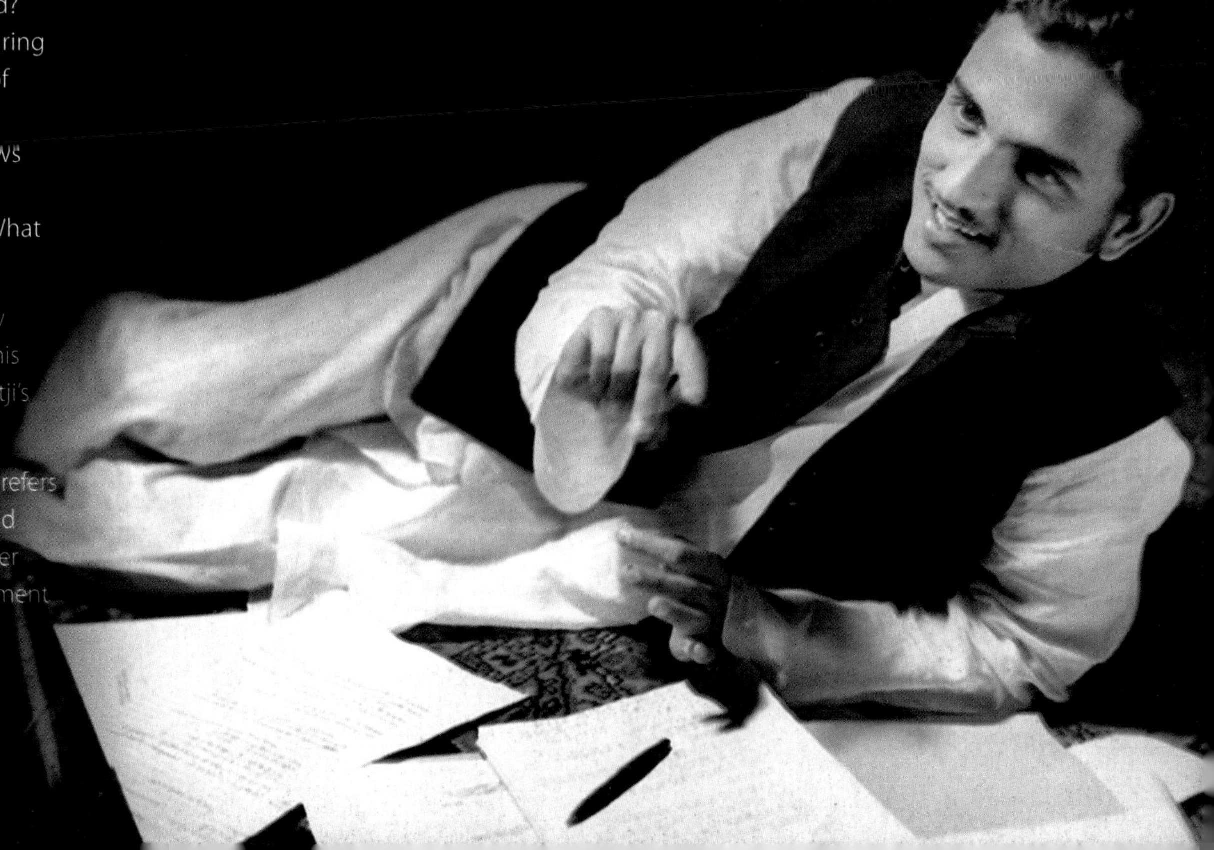

Panditji making notes during his work on the music for the film 'Ahimsa'

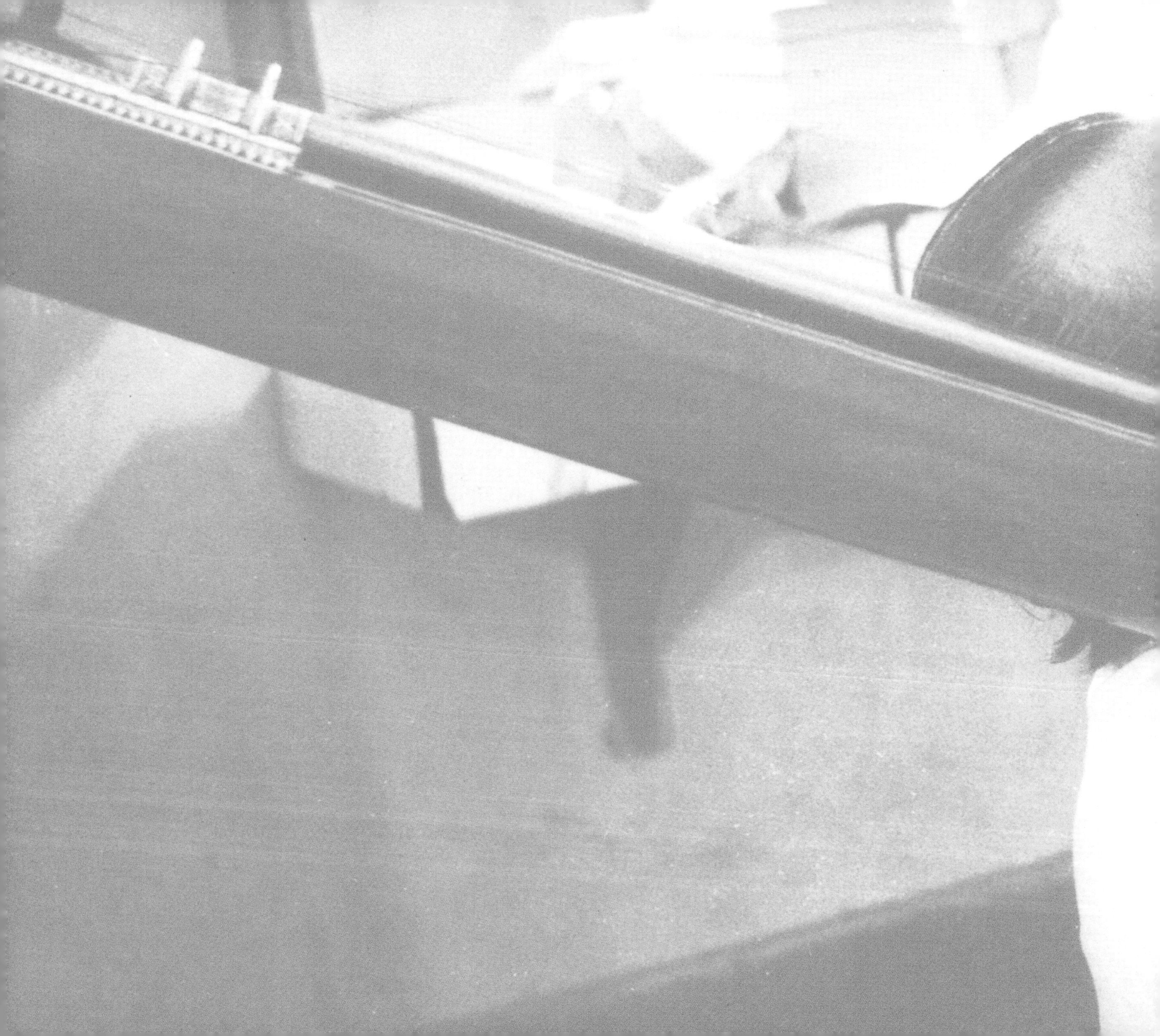

प्रारंभ

PRĀRAMBH

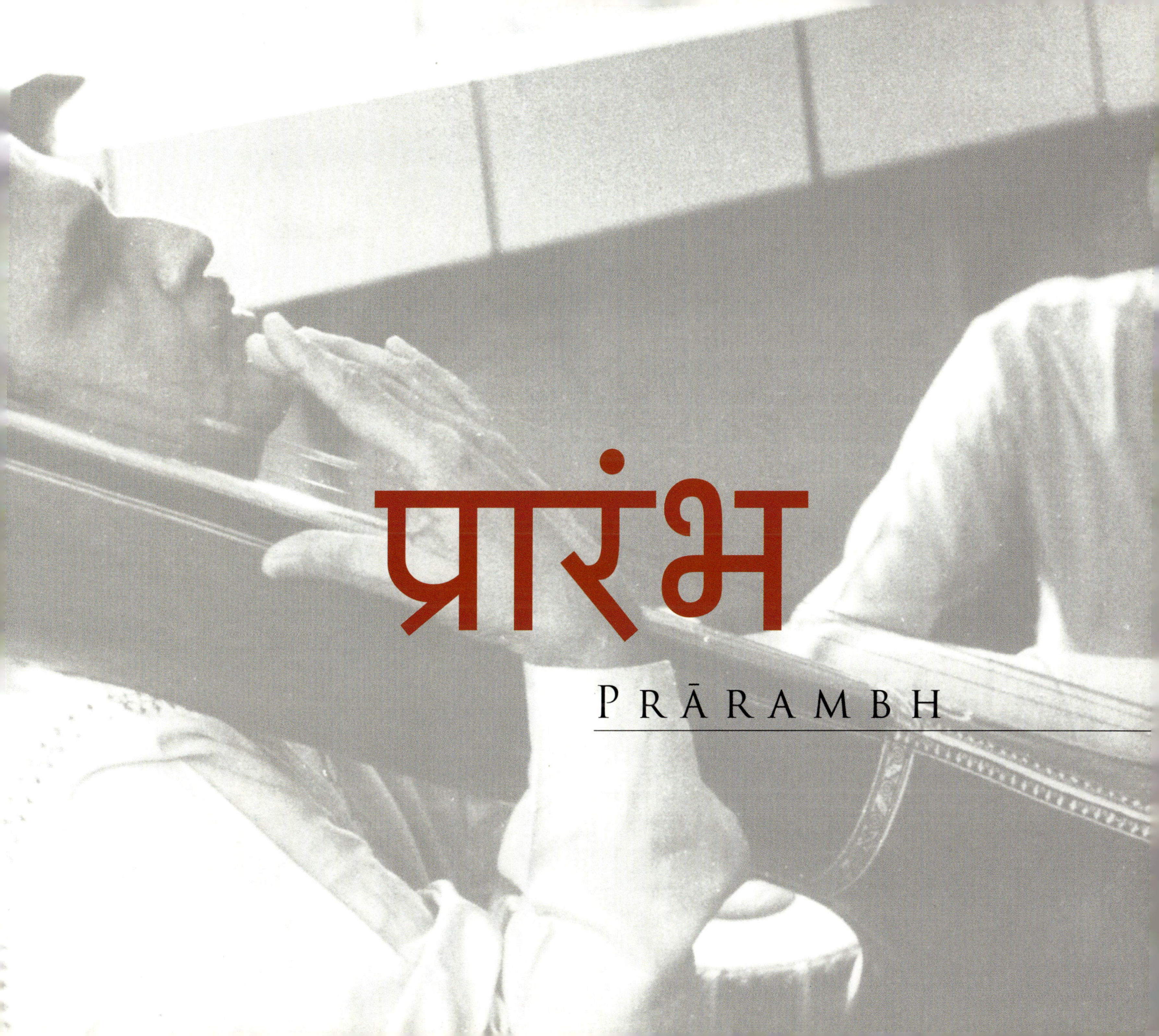

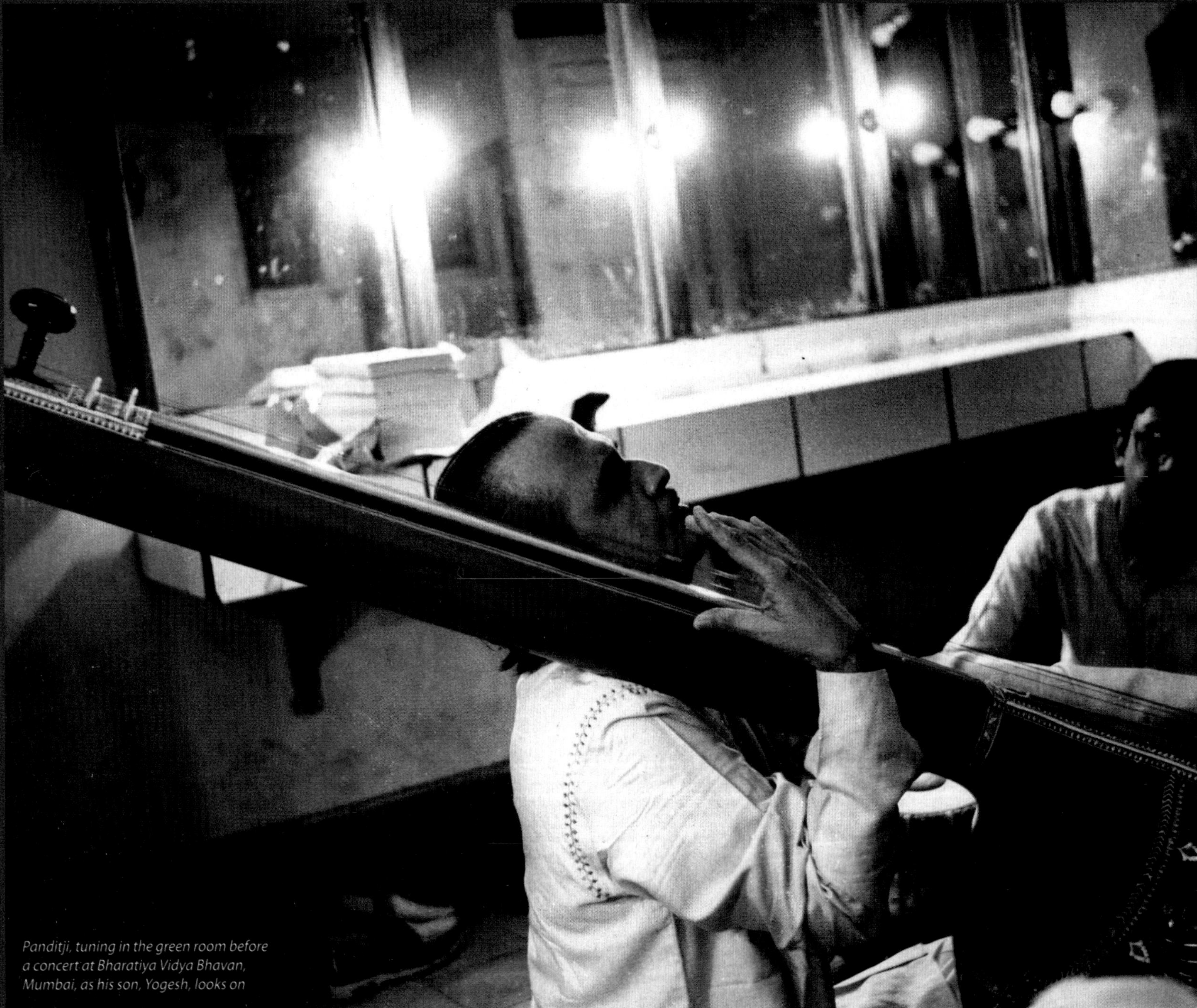

Panditji, tuning in the green room before a concert at Bharatiya Vidya Bhavan, Mumbai, as his son, Yogesh, looks on

SOUND OF MUSIC

"There is only one thing common between human beings, and that is emotion. All the rest differs - height, colour, language - but emotion at the core is the same. This emotion is connected to the soul, and that is what touches listeners. Good music is never enjoyed by the mind - only by the soul. Our music is not manoranjan - it is ātmaranjan."

In my attempt to understand music from its very source, I began our conversation with the fundamentals. Examining the qualities of music requires understanding the inherent nature of sound. What is it? How do we describe that which is perceived by our ears? We identify what we see with our eyes by its physical qualities - its size, colour, or shape. We identify what we touch by its texture - smooth, coarse, or jagged. When we eat, our taste buds detect sweet, salty, sour or spicy. But unlike the tactile nature of the others senses, sound possesses intangible qualities. How do we describe these? How do we confirm what we believe about sound? Scientifically, there are definitions that reduce it to vibrations in the air. But how are these vibrations produced? Is it an innate human quality to produce sounds? Does the creation and existence of sound depend upon hearing it for verification?

Various disciplines define sound by the parameters and tools they are given. Physicists may measure exact frequencies and wavelengths to precisely identify sounds. I was, however, interested in understanding sound from the perspective of a musician. After all, who else is better to deliberate on this than one who has spent most of his time perfecting the art of creating pleasurable sounds? Here, we abandon the technicalities of scientific studies and rest on a more philosophical, even spiritual, plane.

"Sound is cosmic energy. You may call it by any name, God, Saraswati, Ganeśa, but to me God is a supreme energy, and sound is equivalent to that," Panditji told me.

In the philosophy of Indian music, as studied by Panditji from the works of Pandit Vishnu Narayan Bhatkhande, the word nād comes from the letters "na," meaning air, and "d," signifying agni, or heat. When the two are struck together, sound is created. Sound is divided into two categories: anāhāt nād and āhat nād. Āhat nād is intentionally created, struck sound - the sort that fills a typical day, ranging from daily chatter to musical symphonies. Anāhat nād, also known as cosmic or un-struck sound, is believed to be the original source of sound. It is not audible,but its vibrations permeate the atmosphere and are associated with the origins of the universe and the sound of the word Om. Yogī-s and riśī-s in extreme meditation can reach the point of being one with this sound vibration. Experiencing anāhat nād, according to Panditji, is a source of great spiritual strength. It requires tremendous focus and oneness with the cosmos to access this energy.

Panditji's experience of musical ideas was much like the vibrations of anāhat nād. While most people can access obvious day-to-day sounds, more refined sounds such as musical thoughts are accessible only to those who are very finely tuned into this blanket of energy. "All the musical ideas and compositions, including the sāhitya and literature, I can feel them in that cosmic energy. It is already there in the atmosphere - I am the medium, and it comes to me as if I'm the receiver. According to me, all the music is already there."

If this cosmic energy is all pervading, then it is logical to ask, is there such a thing as silence? If anāhat nād is an enveloping blanket laden with the sounds of the universe, then is what humans perceive as silence merely an inability to connect into this energy source? "If we concentrate with no sound at all, we can hear music. That is the music of silence. In that state of mind, when you give form to the energy that you perceive, it starts becoming music." Thus, in a meditative state of mind, concentrated and liberated of earthly concerns, the elusive patterns of music are floating about and can be captured and released into the realm of āhat nād.

Hindustānī Rāgsangīt

Svar

Āhat nād can include a gamut of sounds, but here we are concerned with musical sounds, those that are sangīt prayogī. What differentiates all sounds from those that are musical? "Musical sound," according to Panditji, "gives us pleasure, and is intentionally produced. There is a thought process behind it." How did the evolution of sound progress from unintentional reverberations to those that were deliberate and enjoyable to the ear?

Here, anāhat nād plays a crucial role as a starting point of Indian classical music. The primordial sound, Om, which was heard by the yogī-s of ancient times, was a tone that was the underpinning of all others to follow. Its sonority occupied their meditative minds, and thus they used it as the initial pitch on which they chanted the Vedas, the sacred Sanskrit canons of Hinduism.

The Vedas comprise four major samhitā, or collections: the Rig Veda, Yajur Veda, Atharva Veda, and Sāma Veda. The chanting of the Rig

Veda was the first form of intentional tonal expression. Using the pitch of omkār as their tonic, or svarit, the sages chanted the text in this single tone. According to Panditji's own theory on the evolution of the scale, while chanting texts in one pitch, a phenomenon occurred in which there was a subtle touch of a lower tone while uttering the svarit pitch. "This is a very natural occurrence. For instance, if you are shooting an arrow, you must pull your arm back first to gain the momentum to release and shoot it forward. In the same way, while chanting the Rig Veda, to sing one note, the slight help of the lower note was taken." This pitch that was slightly lower to the svarit tone is known as anudāta.

Taking the support of these two pitches, the Gāthā Gān period followed. Gāthā Gān was oral recitation of the history of India and other purānic or epic stories in a particular meter in the svarit and anudāta tones. In this ballad form, it was easier to memorise and pass down this history. Much like the Indian musical tradition that would develop, Gāthā Gān was a śravan vidyā in which learning was primarily through listening and only later through written documentation.

In the Yajur Veda, in which sacrificial offerings were made, chanting occurred in four groups. The first group would begin reciting the Sanskrit couplets, after which the next group would pick up immediately. To differentiate between the groups, they started to take the help of a pitch slightly higher to the svarit known as udāta. Much like anudāta was uncovered in the Rig Veda, the idea of using another pitch in relation to the svarit

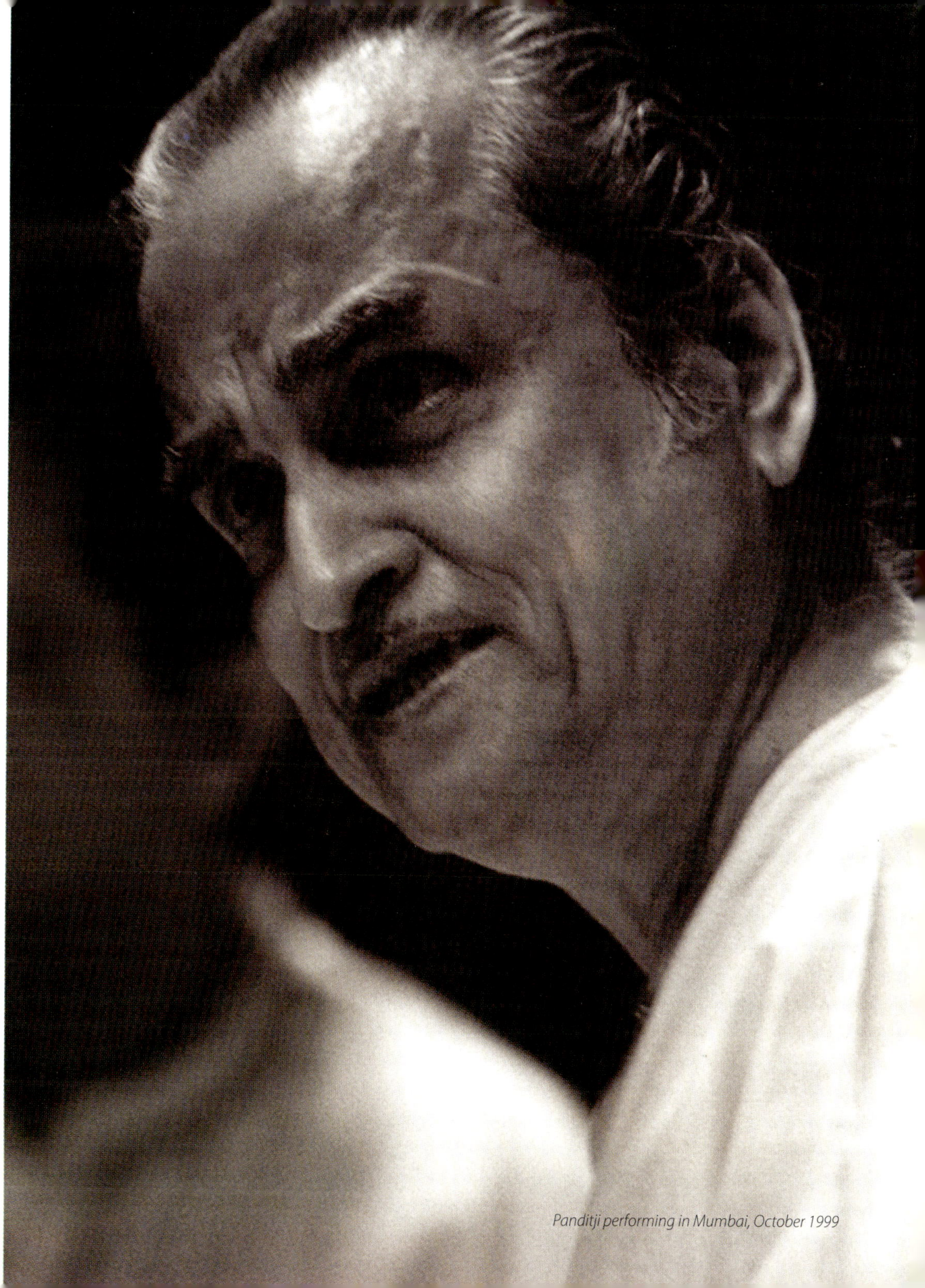

Panditji performing in Mumbai, October 1999

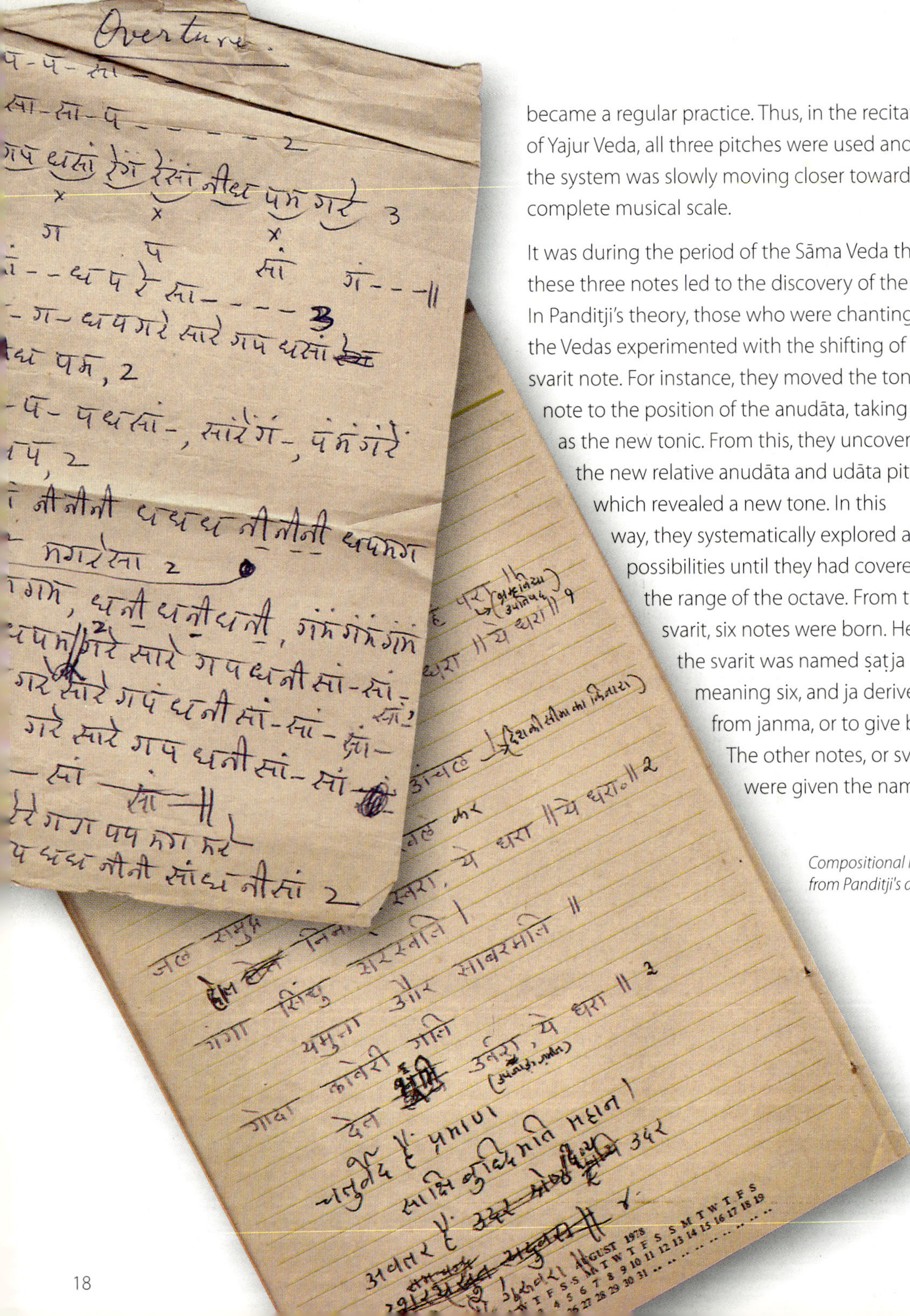

became a regular practice. Thus, in the recitation of Yajur Veda, all three pitches were used and the system was slowly moving closer towards a complete musical scale.

It was during the period of the Sāma Veda that these three notes led to the discovery of the rest. In Panditji's theory, those who were chanting the Vedas experimented with the shifting of the svarit note. For instance, they moved the tonic note to the position of the anudāta, taking it as the new tonic. From this, they uncovered the new relative anudāta and udāta pitches, which revealed a new tone. In this way, they systematically explored all possibilities until they had covered the range of the octave. From the svarit, six notes were born. Hence, the svarit was named ṣatja - ṣaṭ meaning six, and ja derived from janma, or to give birth. The other notes, or svar-s, were given the names:

Compositional notes from Panditji's diary

riśabh, gandhār, madhyam, pancam, dhaivat, and niṣād. All seven notes together are called a saptak. Music took a more concrete form in the Sāma Veda, by utilising all of these svar-s and concentrating on breathing and elongating the notes.

More exploration of the notes of the saptak led to realising that some could be altered, either by increasing or decreasing the pitch. The notes re, ga, dha, and ni could be taken from their natural, or śuddh, position and made komal, or lower. The note ma can be raised and made tīvra, or higher, and sa and pa are immovable. In this fashion, the total number of possible tones of the seven svar-s becomes twelve.

The twelve-tone basis of music is common between Indian and Western classical music, but what distinguishes Hindustānī Rāgsangīt is the concept of microtones. Microtones, or śruti-s, are the subtle shades of a note that exist between each tone. For instance, there is an infinite musical space between komal re (flattened re) and śuddh re (natural re). The differences between these tones are extremely subtle, requiring a keen ear and rigorous practice.

There are twenty-two discernible śruti-s, according to Bharata's Nātyaśāstra. Depending upon the skill, musicianship and aesthetic sense of the performer, he or she will be able to evoke a different emotion by producing the correct shade of a particular note. We will visit this concept later in greater depth in our journey through Hindustānī musc.

Laya

We have traced the origins of svar, but what is laya and its related concepts, and what is its source? Is it also manmade, or like nād, does its existence precede and supersede human perception? And what role does it play in the context of music?

"Laya is time. Man may produce sound, but he cannot produce laya," Panditji said. This concept, that we are so familiar with, is actually at the basis of musical movement. Time is a continuous, abstract entity, independent of all other factors, even of music itself. The clock continues to tick, regardless of what occurs during the interval of each second, minute or hour. Humans cannot control this continuous function, so in what way can they engage with it? "Man has no control over laya - he can only divide it to suit his needs. When you divide laya aesthetically, it becomes music." Thus, we cannot change the fact that time is being expended as we speak, but we can control how we choose to measure, divide, and use it. For example, take the natural cycle of night and day. Man has decided to split twenty-four hours into night and day. Within these, man has subdivided time further into minutes and seconds. These are all divisions of laya. As you see, all humans must interact with laya in order to function in daily life. Laya is a part of life, in the background of life, and at the same time the only concrete demarcation of life itself.

In music, this same concept is applied at a micro level. The moment a note is uttered, sustained and ended, one has defined the laya, or timing, of that note. Sound is the medium through which laya is demarcated. This is perhaps the most fundamental understanding of laya.
There is no need to introduce a rhythm pattern or cycle to have a measure of time in music. "Laya itself cannot be reproduced, unlike sound. We cannot go back in time - once the time has passed, it is gone. We can only use sound to recreate a moment." Thus, as Panditji described it, laya is a constant abstract continuum, independent and irreversible.

Moving from Abstract to Concrete

I was perplexed by the eternal presence of sound and its manifestations in svar and laya. It felt as though we were still floating in areas of abstraction. We cannot produce laya, only divide it. We can create sounds, but are limited by our ability to tap into the energy cosmos. Is there anything more concrete about music? As our conversations progressed towards structured music, more boundaries were defined that served as reference points. To place a single note in a context, we need more parameters. In what ways are these svar-s arranged? At this juncture, Panditji spoke at length about the concept of rāg.

What is a rāg? A textbook may provide definitions such as "a scale of notes creates a rāg," or "the counterpart for key" in Western classical music. But it became apparent that in Hindustānī Rāgsangīt, understanding a rāg means looking past the notes that it comprises and viewing it from a holistic perspective.

"A rāg is the arrangement of notes into a defined form. It is like a personality, having likes and dislikes, salient characteristics and features." While in a person we may identify a pointy nose, a hearty laugh and gregarious nature, how would we understand the personality of a rāg? Clearly, the "features" of a rāg are abstract, and cannot be humanized. One may say that rāg Aḍāṇā is a bold and forthright rāg, but this is only one interpretation of what is meant by the personality of a rāg. While these adjectives attribute human qualities to a rāg, its personality must also be described and understood in musical vocabulary, thus making it a more specialised and subtle concept. Its primary features are: śruti (the notes and microtones that comprise the scale), ākṛti (shape), bhāv (emotion) of each svar in the rāg, the relation between each svar, the laya or timing with which one moves from one svar to another, the nature of this movement (i.e., curved or angular), the characteristic phrases (rāg ang), and the note combinations that suit all these conditions (rāg vistār). A slight variation in any of these factors could be the difference between two rāg-s. "All these characteristics combined constitute the form of a rāg - it is up to the musician to work within this form, but at the same time not be constrained by it. Musicianship lies in the ability to capture and maintain the essential spirit of the rāg while creatively varying the approach to avoid monotony."

By adding the notion of rāg, I found more definition to the framework of Hindustānī music. But within the confines of a rāg, how does a vocalist go about unfolding and elaborating? Ālāp is a free form, improvised elaboration within a rāg that delineates the mentioned features and captures its essence. Upon listening, it seems that an ālāp is only melodically driven - there is no sense of time or rhythm. However, Panditji emphasised that even within the ālāp there is laya, an "abstract cycle" that shapes the timing of notes, phrases, and the overall movement. In addition to svar, laya, and rāg, the ālāp also takes the support of a new feature, phonetics. Often, when listening to an ālāp, we may notice the type of sounds that the vocalist is utilising, usually prolonged vowel sounds. A phrase may be developed in ākār, using the "ā" phonetic, or perhaps using "ī" or "u." Here we see the initial introduction of language in the form of phonetics. While an ālāp does not have a text, it has a language of its own, a language of vowel sounds coupled with specific consonants. These are derived from the chant "Hari Om Ananta Narāyanā." Often a phrase will start with syllables like "na," "ri," "ta num." This style of rendition is known as the "Nom-Tom ālāp," originating from the dhrupad style of singing. Using these syllables, musicians explore the rāg in great detail. But what do these syllables mean, if anything, when taken out of the context of the original phrase? As Panditji illuminated, "For me ālāp is poetry - I give it its own emotional meaning. If I want to convey the emotional content that occurs to me, I mould whatever vowels or phonetics I require to successfully fulfill my intention." Just like the notes, these phonetics are the vehicles through which musicians paint a portrait of the personality of the rāg.

From phonetics, my line of inquiry progressed to language. What is language? "Language is the arrangement of phonetics used to convey a specific meaning," Panditji said. In the ālāp, phonetics are arranged to suit the desire of the musician, and their meaning is an intangible sentiment that may or may not be conveyed as envisioned in the mind of the musician. With the introduction of language, we are no longer saddled with such ambiguity. Words depict specific meanings and emotions, and when they are strung together in sentences, verses, and full compositions, they can describe a moment, event, or even tell a complete story.

In Hindustānī music, language is introduced in the composition, also known as the cīz or bandiś. The introduction of śabd, or words, serves as a framework around which the musician elaborates. With the bandiś, the artiste takes a huge leap from the open space of conceptual freedom to a defined workspace that sets a definitive tone. In addition to language, there is one more essential added boundary in the bandiś that makes it rigid: tāl. Tāl is a fixed cycle of beats that repeats continuously throughout the entire bandiś - it is a particular division of laya. It has a defined beginning and end, and the composition is placed precisely within this cycle. The word "bandiś" itself is derived from the verb "bāndnā," which means "to bind."

"What is being bound in a composition?" Panditji asked. "The laya, specifically the tāl cycle, is binding the words and the svar together to form one unit. If the cycle is not there, there is no bandiś - it will sound like an ālāp. You sing the bandiś within the definite, equal timing of the cycle. It is like playing tennis. You can't just hit anywhere and score points - only within the lines. That is the cycle of tennis."

Our discussion had progressed from the vibrations of cosmic energy, to nād, laya, rāg, śabd, tāl, and the bandiś, to unearth the numerous elements that are the foundations of Hindustānī music. Just as I had started to think that I had understood the nature of the various components, some being abstract and others concrete, Panditji introduced his theory of fluidity between these realms. "Musicianship lies in transforming the concrete into abstract, and abstract into concrete. Laya is totally abstract, sound is semi-abstract, and śabd is concrete. But each of these can be made either abstract or concrete." While śabd may seem like the most concrete element, it can be taken to an abstract space through various emotive interpretations, done through the creative use of svar. A simple word, such as "jāo" (a command to go), could be sung with authority, tenderness, cajoling, or anger, depending on the intention of the artiste and the context. It is up to the artiste to take the word to the abstract realm and imagine and execute its various depictions. The use of svar is also fixed, given the definition of the rāg; however, the finer śruti-s to be discerned by the musician allow for a more subtle way to experiment with the desired outcome. Laya, finally, is abstract in its constancy and independence, but is brought back to the concrete world by dividing and manifesting itself through sound, such as in tāl. It is through the constant interplay between these spheres - the abstract and concrete - that a creative and fluid art form thrives.

After taking some time to contemplate Panditji's philosophies, I found myself drawn back to our starting point. He had traced the intricate evolution of sound into the complex system of Hindustānī music. But I was still curious to know:

What is that compelling quality about music that distinguishes it from other sounds? How does it lure listeners in and sustain their attention?

> *"Sound may have an effect on the mind and body, but music has a pleasant effect. After all, it is with breath that we create sound while singing. Breath literally gives life to sound, and that is why it is effective. There is only one thing common between human beings, and that is emotion. All the rest differs - height, colour, language - but emotion at the core is the same. This emotion is connected to the soul, and that is what touches listeners. Good music is never enjoyed by the mind - only by the soul. The mind is always preoccupied with so many ideas, but the moment something enters into the soul, there are no two opinions about it - it is being enjoyed. Our music is not manoranjan [enjoyed by the mind], it is ātmaranjan [enjoyed by the soul]."*

This idea reminded Panditji of the numerous concerts and lecture-demonstrations he had given throughout Europe to audiences with little or no exposure to Hindustānī music. The response was tremendous, and he was convinced of this universal connection that music could make. "Whenever you sing through your heart, it reaches the human emotion of any region, race, colour. When I sang a Nom-Tom ālāp of 25 minutes in Yugoslavia, there were 300 music students and professors in the audience. They were so taken by it, that they asked me to repeat what I had just sung, and I explained that this type of music cannot be replicated. Each time I sing a rāg, it is improvised and will be different. But nonetheless, I sang again for 15 minutes, and they appreciated it so much that they were standing on the chairs and applauding! 'What did they like?' I wanted to know for myself. Then I came to the conclusion that when you approach music very sincerely, authentically and with a focused meditative quality, you will find that it reaches anyone. They may not be able to understand rāg or tāl, but they do appreciate this meditative quality and the human touch."

Panditji remembered his realisation of this idea at the most personal level, with his own father. "My father was totally nil as far as music was concerned. He heard me for the first time in a mehfil [an intimate chamber concert] at somebody's house in Bangalore. He happened to be there, and after he heard my concert of three and half hours, we both sat on the sofa, father and son. He said, 'Dinkar, now you have become a gavaiyā, an Ustād. You sing like a big Muslim musician.' I had already given so many concerts and was well known as a singer, but my father told me when I was 50 years old that my singing was like a stalwart. That is not because he was my father - it is because that music had that effect on him. That is the power of music."

Panditji in concert, Delhi, 1955

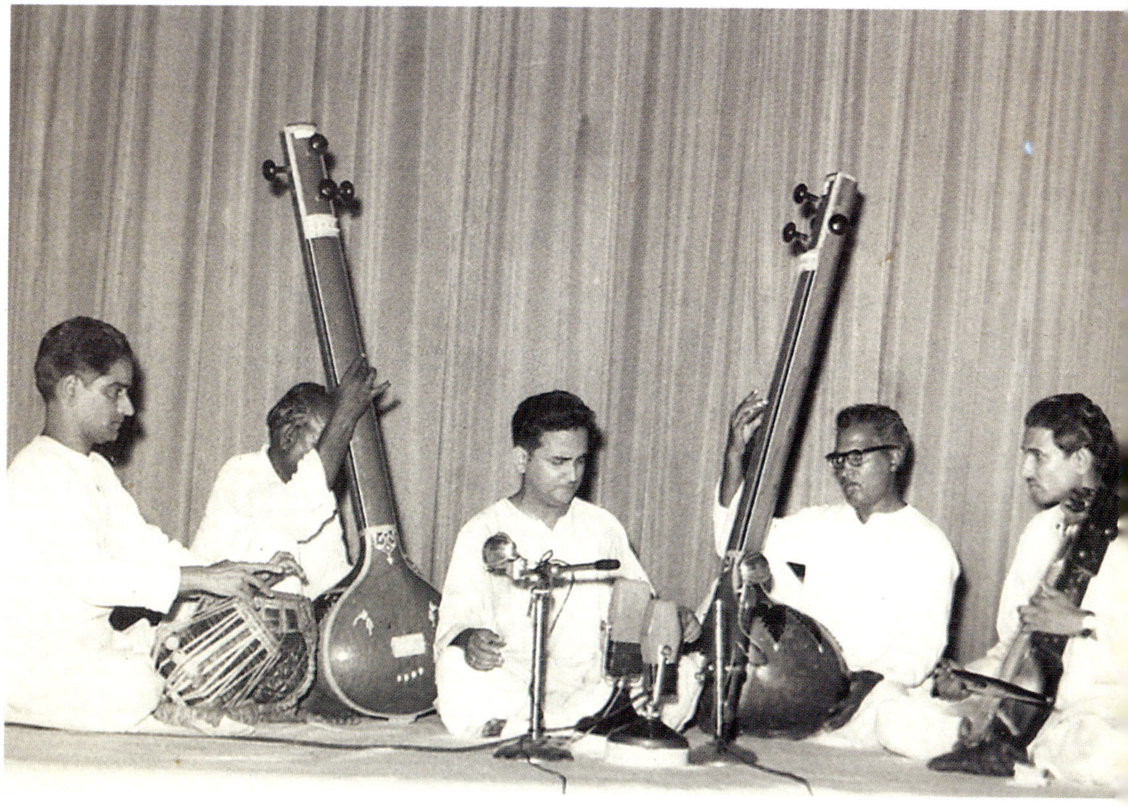

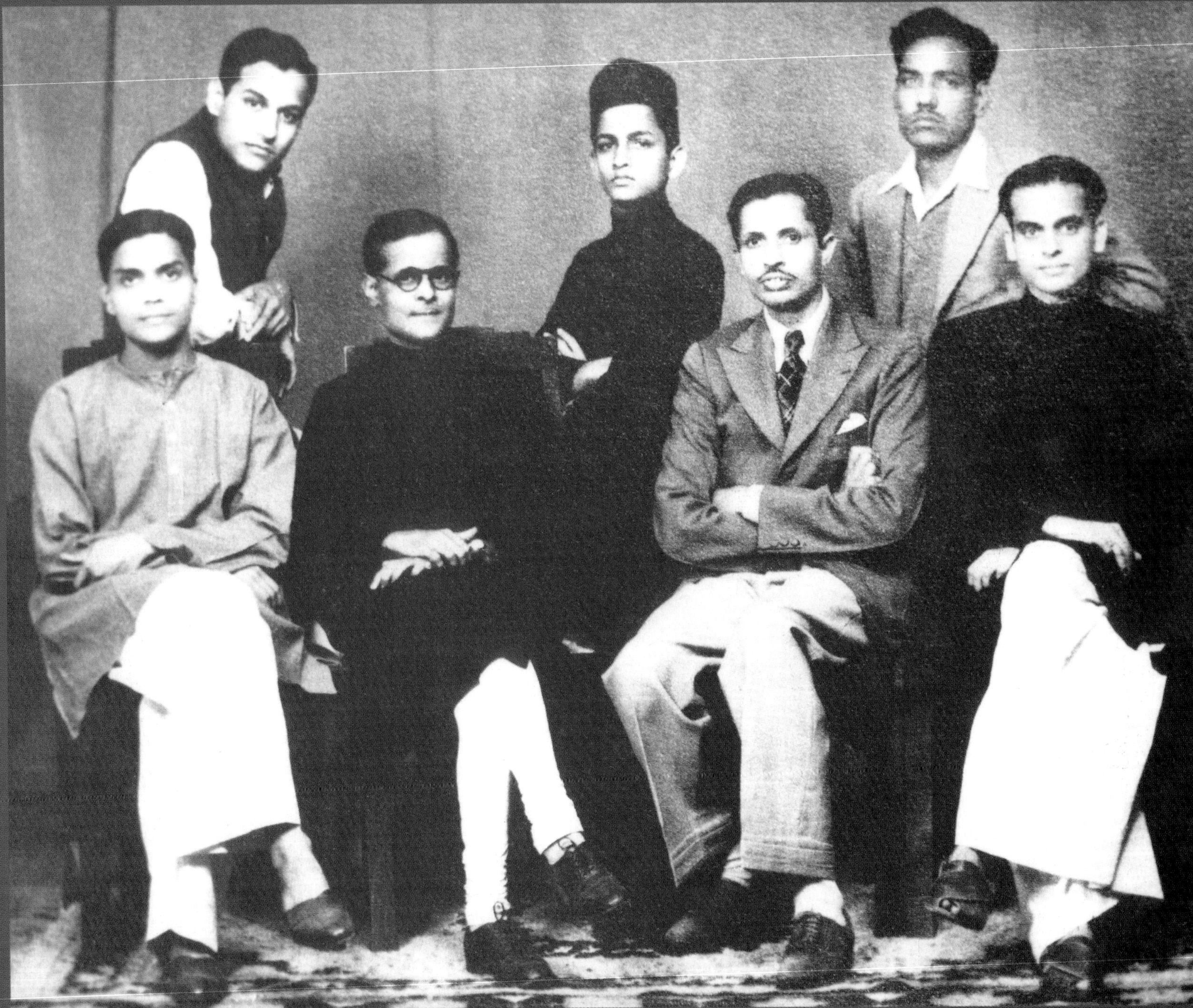

Young Dinkar (at back and centre) with his guru and gurubhai-s in Lucknow, 1944. From left to right: Pandit K.G. Ginde, Pandit S.C.R Bhat, Pandit S.N. Ratanjankar, Pandit Dinkar Kaikini, Pandit G.N. Nathu , Sri Vadilal, Sri Mohanrao Kallianpurkar

EARLY SANSKĀR

"For the first time in my life I saw drops of tears on his [Anna Saheb's] caśmā. Even now that picture is vivid in my mind. For me that was equivalent to receiving a Bharat Ratna - my guruji appreciated my music so much that tears came out of his eyes."

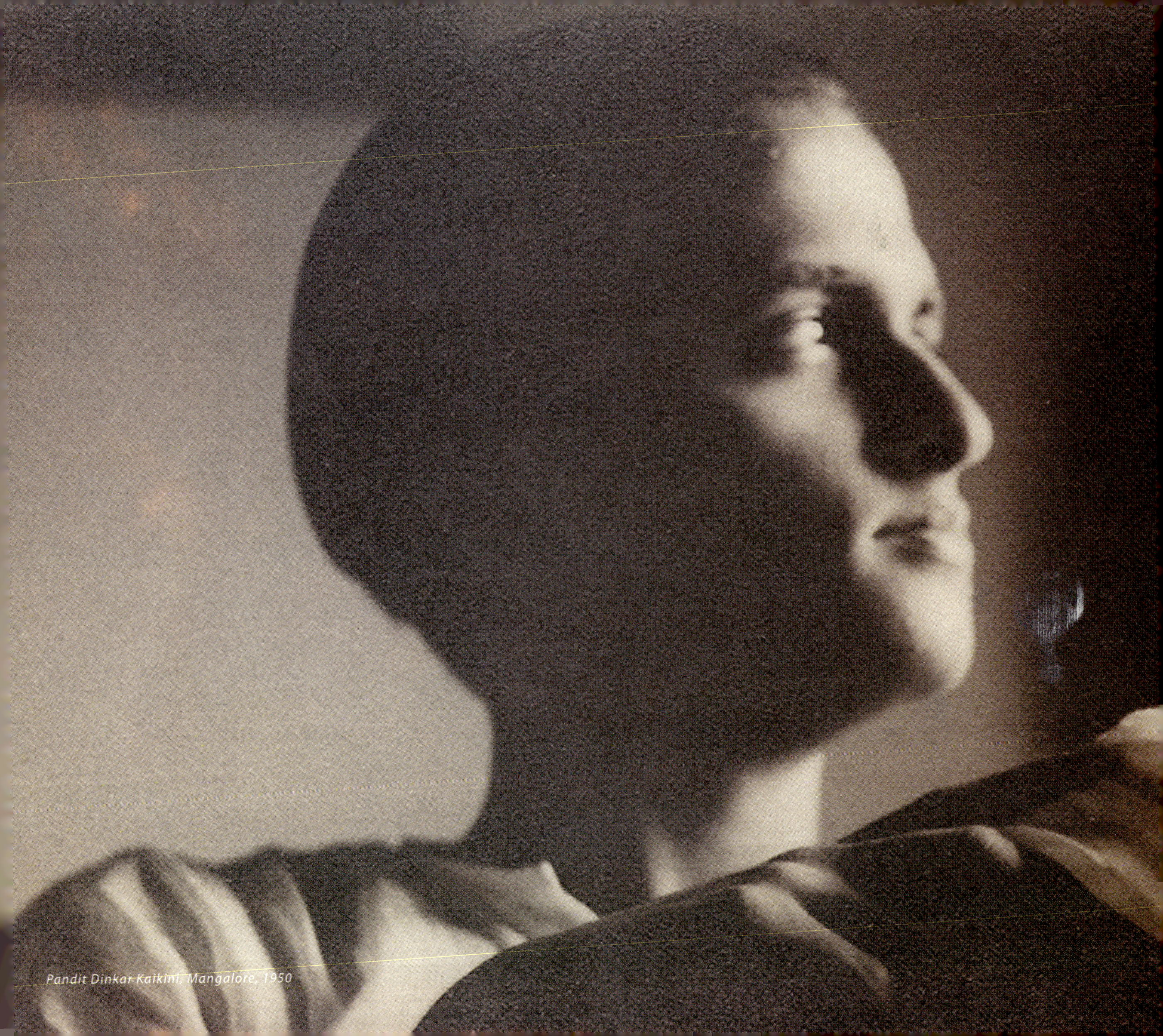

Pandit Dinkar Kaikini, Mangalore, 1950

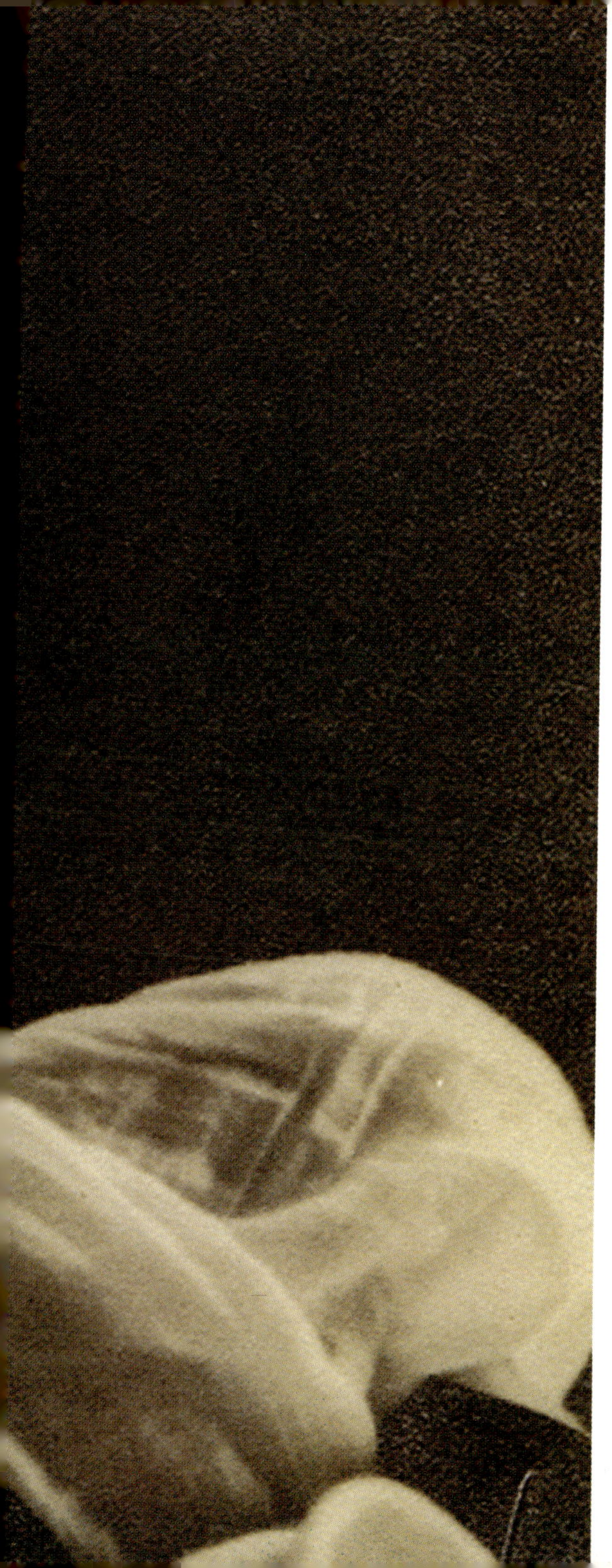

As a seeker of knowledge, learning was only one aspect of the process. It was equally important for me to understand the path. What is the road to tread? How should this wisdom be transferred, and what are the ideal conditions for being a recipient? Hindustānī Rāgsangīt has historically been an oral tradition, passed on from generation to generation in a very close, intimate setting. Originally, the expertise was shared only within families, hence the birth of the Gharānā system. While the system eventually expanded outside the family structure, the values and expectations of family were still extended to students. Music was a way of life, not just a discipline, and students imbibed all aspects of this lifestyle, musical and otherwise. These values and practices are known as sanskār-s and are critical in shaping the mind of a musician. As Panditji said, "Teaching is not just about rāg, tāl and composition, but also about creating an open dialogue about history, philosophy and personal experience." He then proceeded to tell me about the path he had taken.

Panditji began his musical quest at a very young age. His parents, Dattatreya and Krishnabai Kaikini, realised early on that their third child was inseparable from music. Though they themselves were not musicians - his father held a variety of jobs over the years to support the family and his mother was a housewife and a fine Bhajan singer - they recognised that Dinkar was a very special child after several revealing moments in his childhood.

His father had taken him to see the film "Sant Tukaram" - a Marathi film that told the story of the 17th century Marathi saint and poet. The film featured a very popular and appealing soundtrack of abhang-s. One day, Dinkar heard his neighbour, a harmonium player, playing the same melodies on his instrument. Excited, he joined in and sang along, recounting all of the songs from the film perfectly. He had only seen the film once.
He became a phenomenon of sorts, and his neighbour encouraged his father to teach him music seriously.

One of Dinkar's most pivotal epiphanies came at the tender age of seven. At the time, he was taking music lessons from a harmonium player in his neighborhood. On one such occasion, when he came for a lesson, he found his teacher stepping out. "I'm going to an important concert now at the Blavatski Lodge - I will come back later," he told him. Rather than running back home to play like most children his age, Dinkar decided to follow his teacher. Where was he going? Who was he going to hear? He stealthily made his way to the concert, where he sneaked in and sat right in the front. He did not know that he was about to hear music that would change his entire life. The concert featured three Hindustānī legends: Ustad Alladiya Khan, Ustad Faiyaz Khan, and Ustad Abdul Karim Khan. At the conclusion of this grand musical feast, he had made up his mind that he must become a musician, and he must sing like none other than Ustad Faiyaz Khan! Faiyaz Khan Saheb had a powerful and at times flamboyant presence, a highly emotional style of rendition, and an unforgettable demeanour: with his regal appearance, his display of medals on his vest, his authoritative moustache and arresting and sweeping voice, he made a lifelong impression on the young child.

After Dinkar announced his intention to become a gavaiyā like Ustad Faiyaz Khan, Dattatreya became even more serious about his son's talent and narrowed his search for a guru in the same style of Khan Saheb. It took time, patience, unrelenting effort, and an uncompromisingly strong desire for high quality Hindustānī Rāgsangīt before a suitable guru was found for Dinkar. He studied with local music teachers that his father found, depending on where they were living at the time. While he approached stalwarts who came through the city to perform, either he could not convince them to take on such a young child as a disciple, or he was not able to afford their fees. For a brief period, he studied with Pandit Omkarnath Thakur, an experience that exposed him to the various temperaments of musicians at a young age.

"For two years I learned with Karekette Nagesh Rao, three classes a week for five rupees a month. Then my father took me to Omkarnathji. He tested me and said, 'Yes, he has a good voice and he is intelligent. But I can't teach him because I charge Rs 15 and you cannot afford that. He can join the class of my student, Shirin Engineer.'" Panditji joined this class for about one month before he came home and told his father that this was not meant for him. This was not like the music he had heard at Blavatksi Lodge. Omkarnathji noticed that Dinkar was not coming to class anymore and approached his father. When Dattatreya told him that it didn't suit his son, he asked him to send Dinkar to his class without an increase in fees.

"I started and continued learning from him for about one and half years," Panditji said. "I was uncomfortable with the way he spoke about Muslim artistes, including even Abdul Karim Khan, though he used to copy his style of singing. One day, he began a rant in which he cursed Muslim musicians, especially Abdul Karim Khan Saheb and Faiyaz Khan Saheb. Then he proceeded to sing 'Gopalā karunā kyun nahi āye,' a bandiś which Abdul Karim Khan Saheb had recorded. He sang one phrase and said, 'You see, this sangīt is such that it doesn't come just like that. You have to do sādhanā and have bhaktī.' He gave a philosophical lecture on the matter, just after he had abused the others. Then he sang a phrase and said, 'If I ask this boy to sing, do you think he can sing that? Sing!' he said to me. And I imitated the phrase exactly. Immediately he said, 'Chup!' I was very good at imitation and I didn't know why he got so angry. He asked me to sing and repeat after him, and I did just that. I immediately got up, and he told me never to come to his class again."

It was just a few days later that a neighbour informed the Kaikinis of a concert by a relative, Sri Chidanand Nagarkar. After attending this concert, Dinkar recognised that the style was the same as Faiyaz Khan Saheb, and asked his father to approach him to be his guru. When approached, Nagarkar advised that they seek training from his guru, Pandit S.N. Ratanjankar, who was teaching him at Marris College in Lucknow.

Anna Saheb, as Pandit S.N. Ratanjankar was fondly known, was a musical scholar and prolific composer who had studied with Faiyaz Khan Saheb and his primary guru, Pandit Vishnu Narayan Bhatkhande. He was in Mumbai during the college holidays, which gave Dattatreya a window of time to meet and convince him to accept Dinkar as a disciple. Like many other such visits, he went with his son to plead his case. Anna Saheb responded like the other musicians: the child was too young and he could not be responsible for him. As it was, he already had two young students living with him.

Dattatreya did not give up so easily - despite Anna Saheb's response, he requested that he listen to Dinkar and assess his abilities. Anna Saheb indulged him, and Dinkar soon sang the bandiś-es that he had learned until then. To test his quickness in learning, he sang phrases and asked Dinkar to repeat them, which he did with effortlessness. Anna Saheb was impressed with the child's remarkable talent and was appeased – if his student Chidanand would take responsibility for the child, he would allow him to come to Lucknow and train under him. Nagarkar agreed to do so, and father and son were overjoyed by the opportunity.

Organising the funds for Dinkar's education was not an easy task. His father applied for a scholarship for him, but it was a scholarship for academics and music was not a valid subject. After debate over the merit of giving a music scholarship, it was decided to give him a loan of eight rupees per month and Dinkar's dream soon became a reality.

Krishnabai wept as she packed her child's bags for Lucknow. She was very fond of him, and the thought of him leaving his family at such a young age was distressing. However both parents had the courage to send their son away, with the faith that he was born with a God given exceptional talent, and that he was to be guided by a knowledgeable guru.

The formative years of Dinkar's tutelage would test his commitment to music. Upon his arrival, he was placed in a hostel full of teenage university boys in an atmosphere of debauchery. Although he was at school during the day, he would return to a hostel of students who seemed more concerned with drinking and smoking than music. "For me it was a rude shock, as a Sāraswat Brahmin boy. For a couple of months I stayed there, but I thought, 'I've come here to do music, and nobody here is doing music!'" After tolerating these conditions for a few months, Dinkar went to his guardian and senior gurubhai, Chidanand Nagarkar. "I don't want to stay here, I want to move to Guruji's house!" he begged. Although his gurubhai empathised, he did not say anything to Guruji for several days. Sensing his hesitation, Dinkar decided to take more drastic action: he went on a hunger strike. He fasted for three days, growing weaker and eventually fainting. Nagarkar was shocked by the child's unusual will power and scared into action, immediately went to Anna Saheb and threatened to take his own life if the young boy was not allowed to live with him! Under these drastic conditions, Anna Saheb consented, and from then on, the determined eleven year-old Dinkar lived with his Guruji and two other students: Pandit S.C.R. Bhat, who would be like a father to him and Pandit K.G. Ginde, who would be like a brother. He also received support and encouragement from Sri Mohanrao Kallianpurkar, the head of the Kathak section and a close family friend. His behaviour evinced

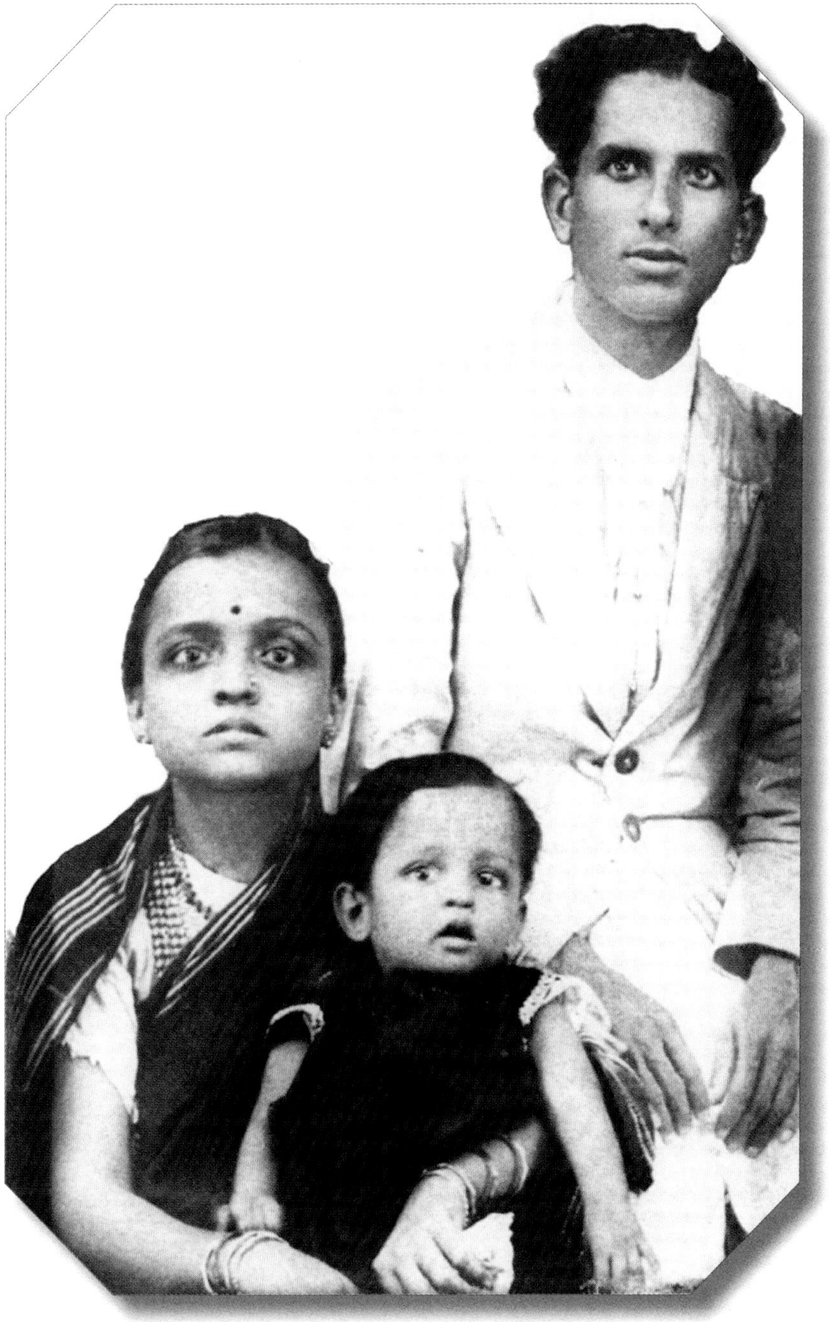

Baby Dinkar with his parents, Krishnabai and Dattatreya Kaikini

the early signs of Panditji's tenacity and resilience, values that would carry him through his life as a musician.

Initially, Dinkar went virtually unnoticed in his new setting. For the first two hours, upon entering the room where he was to stay, his other two gurubhai-s were too engrossed in a game of chess to even acknowledge his presence. Two months later, Gindeji casually asked the young boy if he had prepared for the exams for the next day. "I did not know we even had exams," Panditji remembered. Gindeji advised him: "Tomorrow is the exam - practise and memorise all the songs." He followed the instructions and diligently went through his book to memorise all the text like prose. The next day, in the exam, the adjudicators had written various notes on the board and asked him to sing them. Again, like prose, he read the names of the notes! The examiners then asked him to sing, not read, them, so he sang everything perfectly and was able to identify any note that they sang. The normally stingy judges gave him marks with distinction and full scholarship, and slowly the atmosphere began to change for young Dinkar.

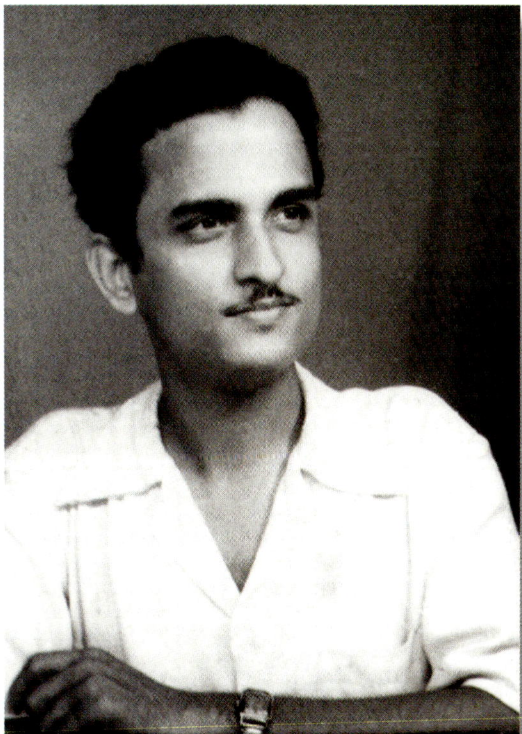

Portrait of a young Dinkar

While Gindeji was the protective elder brother figure for Dinkar, Pandit S.C.R. Bhat looked after the frail yet persistent child like a son during his stay at Lucknow. As they all slept in one room, with Anna Saheb in the room next door, Bhat Saheb would be the one to wake Panditji by 4 a.m. to begin riyāz. During a near-fatal attack of typhoid, it was he who nursed Dinkar back to health, patiently and tenderly, with the few resources they had. "Bhat Saheb was my gurubhai as well as my guru - he conducted my classes and in the fourth year, I studied under him. And more than that, I have fatherly love for him. He was my guru, he was my everything," Panditji said.

His early days were filled with school, music, his gurubhai-s, and the cultivation of his relationship with Anna Saheb, an orthodox traditionalist whose life was completely consumed by music and scholarship.

"Before going to school I used to prepare his things for the day ahead.
When he went for a bath, I used to lay out his kapḍā. He was in the habit of taking pān, and in Lucknow it is considered etiquette. They won't ask for tea or coffee - pān lījiye? He had one silver container in which I used to make 40 pān-s every morning, because he used to consume at least 20 in a day and then offer to others who came to meet him. I went there when I was 11, so after two years, I thought, why don't I also try one?

Anna Saheb was a very short man with a thin voice and was a staunch puritan in his beliefs. Not only did he dislike drinking, but harshly judged those who drank as well. He was a strict Hindu Brahmin with austere, conservative values. Naturally, this reflected in his musical style as well. He was a direct disciple of Bhatkhandeji, and a very strong believer in adhering to everything Bhatkhandeji had said or written.
At times, this along with his rather curt nature, made him unpopular among other musicians and social circles."

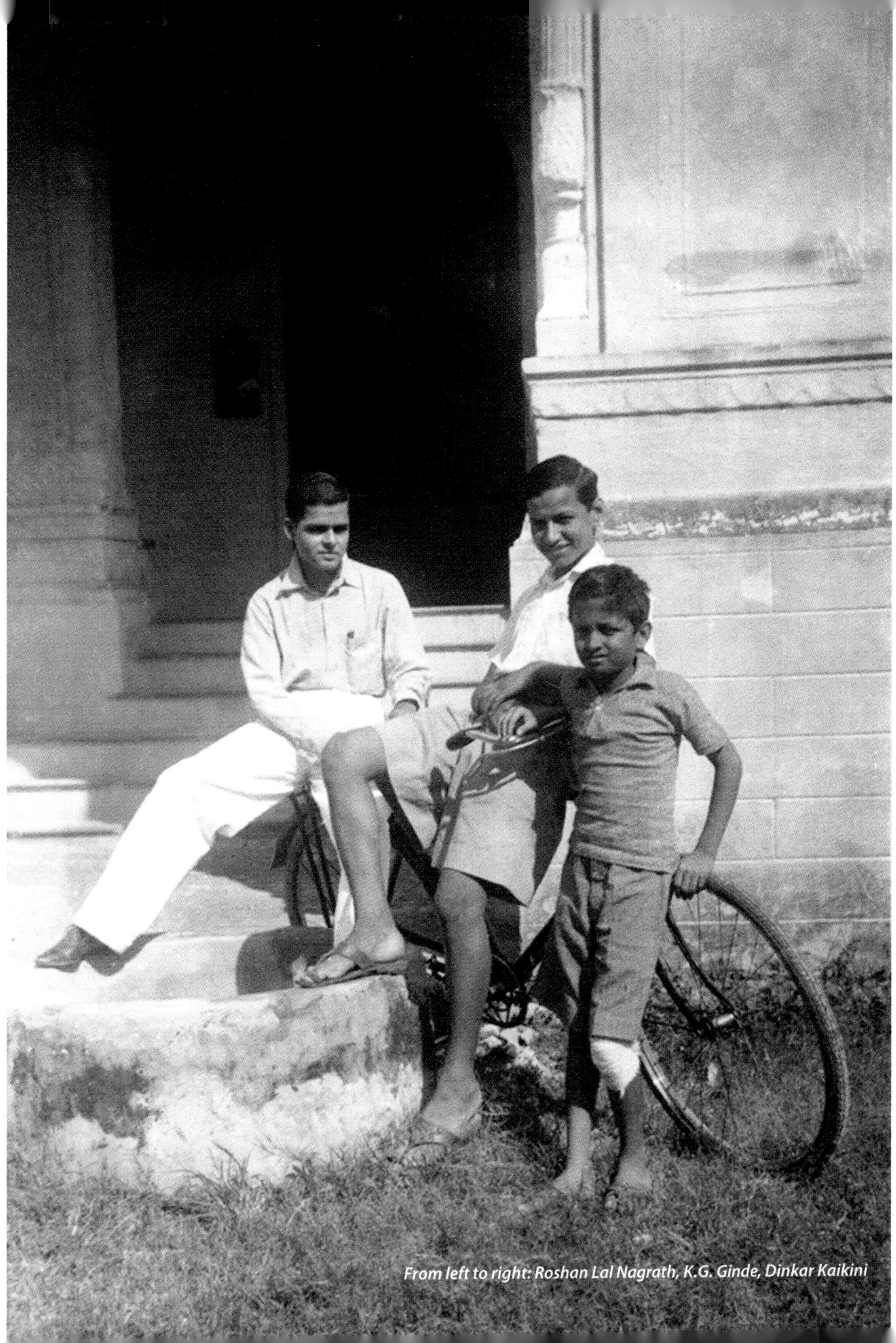

From left to right: Roshan Lal Nagrath, K.G. Ginde, Dinkar Kaikini

As Panditji would say, sanskār-s are both positive and negative, and it is part of the student's intuition and learning experience to choose which values he will adopt. "It is my nature to take what appeals to me and let the other qualities be." While his tālīm (training) was extensive and thorough, his living conditions were abysmal. He was a malnourished child, who received at most one edible meal a day at the University, which was often frozen in the Lucknow winters by the time he was able to eat, left out on a plate that attracted rodents.

"As a 12 year old boy, I had a cup of tea in the morning at about 6 or so, and then I would have lunch at 3 p.m. Sometimes I couldn't concentrate in the class because of hunger. I didn't realise that it was due to hunger at that time. At the same time, I was getting up at 4 to practise. That was of course my duty, and if I didn't do it, Bhat Saheb would poke me with the stick until I did. I used to get up and practise, then do some homework, and then rush off to school. At school the other students would have dishes like pūri bhāji during interval and I would just watch with hunger." Even the college peon chose to bear a grudge against Dinkar, treating him like an unwanted orphan by giving him burned roṭī-s and leftovers. He sometimes chose not to eat the food that was offered in that inedible condition, so the peon complained to Anna Saheb that he was being wasteful, trying to propagate an unfavourable reputation of Dinkar.

Despite Dinkar's exemplary success as a student, given all the prizes and accolades he received, Anna Saheb did not show immediate outward affection or pride. In fact, he was sometimes

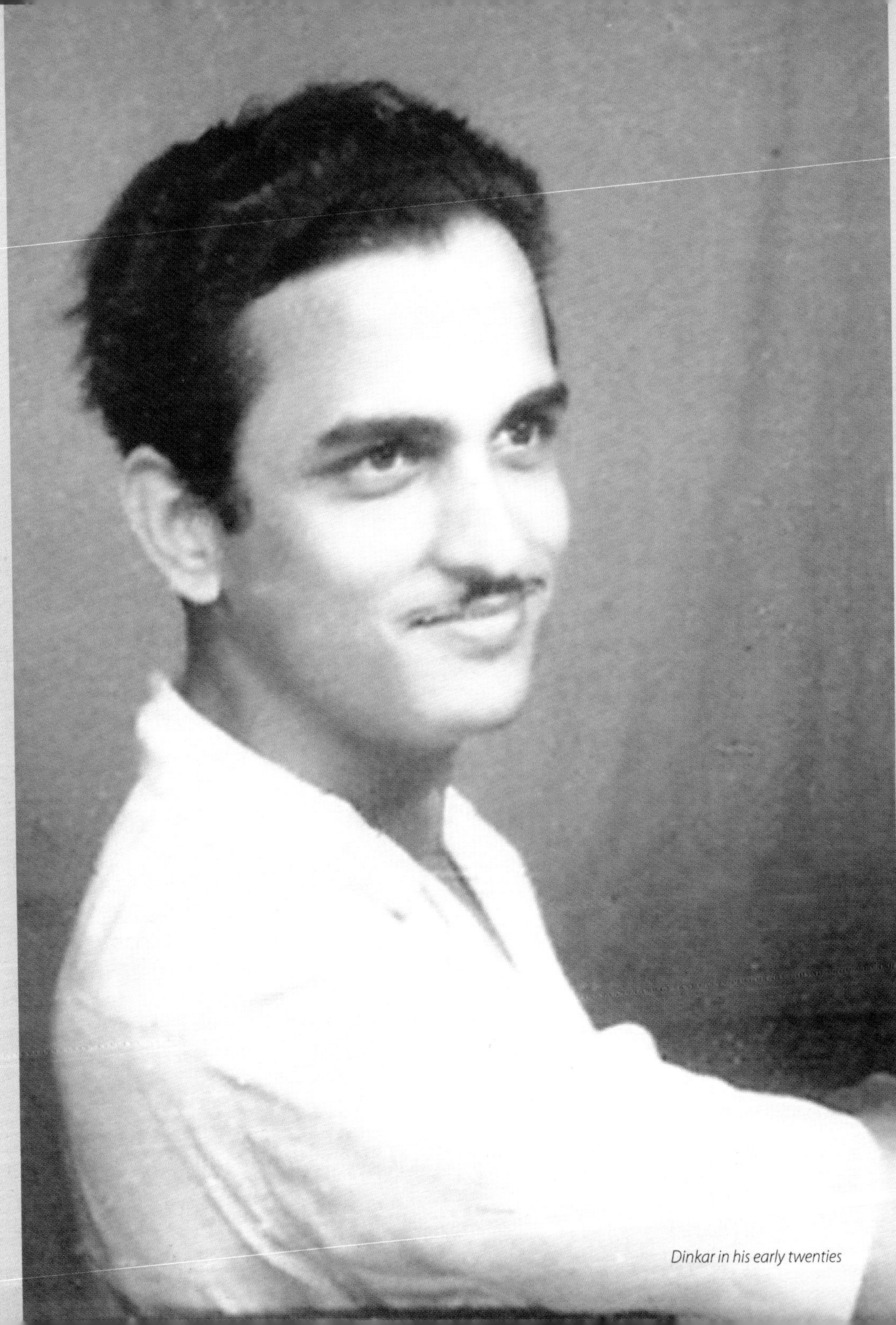

Dinkar in his early twenties

swayed by the negative seeds planted by the peon, thereby creating a barrier between him and Dinkar during much of Dinkar's youth. At his young age, the feeling of being an outsider was sometimes painful. "I was like an intruder in Lucknow. After all, I was forced upon Anna Saheb to stay in his house against his wish. The peons and servants knew this and showed it in their treatment, which used to hurt me." At times, Dinkar longed for the slightest inkling of warmth from Anna Saheb, which was subtly shown to Gindeji, for whom he had a soft corner. "At times that streak of jealousy used to come, it would just touch me and go. After all, Ginde was at Lucknow long before me, and used to stay with Anna Saheb during holidays as well. The feeling remained for some time and later on there was absolutely nothing. Because when it comes to music, you should totally eliminate all these thoughts. My gurubhai-s all had deep love for me."

Dinkar was able to see Anna Saheb for his positive qualities and felt only deep reverence and love for him. "Day-to-day living was not filled with positive sanskār-s for me, but I was able to understand that and remain uninfluenced. At heart, my Guruji was very pure. His tālīm was extensive, his knowledge vast. Aside from his acquired knowledge, he was a prolific composer, fluent in many languages, a voracious reader, and most importantly, he taught from his heart. I used to consider him a guru and a father."

Anna Saheb also fostered an atmosphere of tremendous mutual respect among the śiṣya-s. He treated all of his disciples like family, never allowing one to speak badly about another, nor did they ever harbour such feelings. His approach to teaching was also very open-minded for his musical generation. At that time, many of the major Hindustānī artistes in India would visit Marris College to perform; one of the major broadcasting stations was in Lucknow, and Anna Saheb always invited artistes to give a performance after their broadcasts. He would ask his students to give vocal support to anyone who came, regardless of the gharānā to which they belonged. This was an unusual practice during this period, as many gharānā-s were highly protective of their gāyakī and would not allow students to give vocal support for other styles.

His openness also extended to the nature of the relationship he developed with his students. While many guru-s during this period did not entertain questions from students, (they were expected to imbibe the knowledge and never ask if they had doubts), Anna Saheb encouraged students to think for themselves and pose questions to the guru. He appreciated that Dinkar was a questioning, honest, and bold individual, and even took the liberty of asking him for his opinion on his compositions. One time, Anna Saheb had composed a bandiś in rāg Jaunpuri and asked him for his thoughts. He told him his frank reaction - while the tune was nice, he felt it sounded more like Nātyasangīt (Marathi light-classical) than Rāgsangīt. Without hesitation, Anna Saheb immediately told him to forget the composition, valuing Dinkar's opinion despite the fact that he was his śiṣya.

There were also moments filled with laughter and levity. Dinkar was famous for his ability to do uncanny impersonations (musically and theatrically). Every year, after the Holi festivities, he was asked by all the other students to do impersonations of many famous singers - right from their gait to the manner in which they sat on the stage, their gestures, and of course their singing. In this fashion, he used to do "nakkal" of many, including Faiyaz Khan Saheb, Raja Bhaiya Poonchwale, Vadilalji, and others. When it came to doing Anna Saheb he felt very hesitant, but he would do it nonetheless, giving even Anna Saheb a good laugh at his own impersonation. Panditji believed that a theatrical sensibility is important for an artiste, and should come to the foreground in a concert to build a sense of histrionics in the musical context.

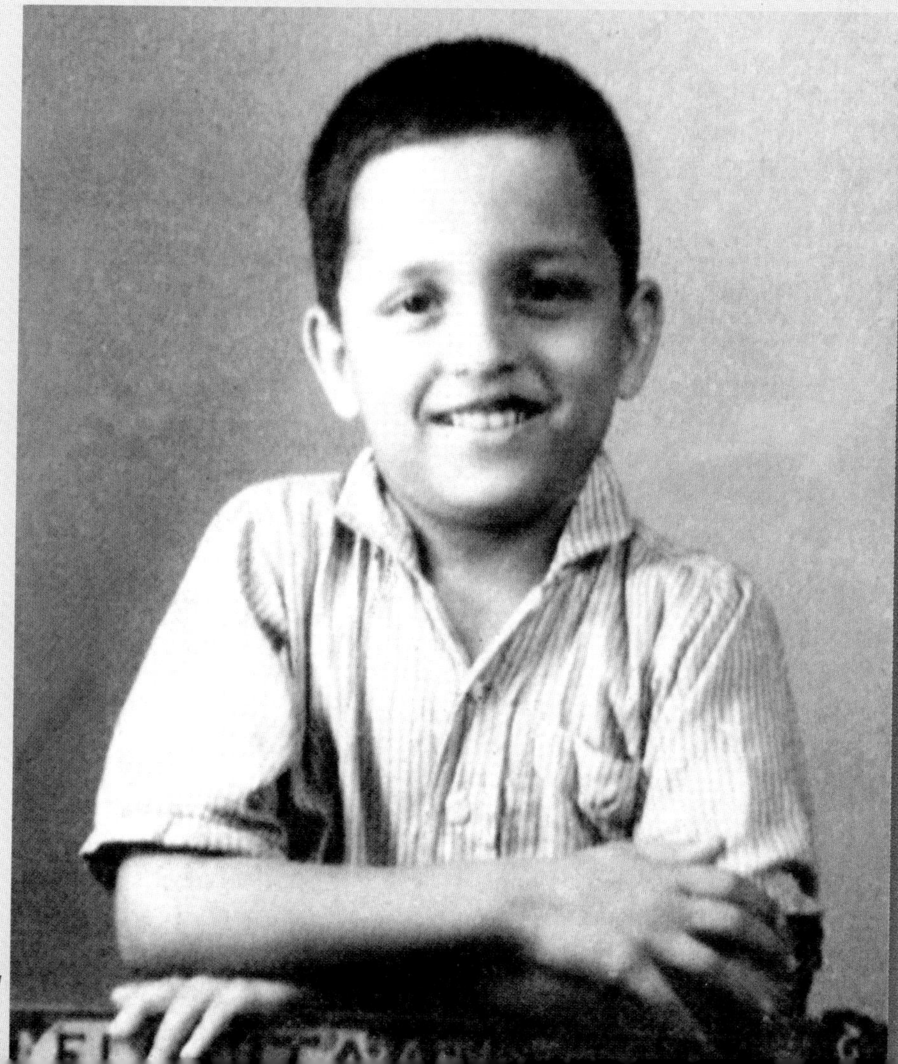

Young Dinkar, age 11

Dinkar's intentions as a student were specific and focused: he sought to imbibe his guru's knowledge and scholastic approach, but to execute in the style of Ustad Faiyaz Khan. Khan Saheb's style was robust, sweeping, and dramatic, and Panditji was enamoured by his voice, exposition and imagination. Anna Saheb, on the other hand, had a smaller voice, and a more conservative style of rendition that paralleled his personality. Dinkar had the utmost respect for Anna Saheb's deep understanding and attention to the purity of each rāg, but always modelled his style of singing after Faiyaz Khan Saheb. He was deeply interested in understanding and mastering his voice so that he could create a sound like Khan Saheb, integrated with the knowledge he had amassed from Anna Saheb.

On one occasion, Khan Saheb was visiting the college and had the opportunity to hear a jugalbandi of the young upcoming vocalists K.G. Ginde and Dinkar Kaikini. Dinkar, excited to sing for his musical idol, became very involved in the music and particularly in executing in Khan Saheb's trademark style. As the concert progressed, Khan Saheb was very impressed with Dinkar's bold rendition in his style, and encouraged him with many utterances of "vāh, vāh." Anna Saheb was uncomfortable with the showmanship that young Dinkar was evincing, clearly inspired and perhaps slightly carried away by the presence of Khan Saheb. In Marathi, he uttered, "Pudhe, pudhe chala," indicating to Dinkar to tone down his theatrics and move on. After the concert, Khan Saheb gave Dinkar a hug and compliment by saying, "Beṭa, tum Agra gharāne ko rośan karoge." At the same time, he spoke his mind to Anna Saheb by saying, "Yeh dekho Sri Krishna, jab śagird gāte hain, tab kuch galtī ho, to apne kamre le jāo, lekin audience ke sāmne is tarah gussa karna achchā nahi hai. Kaise śer bankar gā rahā thā. Tumne ṭokā to lomḍi ban gayā." (Translated: Young man, you will bring fame to the Agra gharānā. . .Look here, Sri Krishna, when a student sings, if there are any mistakes, then discuss it in private, but it is not good to get angry in front of the audience. He was singing like a lion and you interrupted him and made him into a meagre fox.")

Right: Pandit Dinkar Kaikini and Pandit K.G. Ginde at Panditji's Saśtābdhipūrtī. Below: Performing a jugalbandi at the Golden Jubilee of the Bhatkhande Festival, Mumbai, 1985

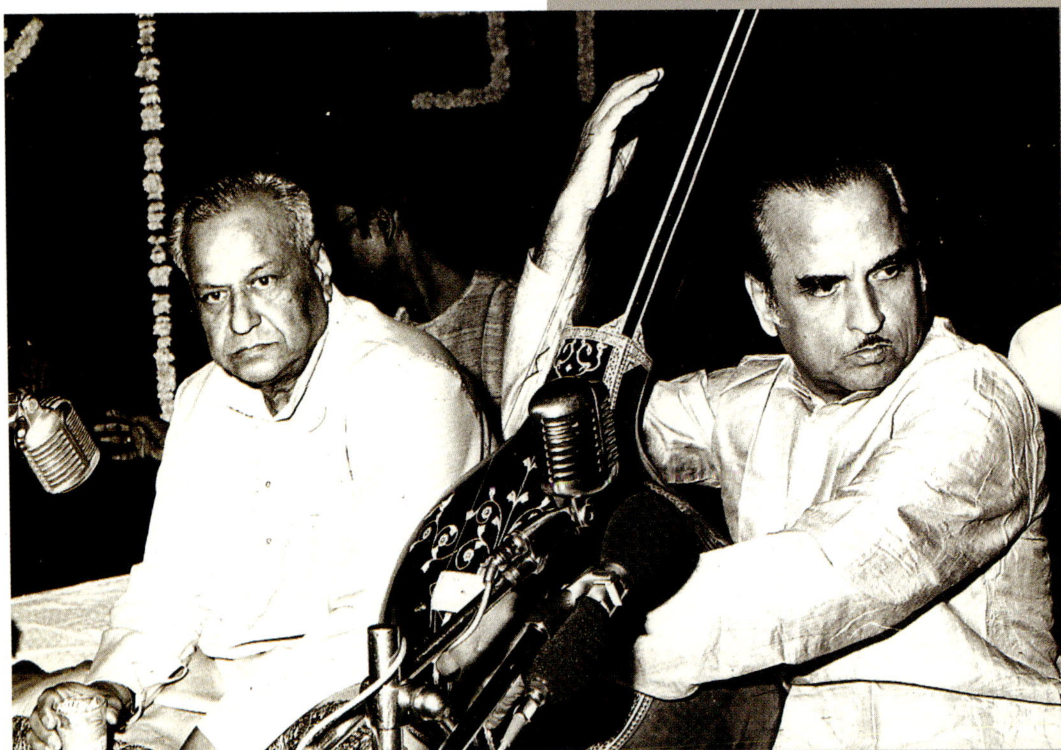

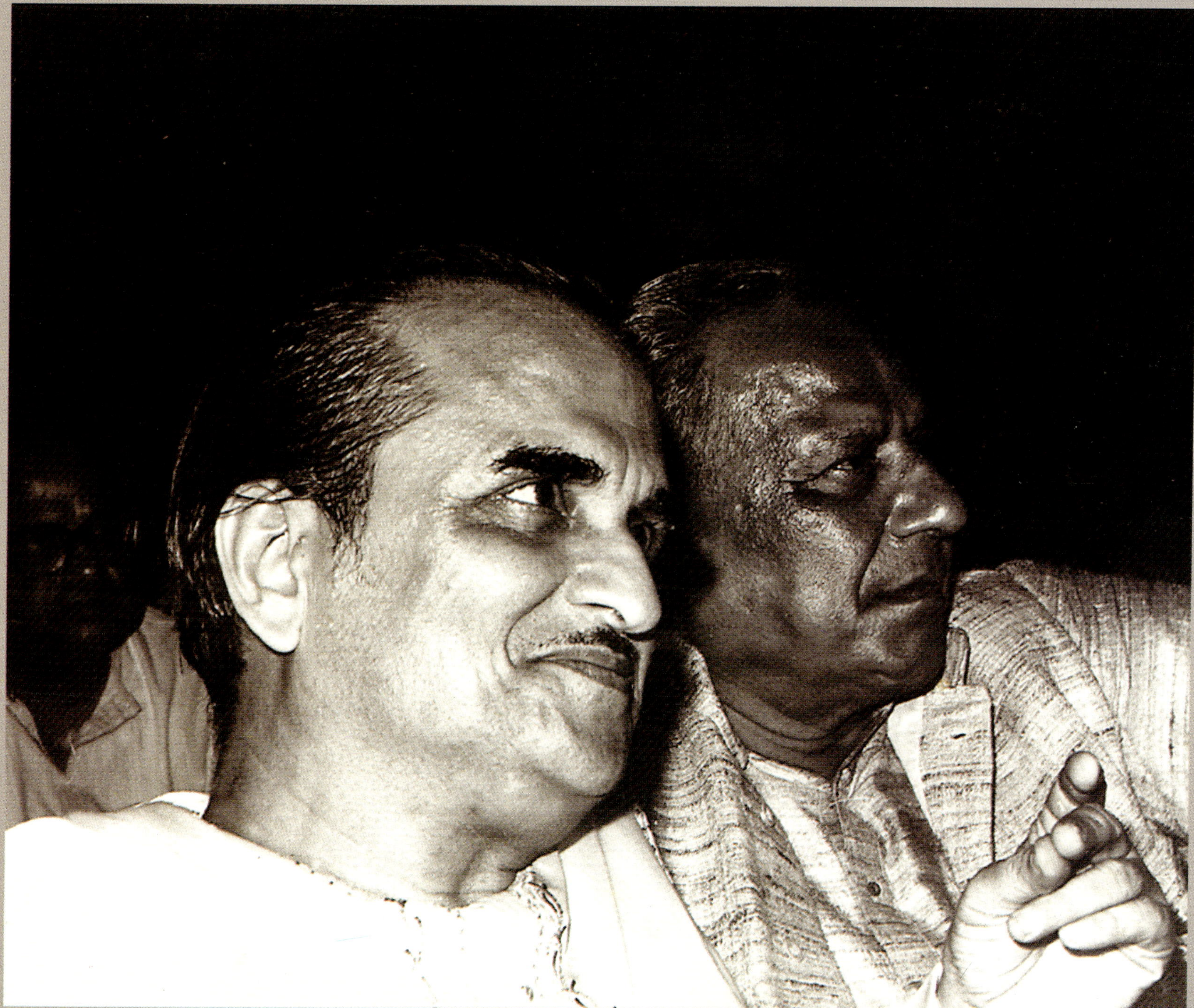

As the years passed, the relationship between guru and śiṣya changed, and Anna Saheb observed from a distance the evolution of his student into a musician. He witnessed the blossoming of Panditji into a successful performer who remained true to the teachings of his guru, while introducing his own personality into his renditions. He also noted the various roles Panditji very capably handled - whether it was as a performer, as a composer for film and theatre, as an administrator, or as a guru. It was Anna Saheb who recommended Panditji for many of the opportunities he would receive after leaving Lucknow, including positions at the All India Radio, Delhi and the Bharatiya Vidya Bhavan in Mumbai. On a few rare occasions he attended his concerts, and at one such performance in

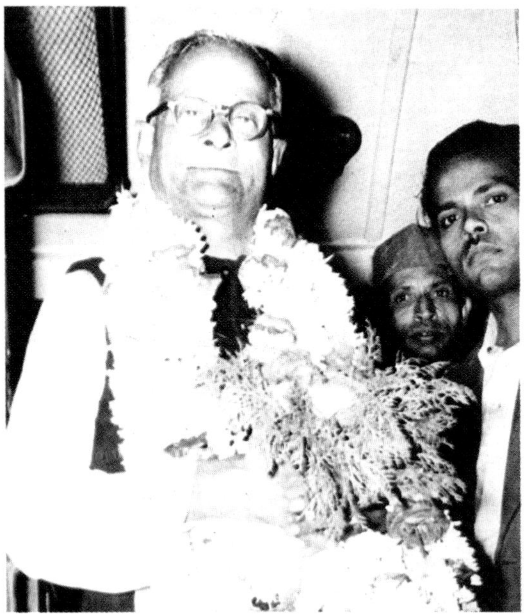

Above and Right: Pandit S.N. Ratanjankar upon his retirement from Marris College, Lucknow, 1959

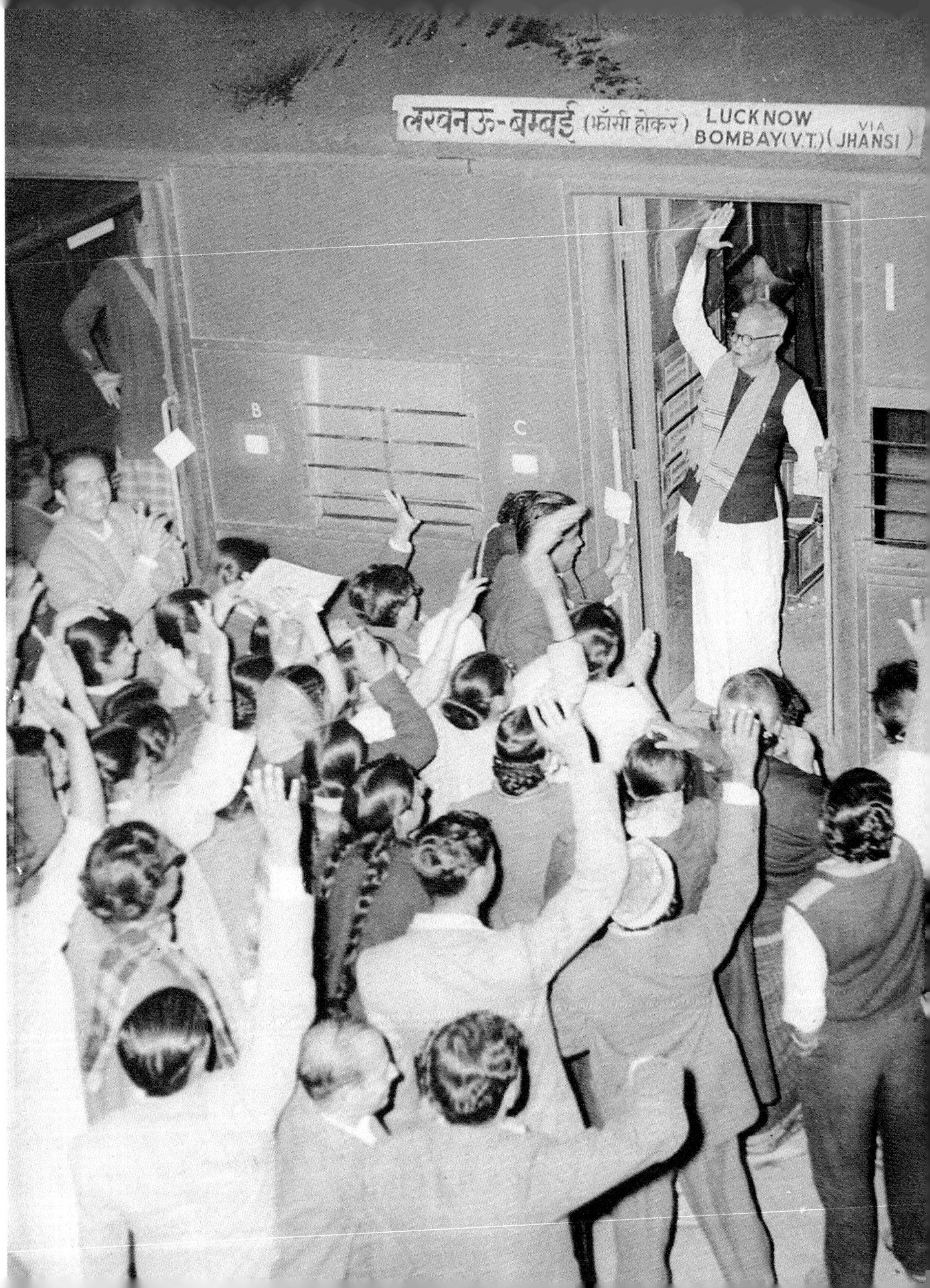

Mumbai, Panditji received the ultimate praise from his Guruji. After a four-hour concert, he looked up for a moment at Anna Saheb. "For the first time in my life I saw drops of tears on his [Anna Saheb's] caśmā. In Marathi, Anna Saheb said, 'Dinkar, now you have become a gavaiyā.' Even now that picture is vivid in my mind. For me that was equivalent to receiving a Bharat Ratna - my Guruji appreciated my music so much that tears came out of his eyes."

The only other such incident in which Panditji received open praise from Anna Saheb was after a national All India Radio programme in Delhi. On the day before the programme, Anna Saheb happened to be in Delhi and met Panditji. He asked him what he was planning to sing, and requested that he sing rāg Shyām Kalyān. Panditji had not learned the rāg, so Anna Saheb taught it to him that day and then left. The next day Panditji performed Shyām Kalyān, and immediately upon hearing the broadcast live, Anna Saheb sent him a postcard stating that he was very proud of him, and that he sang it the way he himself would have. These were the only two instances in which Panditji received outward praise from his guru, and they were forever etched in his memory.

By the end of his tenure at Lucknow, Panditji had completed the Sangeet Viśārad degree and received the high honour of the Bhatkhande Gold Medal. His tālīm with Anna Saheb had been exhaustive, in-depth and rigorous, supplemented by the guidance he received from his gurubhai-s.

25th Anniversary of the Bhatkhande Sangeeth Vidyapeeth (Marris College), Lucknow

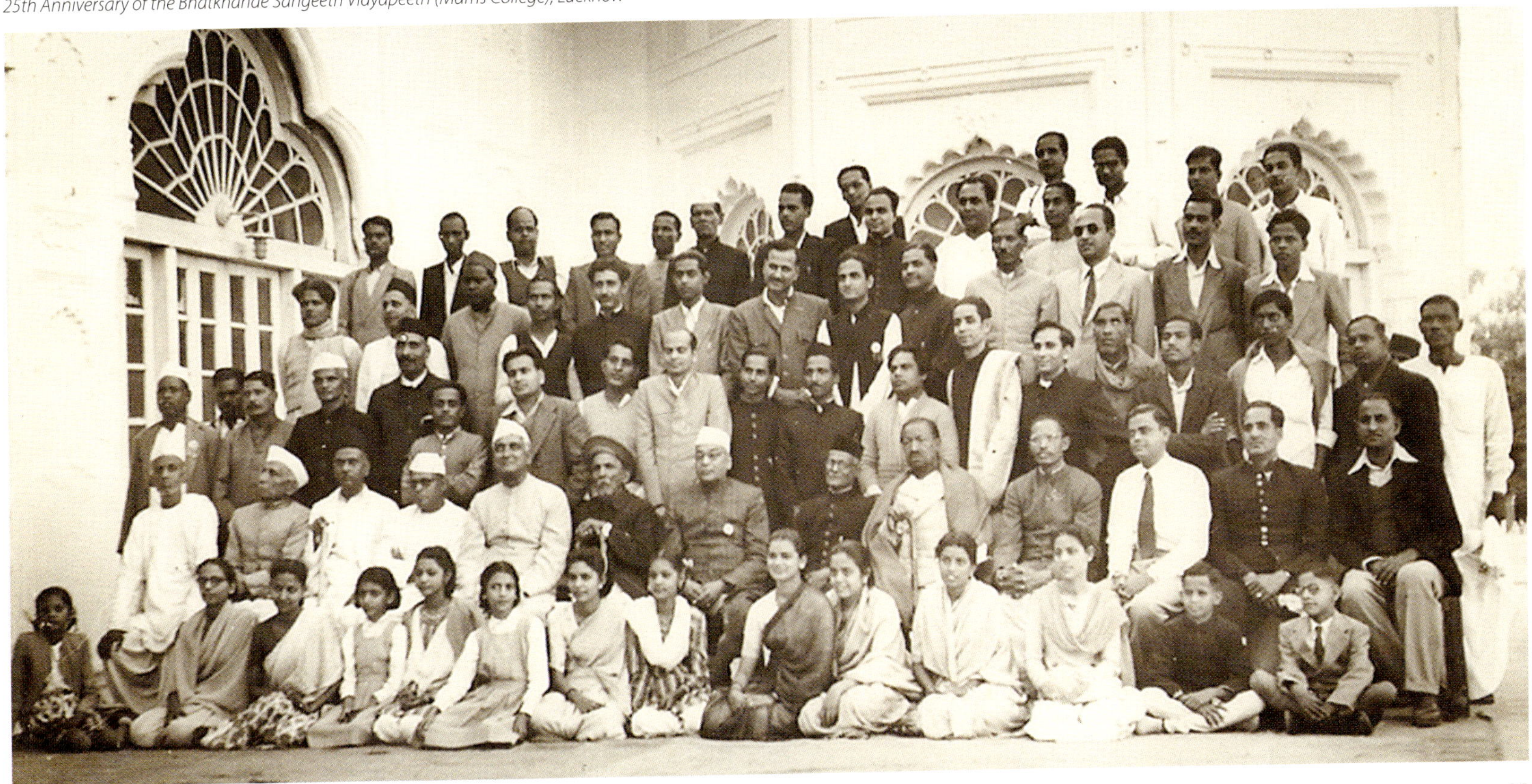

Though the path getting to Lucknow and staying there was fraught with many obstacles, Panditji believed that it is ultimately up to an individual to perceive a situation to his advantage or disadvantage.

"Struggles can be physical, financial, or mental. Feeling like an unwanted child - that is also a mental struggle. All these things can come simultaneously, but you don't stop. You walk. Ekla Cholo Re ['Walk Alone,' reference to poem by Rabindranath Tagore]. Keep walking, alone. You have to walk. Why are you walking? You must know the answer. Where do you want to go? You must know the answer. And all throughout, the joy of walking should not be broken. And when you reach the goal, you find that you have to walk again, because there is another goal. It is a never-ending process. If you think of it as a struggle, if you constantly worry about the struggle, then the joy is not there. You must let the struggle turn into joy."

With his fortitude and invincible positive approach to any and all circumstances, Panditji moved forward from his youth in Lucknow to carve his own distinct place as a musician.

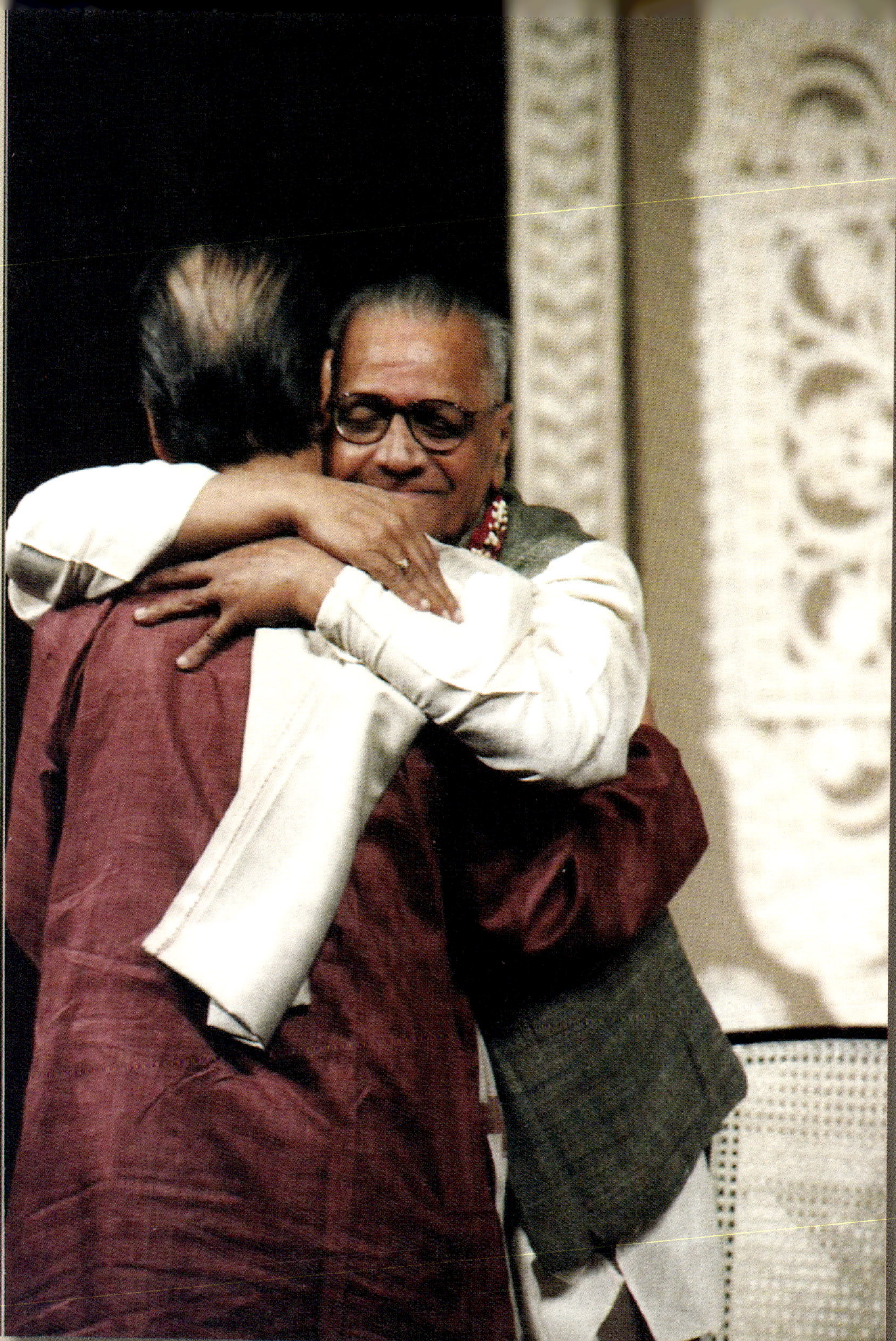

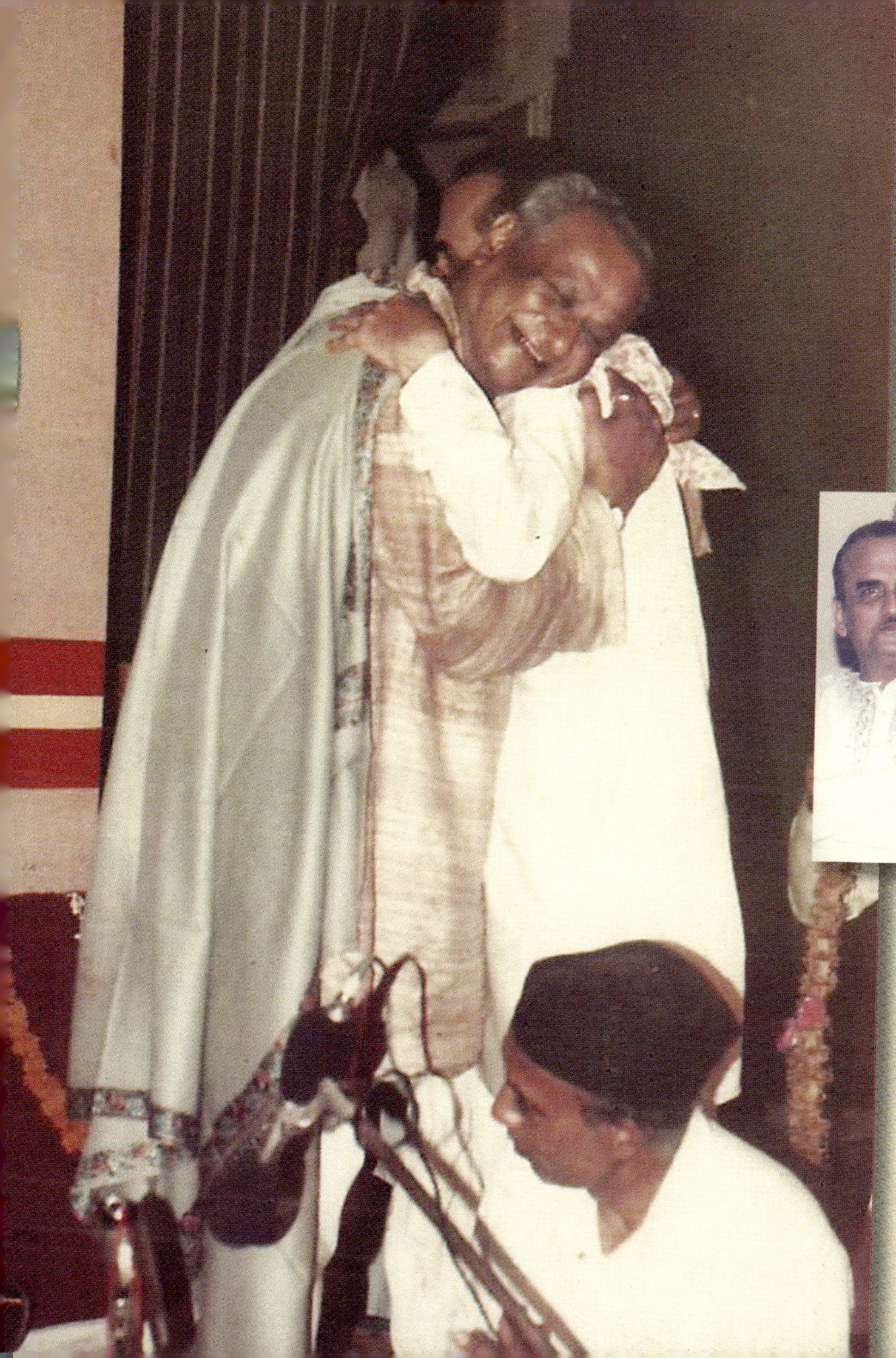

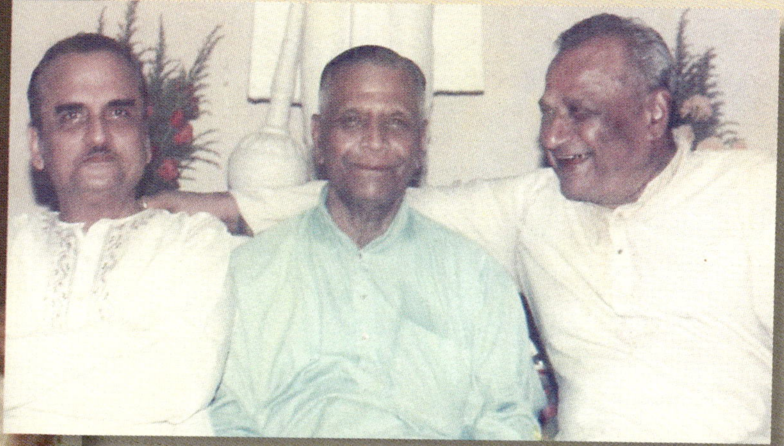

Pandit Dinkar Kaikini, Pandit S.C.R. Bhat, Pandit K.G. Ginde (left to right)

Left: Pandit S.C.R. Bhat embracing Pandit Dinkar Kaikini after receiving the Sangeet Natak Akademi Award; Right: Pandit K.G. Ginde embracing Pandit Dinkar Kakini on his 60th Birthday

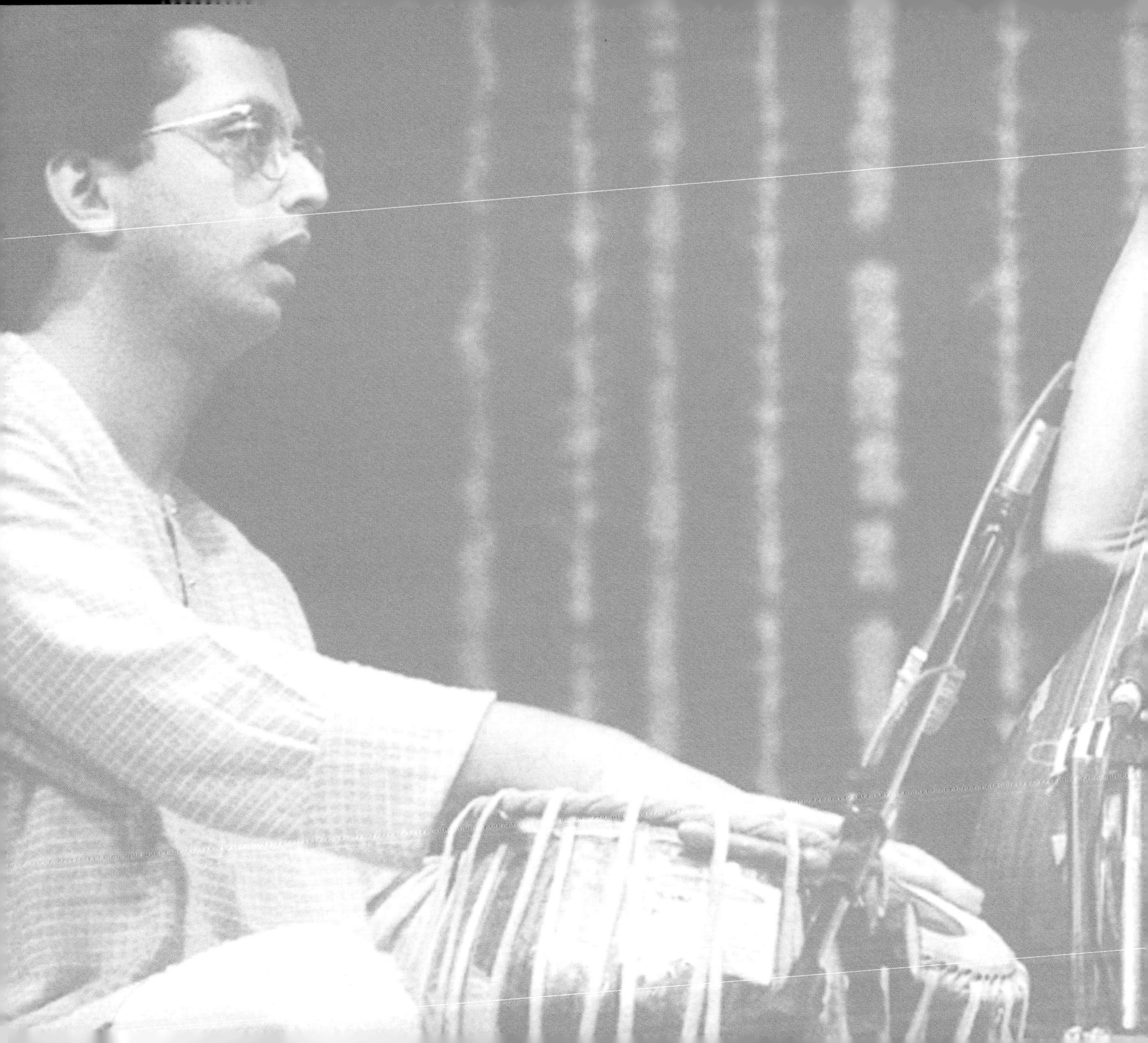

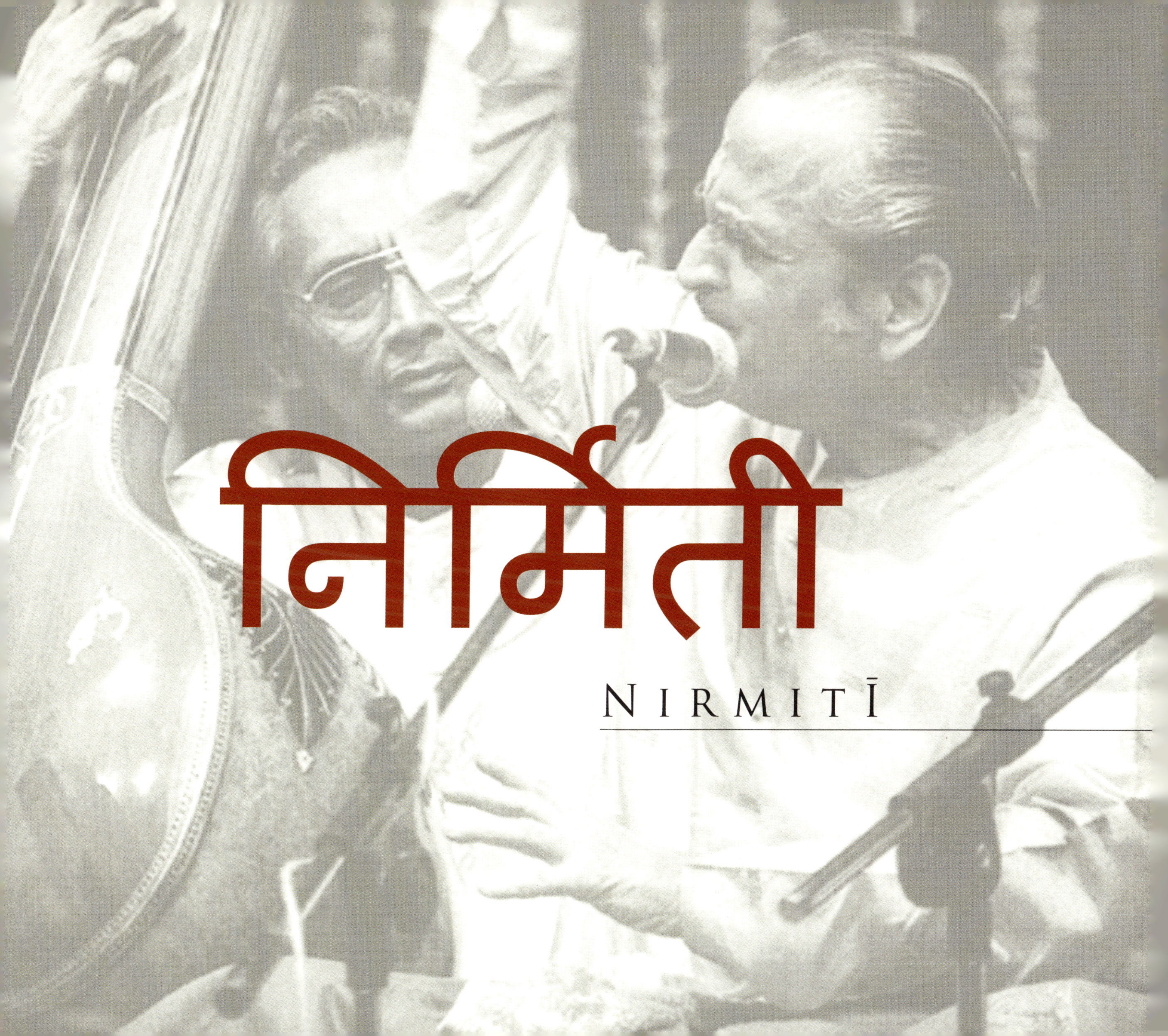

निर्मिती

NIRMITĪ

Panditji in concert, accompanied by his son, Sri Yogesh Samsi, on tablā and his disciple, Sri Sudhindra Bhaumik, on tānpurā

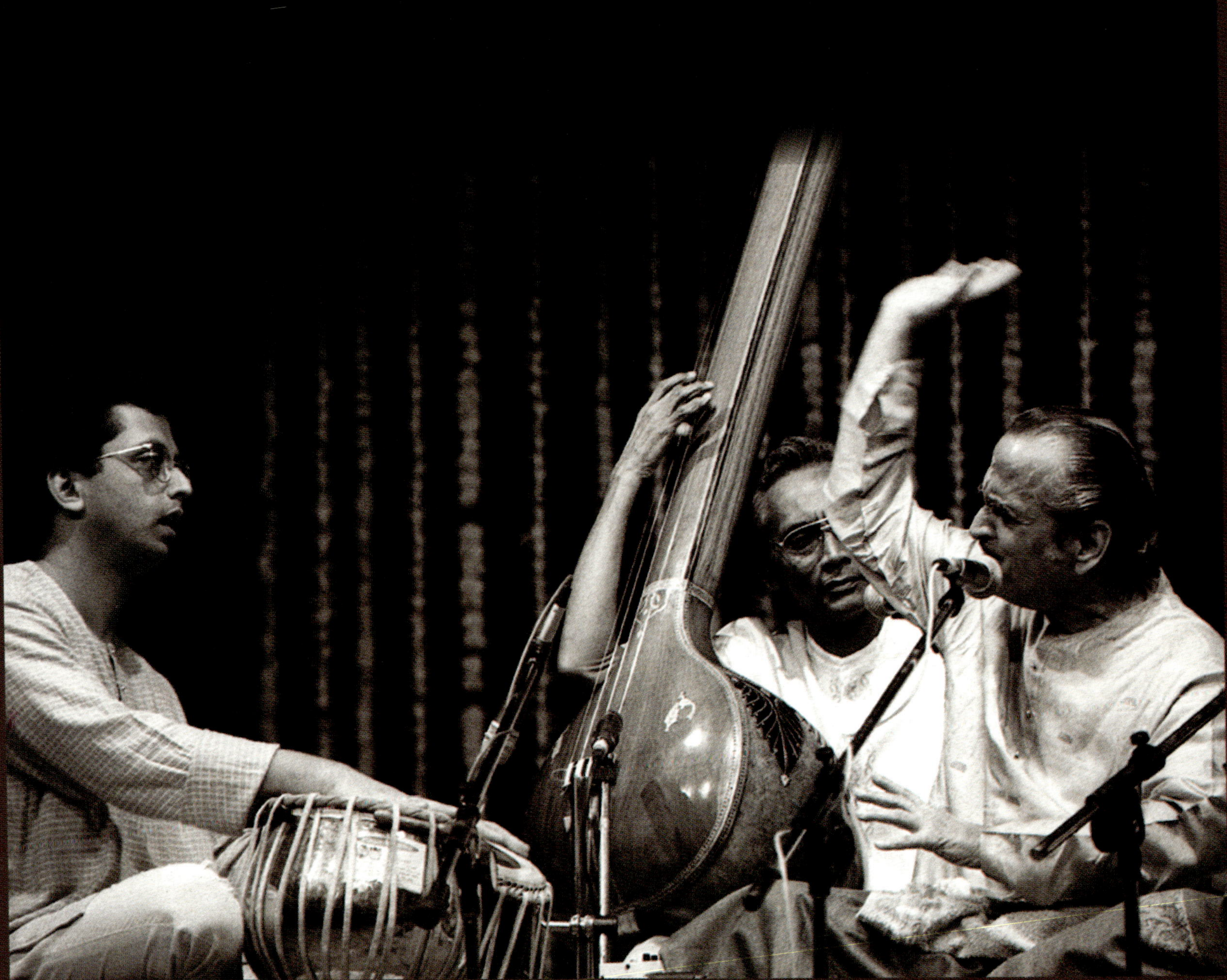

CREATIVITY

"We boast about creativity, but we don't create anything. We only re-create. There is only one creator, and He is God. He has not left anything for humans to create, but only for humans to access through their talents and skills. I should not feel as though I have done something great - I am only the receiver."

Panditji had spoken to me in detail about the building blocks of music, and I was eager to start the construction process. Now that I was equipped with bricks and mortar I wanted to learn how to build a beautiful house. In Hindustānī Rāgsangīt, however, merely constructing a house is not enough; the artiste must also design the interiors, the landscape, and all the details that transform it from a functional unit to a cosy home. Given that it is a largely improvisational style of music, the musician wears the multiple hats of artiste, composer and conductor. "Whatever a musician has learned is vidyā, but when he performs, at that moment, he is composing, creating and conducting himself all at the same time." With all these simultaneous responsibilities, how does one generate this constant flow of musical ideas?

Panditji's philosophy of creativity is very much akin to his beliefs on sound. "We boast about creativity, but we don't create anything. We only re-create. There is only one creator, and He is God. He has not left anything for humans to create, but only for humans to access through their talents and skills. I should not feel as though I have done something great - I am only the receiver." Often, when asked what inspired him to write his compositions, he stated that the thought just "came" to him. On several occasions, an almost supernatural experience took over his mind and body, transporting him to a musical realm. In these instances, I got a glimpse into the moments that have framed his highly spiritual perspective on creative inspiration.

Panditji's encounter with the rāg Jog is one such incident. He was invited to sing at the death anniversary concert for Anna Saheb, and was eager to sing Jog but had never learned it from him. "One night, I had a dream in which Anna Saheb was teaching me Jog, and I learned it for about an hour or so. When he stopped teaching, I immediately woke up… I took the tānpurā and started practising. Generally I used to get up at four in the morning to practise, but that day I had sat to practise by two. I was just delirious with Jog! I began singing, working on the ālāp with the ideas still fresh from the dream." He was determined to sing Jog after the electrifying dream. However, in the dream, his guru had only taught him the rāg ang, its characteristic phrases, movement and development. He had not learned a composition. It was then that he thought of composing one himself, inspired by the entire experience of learning the rāg in a dream. Thus originated the bandiś "Āye sant Sujān det vidyā ko dān, bhanakat mere kān supne me ān," in which he describes the vision of his saintly guru in the dream. He remembers how all the elements required for a successful composition fell into place so naturally. The words must have the capacity to be expanded upon, such as containing ākār vowel sounds. To fit the whole dream episode into two or three lines is difficult business! But it came automatically, and I give the credit to my guru only." He sang a detailed rendition of Jog soon after in Mumbai.

Creative inspiration can also stem from unexpected places. This was the case with rāg Gunaranjani, the haunting morning melody conceived by Panditji. An unusual scale, Panditji actually classified it as a jāti, rather than a rāg. While it had a melodic structure, it did not conform to all the rules of a rāg. Its formation was a highly spiritual journey for Panditji, and took almost twelve years to come to realisation.

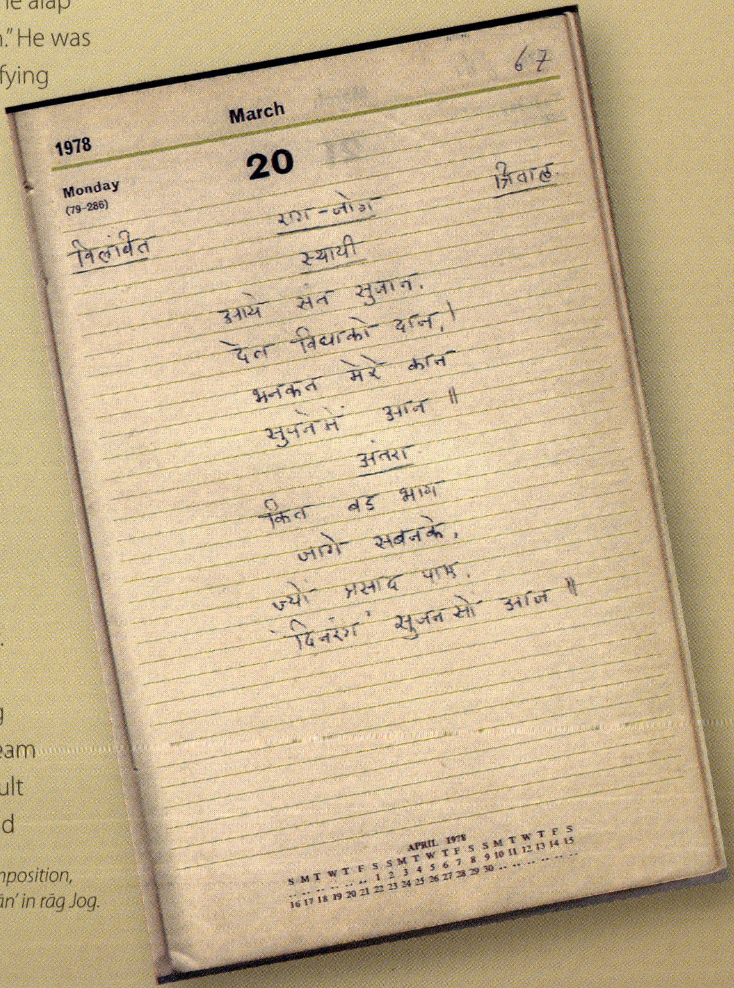

Panditji's composition, 'Āye sant Sujān' in rāg Jog.

He was perplexed by a recurring dream, in which stars fell, almost like fireworks, into the letters of certain svar-s. He spent countless pre-dawn hours ruminating on this combination of notes, consumed by their haunting melody. Over the years of its gradual development, he drew inspiration from various sources until it took a definite form. "When I was in Delhi, practising alone in the house, there was a person who used to ride his cycle outside to sell kerosene. While making his rounds, he used to shout, 'Tel vāllā miṭṭi ka tel, tel vāllā ji…' He used to come by daily.

One morning, I was very engrossed in Gunaranjani, exploring an ālāp in uncharted territories of music. At that time when he shouted, it suddenly disturbed me. I became irritated and said, 'Arre kyā cillāte ho tum? Band karo.' He then replied, 'Nahi sāheb, miṭṭi kā tel.' In just that fraction of a second I thought, I am also shouting while practising. For those who don't understand it, it is shouting! And he is also shouting for his livelihood - he wants to sell and earn. We travel in the same boat - so I have no right to get angry.

Then I said, 'Arre, ek bottle de dena *[Ok, give me one bottle].*' After a moment, I started to think about what svar-s he was shouting – 'sa, ma, ma pa….pa, pa.' I started singing those notes, doing ālāp in these three notes. And my Gunaranjani started to take more shape."

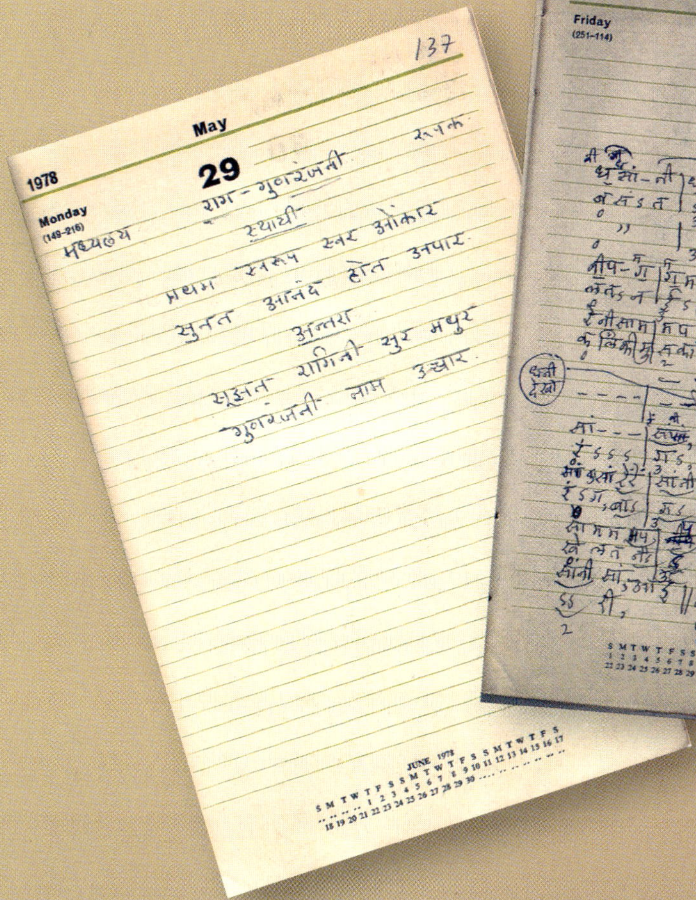

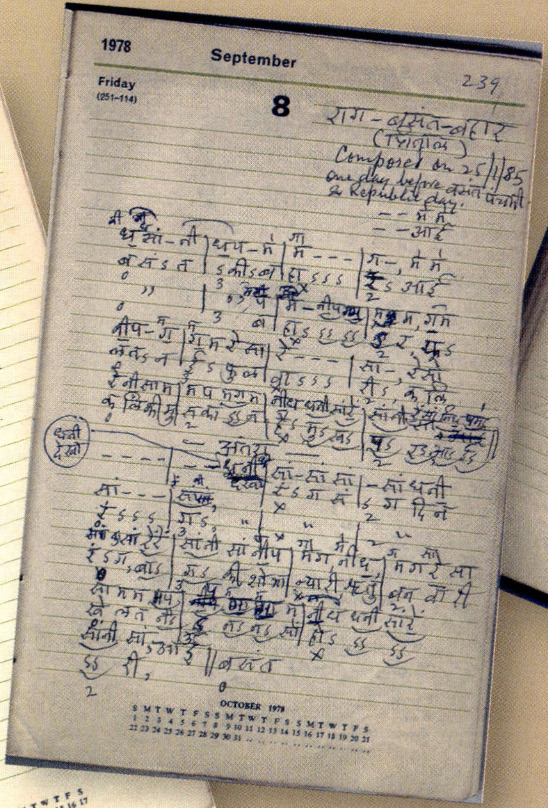

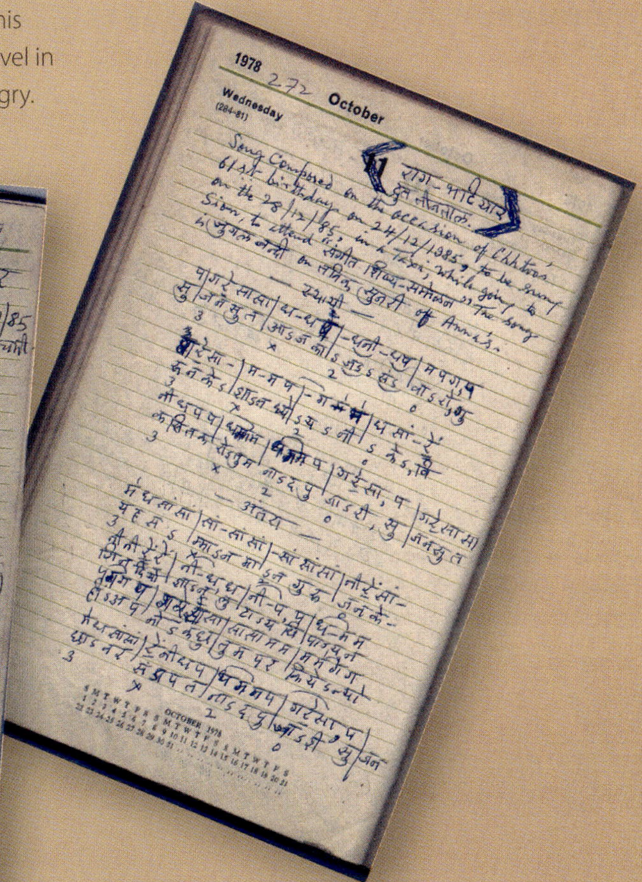

From left to right: Panditji's composition in Gunaranjani, 'Pratham Svarūp'; Notation from his composition 'Āyi basant ki bahār'; Notation from 'Sujan sut āj kāj savāro.' He has noted in the beginning of the last: "Song composed on the occasion of Chhotoo's [K.G. Ginde] 61st birthday on 24/12/1985, in a taxi, while going to Sion to attend 'Sangīt Śisya Sammelan.' The song is jugalbandi on 'Tanik Sunari' of Anna's [Pandit S.N. Ratanjankar]."

Despite the seemingly spiritual nature of creativity, Panditji emphasised that this area can be cultivated with the right tools and concepts. He identified three main components to the creative process: observation, admiration, and indulgence. The first and foremost principle that underlies all creative thought is that of keen observation. Art can only be created by one who can recognise and admire the aesthetic value in any object, and then transfer this appreciation to a new context.

"Whether you hear music, see art, or go about daily life, you must observe your surroundings with a meditative mind. Even right now, I must study the rhythm of how my wife lifted herself and started walking slightly lethargically. When she gives seasoning while cooking, or when she puts salt in the iḍli batter, she never measures it. She just takes the right amount and puts it - that is a meditative quality. For instance, when a child starts crawling, you must observe that laya, the expression in his face, his happiness that he can go forward, the timing. All of this is necessary, so that your mind also gets completely occupied; you are not wasting time or any situation - you are utilising these moments and storing them."

Admiration is appreciating what you have observed. The pleasure you receive from admiring an object should propel you into action to understand more about it. Indulgence refers to the level of involvement that one takes to act upon the observation and admiration - Panditji further expands the three levels of indulgence as mental, verbal and physical. To illustrate this, Panditji describes the situation in which one student sits in to listen to another student's lesson.

"For instance, you have heard the lesson. Mentally have you observed and grasped anything? I was teaching another, but that doesn't mean the lesson was only for him - it was going into your ears, but has it gone into your mind? And does it make you feel like you should also understand the same concept? This is mental indulgence. Verbal indulgence is discussion - asking when you have not understood something from the lesson. Physical indulgence means that you take the tānpurā and sing those ideas that you have understood. If you have not understood it properly, you request and try to understand it. That is why the underlying principle is observation - it should not be casual. When the observation is not casual, that means that you have indulged mentally. Today, I started a poem after seeing a very charming baby. I just saw him more than half a dozen times, but that smile of his was as though he has understood so many things. It was a very experienced sort of smile - I found it very unusual for a child. He just looked like his eyes were telling me something. That inspired me. That is mental indulgence, which immediately inspired physical indulgence, when I started the poem. Those observations are very necessary, especially for an artiste of any line - it is omni-directional observation."

This process was a way of life for Panditji - an aesthetically driven existence. As an artiste, he was constantly a detailed observer of his surroundings, finding beauty and inspiration in things many others may overlook. Whether it was the natural splendour of the environment, the sensual beauty of a woman, or even the pathos of loss, Panditji would find a way to unearth an inherent beauty in all things. Many of his compositions came to life in this manner. He often told the story behind his composition "Panghaṭ pe jal bharan ri mein kaise jāun," a bandiś in Bhairavi. While Panditji was on a bus in Mumbai, travelling from Churchgate to Opera House, he noticed a group of village girls with a lilting walk passing by on the road, carrying earthen pots at their hips with lamps lit inside for the Dussera festival. The bus had stopped for a few moments at the signal, during which he noted the subtle gait of these ladies. Inspired by their swaying movements, he composed the sthāyī of the bandiś instantly, with a similar wave of melodic activity.

In Panditji's ṭhumrī "Dukh ke dinā nahi āve" he evokes a very different shade of Bhairavi, though it was also created in an inspired moment. Panditji was going through a period of helplessness and distress when his eldest son Rajesh was ill. Thoughts of Rajesh's plight consumed his mind, even while he was on the way to a concert hosted by the Suburban Music Circle in Mumbai. In this mental state, he was struck with a sudden self-realisation. "Dukh ke dinā nahi āve, dukh me sukh hove sang hi jāve." Sorrow and joy are two sides of the same coin, and they must coexist. This thought came to him almost as a philosophical and musical message, taking shape as a ṭhumrī. Deeply impassioned by these emotions, he performed a very stirring rendition of the ṭhumrī at the same concert, moving many in the audience to tears. It only revealed that there was not a single moment in Panditji's life that was devoid of an aesthetic outlet: to find a

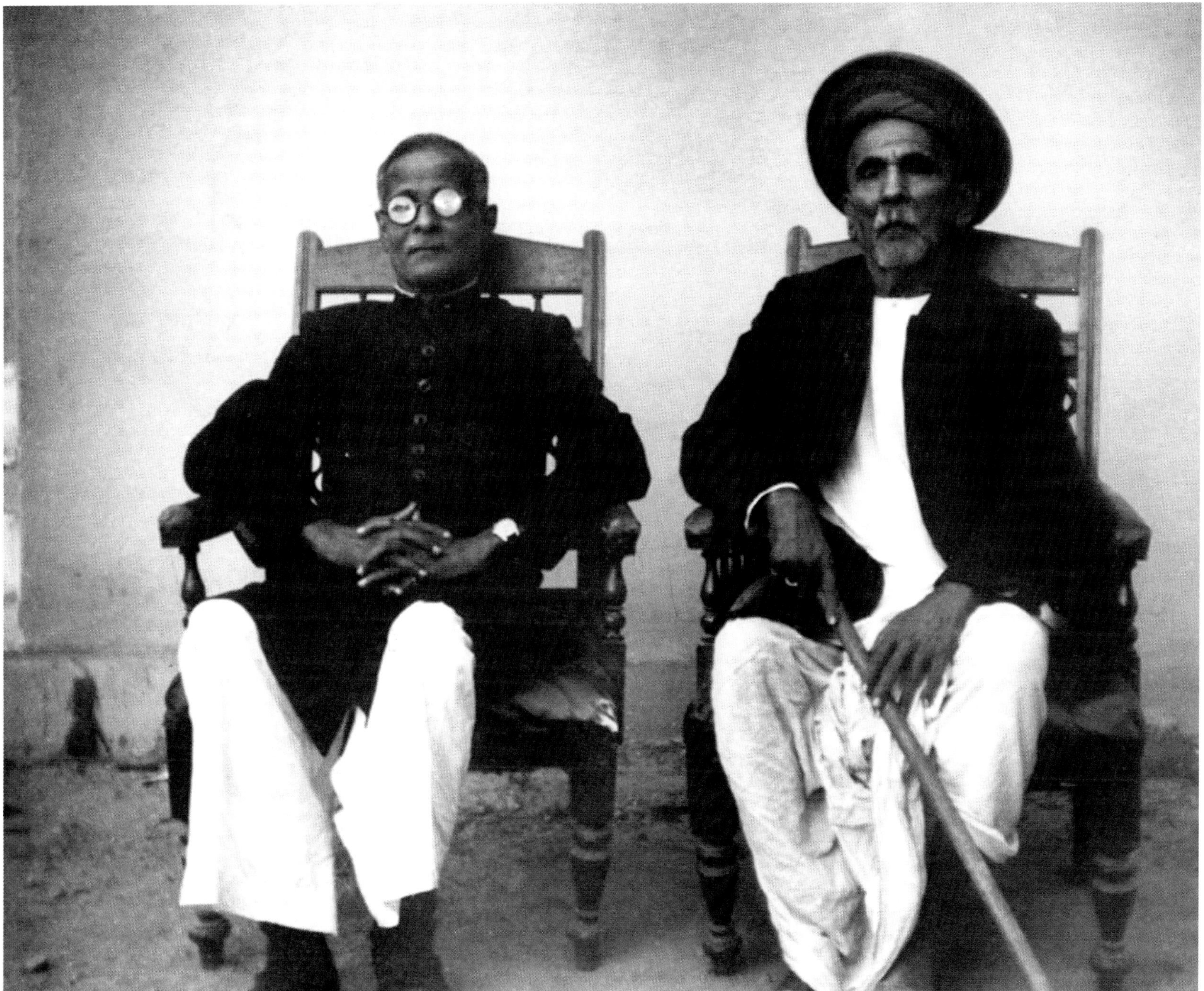
Pandit S.N. Ratanjankar and Pandit Raja Bhaiya Poonchwale

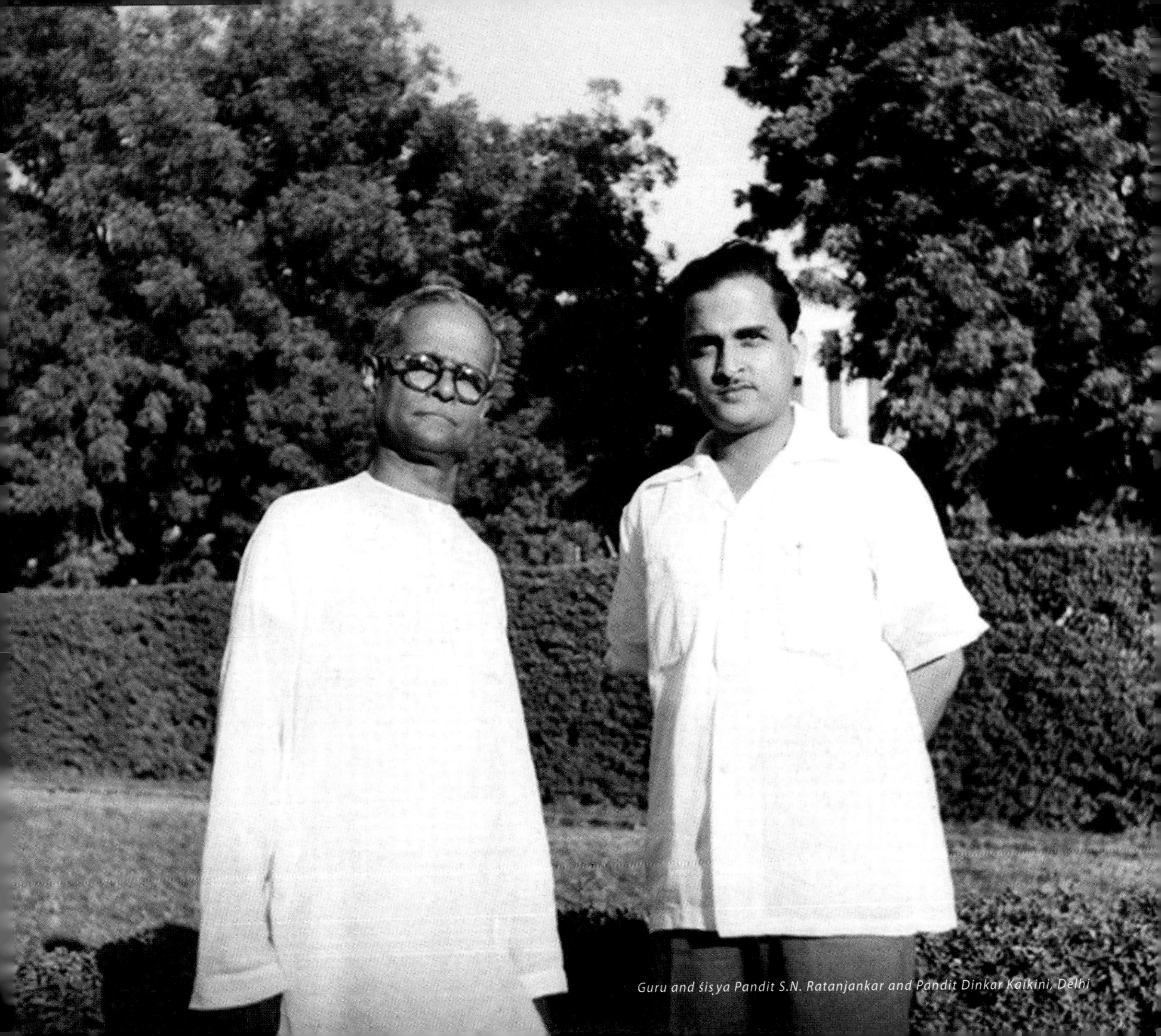

Guru and śiṣya Pandit S.N. Ratanjankar and Pandit Dinkar Kaikini, Delhi

beautiful and profound meaning in his own state of vulnerability, and to channel that into art, was the highest mark of a truly creative artiste.

Creativity Enabling Tools

In Panditji's approach to music, keen observation is a recurring theme that he emphasised in all areas of practice. At the macro-level, observing the world and our surroundings can inspire a wide yet subtle range of ideas or emotions that can be conveyed through music. At a micro-level, he insisted on observing each musical utterance and understanding its purpose. When is a svar introduced and why? What type of development should be used for a phrase and why? Elaboration in Hindustānī music is inspired and spontaneous, but that does not mean that it is random and unintentional. To aid students and musicians in honing these observation skills in a very specific way, Panditji coined terms for musical concepts that are the roots of creative growth. Each concept, when scrutinised closely, guides a musician in exploring the different paths of development of a rāg or bandiś, and the numerous ways to approach a single musical phrase. This is particularly important in an improvisational art form in which it is easy to get stuck in imitation and recollection, especially when students begin learning by repeating after their guru. "You are not a slave to whatever you have learned, you must go beyond that," Panditji said.

The Concept of Ang

The first milestone of development is the "ang." As mentioned earlier, "ang" refers to the essential parts that make a complete whole. In musical terms, an ang can be identified based on its context – in a rāg, khayāl, or svar. At the largest scale, we have rāg-ang. Rāg-ang is a specific arrangement of notes, sung in a particular rhythmic timing, which uniquely defines a particular rāg. This concept was defined by Pandit Bhatkhande in Kramik Pusthak Mālikā in which he documented such phrases for hundreds of rāg-s. A sound understanding of rāg-ang is essential in Hindustānī Rāgsangīt, as one scale does not necessarily make only one rāg. There are many cases of rāg-s with the same scale, but which are distinct from each other because of their particular melodic and rhythmic phraseology – their rāg-ang. The rāg-ang phrases are the signs that allow the vocalist to navigate the map of the rāg. Each phrase is an essential component – it must be visited, but then expanded by the vocalist. The identity of the rāg is already defined, but the "rāg svarūp," as Panditji defined, is "your personal involvement with the rāg."

Panditji took the same concept and applied it to the context of the khayāl. Khayāl-ang refers to the core phrases around which a bandiś is composed. Just as rāg-ang provides benchmarks for unfolding the rāg, khayāl-ang provides anchors for development in the context of the composition. In this way, the unfolding of the bandiś is seamlessly woven with the improvisation.

Finally, svar-ang penetrates to the atomic level of the ang concept. Svar-ang is the specific treatment of a note within the context of the rāg and bandiś - it examines the specific microtone of a svar (śruti), in relation to its neighbouring svar-s and its use in the composition and rāg. "If you're not careful, sometimes you can give the feeling of a different rāg," Panditji said, citing the examples of Bhairav, Ramkali and Jogiya. All of these morning rāg-s share similar scales and the note komal riṣabh, sung in varied śruti-s and timings that are unique to each. The process of mastering svar-ang requires intense concentration and a finely developed ear.

Phrase Development

Taken out of the context of rāg or khayāl, each musical phrase can also be viewed under a microscopic lens. What are the basic elements that constitute a phrase? First, Panditji directs students to the ideas of gṛha, auns, and nyās. Gṛha, literally meaning "home," originally referred to the starting note of a song. Gradually, the term was used to refer to the first note of a phrase. Panditji took this to a different level by applying it to delineation in Rāgsangīt. One should pay attention to the gṛha svar being used in each utterance and consciously vary it to avoid repetitiveness. Many times this svar is very lightly touched, almost grazed, before reaching another svar. Still, this detail should be executed with awareness and intention. Likewise, the nyās svar is the ending note of a phrase, whether prominently pronounced or lightly touched. Varying the starting and ending svar-s of phrases intentionally brings forth the different relationships between notes and breaks the predictability of the development. It also requires complete alertness at all times. Finally auns, according to Panditji's interpretation, is the timing and proportionality of connecting the gṛha and nyās svar-s.

Another lens that can be used to view a musical phrase is that of varṇ. Varṇ refers to the direction of the movement of notes – ārohī, avarohī, sthāyī and sancārī. Ārohī varṇ is the patterning of notes in ascending order, and avarohī varṇ is in descending order. Sthāyī varṇ is the repetition of the same note in its place, and sancārī is the mixed usage of ārohī, avarohī, and sthāyī, and is also the most commonly used approach to phrases in general. Any phrase can be deconstructed in this way - whether in an ālāp or a tān - and it is important to be aware of the pattern's varṇ to avoid mechanical repetition.

"Varṇ is just like painting," said Panditji. "Lines going upward, downward, sideways, left to right, right to left. It is creating an image of a coil or arch, or jagged lines. You can only mould your svarā-s and phrases when that level of awareness and imagination is present." If one visualises the movement of what he or she is singing, rather than getting bogged down in the technicalities, these variations will manifest themselves. Panditji is a strong proponent of drawing upon other art forms, whether it is fine art, theatre or dance, as inspiration for music.

"Even while uttering svarā-s I am painting, not just one colour , but several shades. I may draw a combination of shades or patterns - it is all abstract, but in my mind I give it a concrete shape. The next day when I sing, I will visualise a different shape and sing that, and each time I sing I should feel like producing something new. We should not be like typewriters, always creating letters of the same shape…When we sing, we create an image. The movement of the notes is what delineates these images."

Simeen Oshidar, Mumbai-based visual artist and student of Panditji, has found Panditji's musical lessons intertwined with her work as a painter. She recounts him telling her: "Everything is connected. Nothing is separate; we only perceive it as separate and that is our misfortune. Your music will help you paint and your painting will inspire you to sing." These words still resonate with her thirty years later. "Whenever I sit to work at my paintings, things that he said about form and the fleeting nature of form; the nature of sound, the abstract form that sound takes; the stillness from which all form arises and dies into; all these relate to both our work and to our lives."

Inspiration of Laya

"Laya gives aesthetics to music," Panditji said. Movement, simply put, is what transforms a mere group of notes into a cohesive phrase, sentence, paragraph, and ultimately, a meaningful story. Just as Panditji deconstructed phrases with respect to svar, he has done the same in relation to laya. The laya, or rhythmic timing of phrase, can exist with just a single note - how long is it held? That length is its timing. However, the moment a note is in the context of a musical phrase, its placement must be handled with extreme precision and awareness to convey the desired effect. For example, you can take just two notes, re and sa, and experiment with altering the length of each, changing the degree of mīnd (the depth of the gliding) taken to connect the two notes. It could be a deep, gradual mīnd, or a sharp jump from note to note. This subtlety can often distinguish two similar rāg-s. Changing the timing and mīnd between pa and śuddh re differentiates many rāg-s in Kalyān thāṭ (the family of Kalyān rāg-s), such as Yaman, Chāyānaṭ, and Bhūpālī.

Just as we have discussed methods to form melodic patterns, the same concepts apply in laya patterns. In Hindustānī Rāgsangīt, rhythmic patterns are abstract, as they are conceived by the musician and do not have a detailed method of notation in the way that Western classical music does. The musician must therefore have a clear idea and execution of the pattern. In a fast moving piece, such as a tān, rhythmic patterns are easier to grasp as they are more obvious and concrete. Within eight notes, for instance, one can create different phrases by grouping the notes into two groups of four, one of five and three, and so on. By changing the division and emphasis (known as chand) of a phrase, its entire character and effect changes. Even in an ālāp, a phrase has a certain timing, and the rhythmic movement of these slower phrases should be observed closely and varied. This is what Panditji termed "abstract laya," where the division of time and the meter is up to the artiste to visualise and execute. There is no external guide - like a tāl cycle - for the artiste to use as a reference. This laya must be felt internally.

When one combines rhythmic variations with melodic patterns, there are a boundless number of combinations. One such example is the idea of "samaprakritic phrases," as coined by Panḍitji. These phrases are melodically and rhythmically symmetrical. For instance take the Kalyan ang phrase: pa re ga re ni re sa. Its counterpart phrase in the other half of the octave would be: sa dha ni dha ma dha pa. This transposition of notes is melodic symmetry - if the same timing is maintained for both phrases, it would have laya symmetry as well. Similarly, the timing of two phrases can be maintained while the notes are asymmetrical, so they are symmetrical only with respect to laya. Identifying these relationships between phrases opens up possibilities for rāg and composition development.

Nava Rasa

All of the mentioned concepts are aids that will guide a singer to creative independence and freedom, the highest goal in the process of musicianship. But, one should never lose sight of the first and foremost intention of music - "the purpose of Rāgsangīt is to express human emotions. That is the main characteristic of Indian music." In the ancient text, Nātyaśāstra, Bharat Muni outlined the nine main states of human mind for enhancing the understanding of theatre. The nine emotions, or nava rasa, are: sringār (romantic), karunā (pathos), bhakti (devotion), vīr (heroic), raudra (anger), bhayānak (fear), vibhatsa (disgust), hasya (humour) and śānta (peace). While all of these emotions can be visually exhibited in theatre, in vocal music only sringār, karunā, bhakti, vīr, and śānta can be sung. In a bandiś, the vocalist must pay attention to the rasa of the text. Each word should be analysed and various depictions conceived. If the nāyikā, or the heroine, is asking a question, for instance, in what way is she doing so? Is she demanding, pleading, hesitant, forlorn? This is up to the vocalist to imagine and execute, using the previously mentioned techniques. Emotional variation can be expressed even without the support of words or complex phrases - the gradations of śruti-s are the source of emotional content, and the very subtle use of these can convey a different emotion.

Stages of the Creative Journey

While these tools are certainly helpful, the creative journey is long and enduring. Panditji classifies the stages of creative progress in three phases: recollecting, recreating, and creating. "When you are focused on remembering what you have learned and repeating that, your mind is busy recollecting those ideas. In this phase, the mind is so busy recalling and replicating that there is no room for new thought - the ideas become stagnant, and it becomes difficult to think differently. Once you are used to recollecting and you have performed enough to gain familiarity, you are in the re-creative phase. You are able to re-create those ideas without the effort of recollection because they have been internalised. The final and ultimate phase is creation, in which the thought and execution of ideas are born in the present moment. Here you are no longer a slave to what you have learned."

Breaking Rules

Inundated with guidelines, I asked Panditji how rigid these boundaries were in Hindustānī Rāgsangīt. He reminisced about his idol, Ustad Faiyaz Khan, when he gave me his response.

"While we must adhere to certain rules in our elaboration, liberty can occasionally be taken to cross those rules for the sake of bringing more abstract beauty to music. For instance, my Guruji used to respect Faiyaz Khan Saheb very much, and once we went to hear a concert of Khan Saheb's together. Guruji was never in the habit of saying vāh, āhā, or such praise. He would just close his eyes and listen, regardless of whether the music was good or bad. Khan Saheb started with a Nom-Tom ālāp in Megh Malhar, and at a certain point he surprisingly sang komal gandhār.

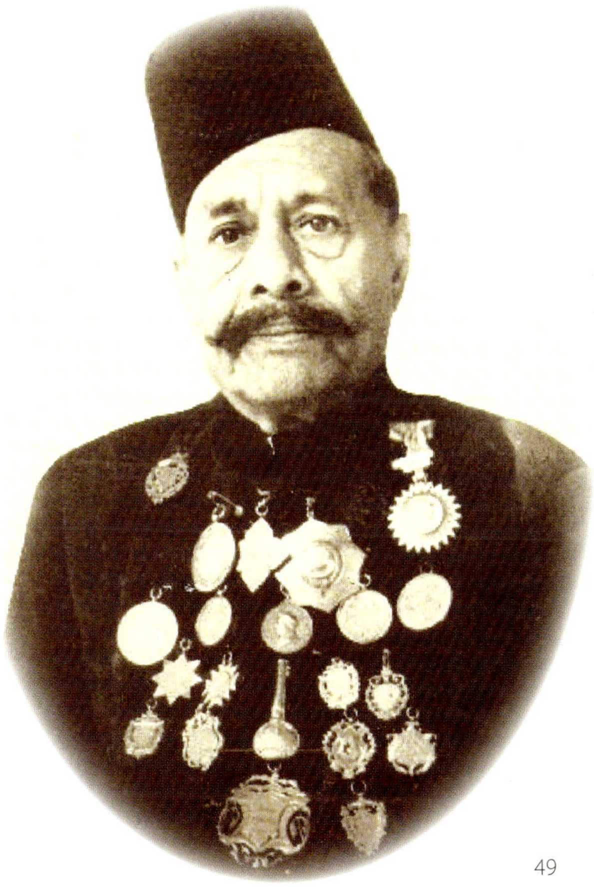

Panditji's idol, Ustad Faiyaz Khan

My Guruji immediately opened his eyes, because komal gandhār is not included in Megh Malhar. Khan Saheb immediately noticed his reaction and said on the stage, 'Sri Krishna, yeh tumhāre liye nahi, hum logon ke liye hai.'

"He had confessed that he was doing a musical experiment at the moment that was meant for the enjoyment of listeners, not scholars. If you add komal gandhār to Megh Malhar, there is no difference between Kānadā and Malhār. But he simply added it like mukhvās, just as we might have pān after eating a good meal for a pleasant taste. Nowadays, however, many Agra Gharānā singers use komal gandhār in Megh Malhar excessively and it has blurred the distinction between Malhār and Kānadā. That is where śāstra is important - aesthetics should not be devoid of śāstra. While teaching a student, you must teach them absolutely pure music. If the teacher starts doing such experiments and doesn't explain the reasoning, the students will blindly imitate. For instance, I've composed a bandiś in Bihāg in which I sometimes sing komal niṣād, a svar that does not come in that rāg. From a śāstriya point of view, if I teach anybody this song, I won't use this komal niṣād. This is meant to be done only at the performance level, when the artiste is in the full creative mood and is inspired at the spur of the moment to boldly take a creative risk. It is a beauty spot - it is meant to be shown, but not elaborated. One such is nice, but if there are five or six it spoils the beauty."

Aesthetics

With all these tools and concepts that help generate various permutations and combinations of notes, how do we know which ones to use? This is where aesthetics plays a key role in distinguishing a vocal acrobat from a soulful and sensitive musician. Being able to sing infinite combinations of notes or phrases shows skill, but the ability to present the winning phrases among these, and to use these at the right moments and in the right proportion, is musicianship.

"Aesthetics is beauty, and without aesthetics music lacks imagination and is not artistic. When a musician begins rendering, it is not enough just to follow the rules and develop a rāg within the boundaries. Whatever is uttered must have beauty - a delicacy and attention to the way it is uttered."

The role of an artiste is to create the appropriate conditions for the inherent beauty of the art to shine through. "If you set a diamond in a very shabby way, the beauty of the diamond is marred by the setting. In music also, I must create a place for the combinations that I feel are beautiful. That place that I create and the supporting phrases should be thoughtful so that the intended beauty comes out. How can you beautify beauty? That is the artiste's job."

How can this type of aesthetic sensibility be developed? Again, Panditji refers to his belief in observation and questioning. "If you observe something and appreciate it, ask yourself, 'Why do I like this?' What attractive qualities does it possess? Or, if you don't like it, what is it you don't like about it? And what could be done to make it more appealing?" This line of thinking cultivates an attitude towards aesthetics in all disciplines. "In performance aesthetics comes first, and then comes the imagination. You should form a habit and attitude that whatever you do should be beautiful. After all, art is beauty, which penetrates within you and reaches the soul."

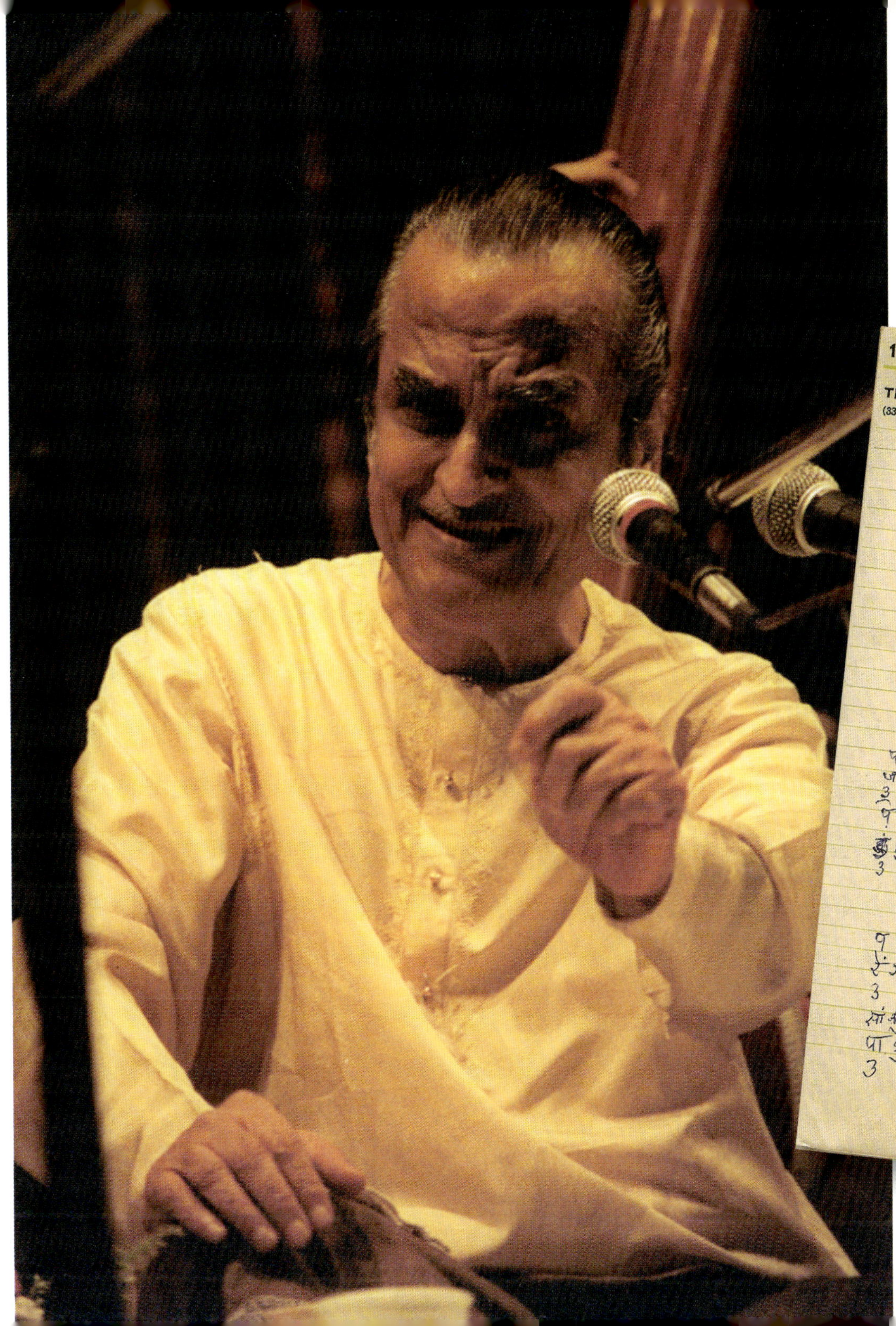

Panditji performing in Mumbai

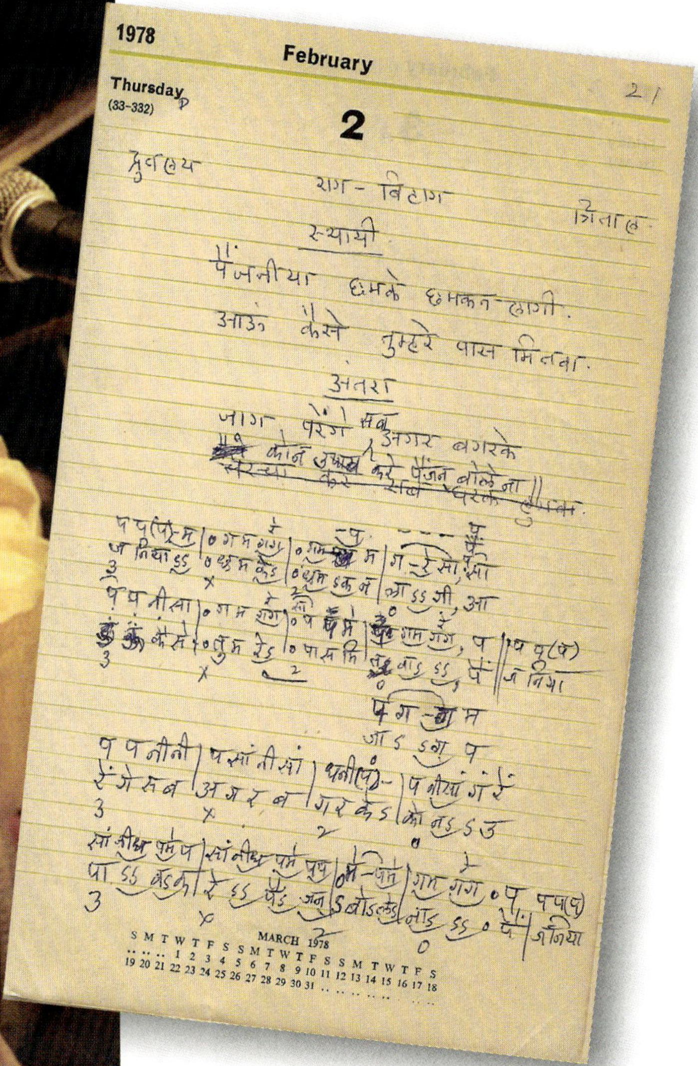

Notation for 'Painjanīya chamake,' in rāg Bihāg

Panditji being felicitated by Professor B.R. Deodhar

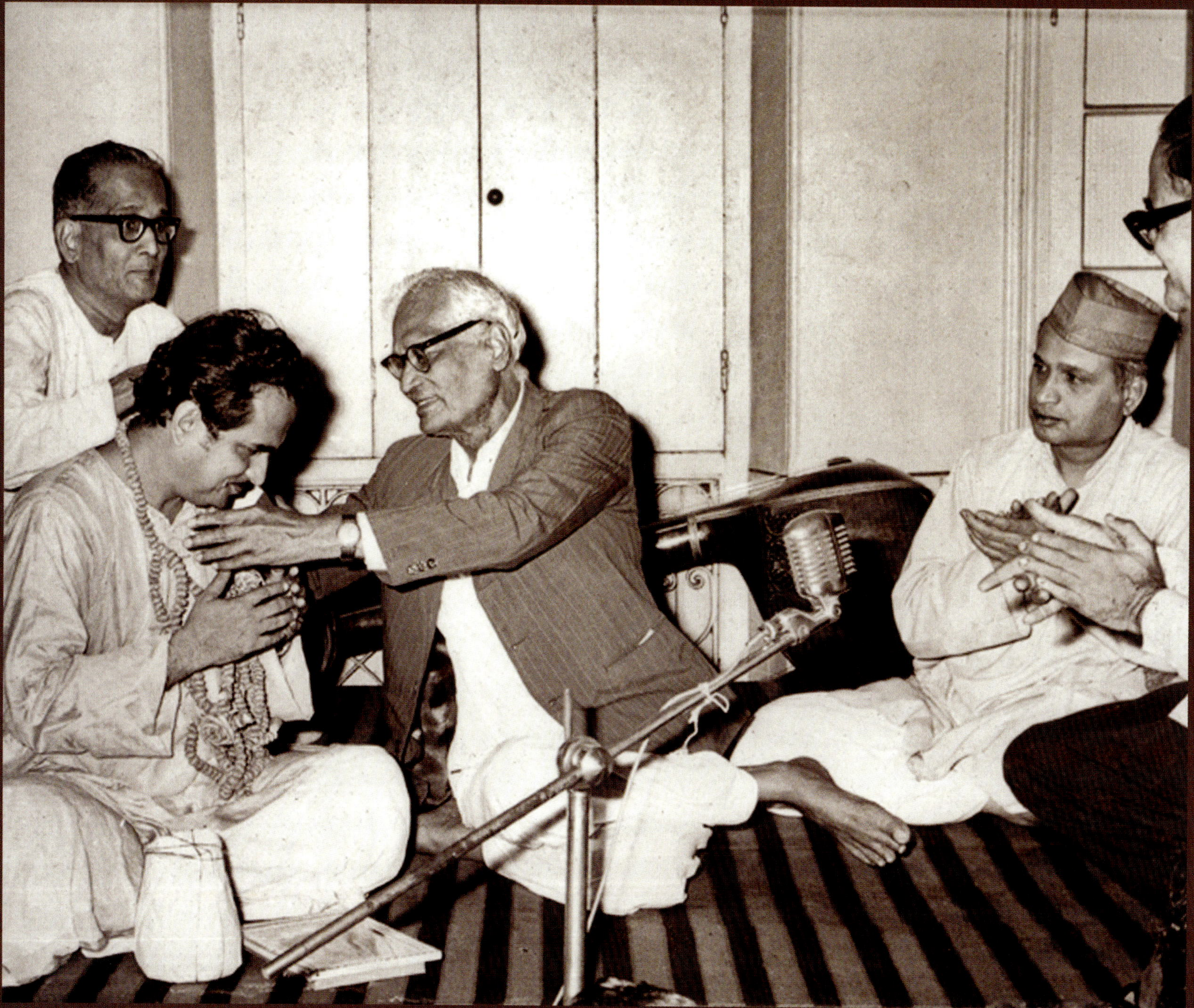

BLOSSOMING OF A MUSICIAN

"I prayed to Tirupati Balaji that I should get a wife like Shashikala, and it was miraculous."

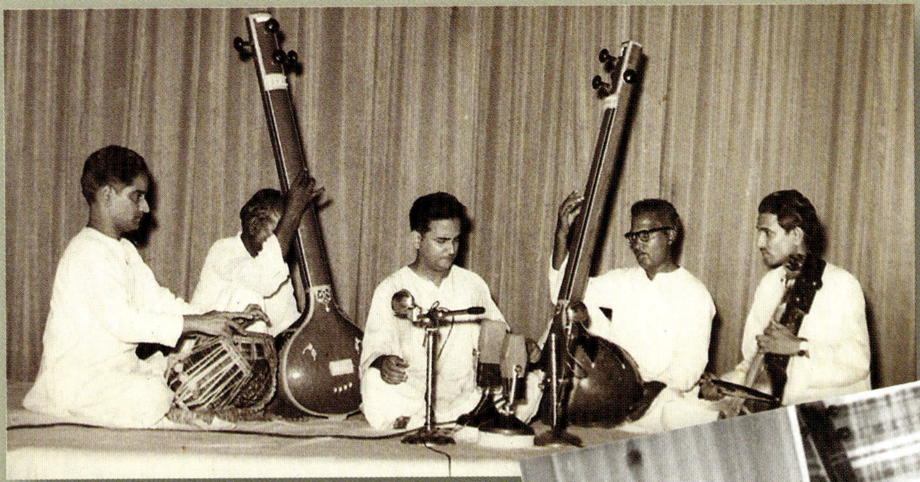

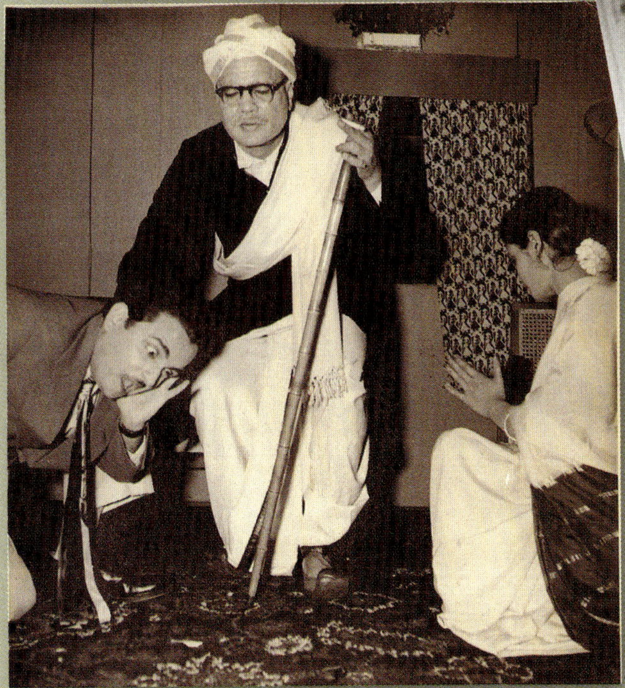

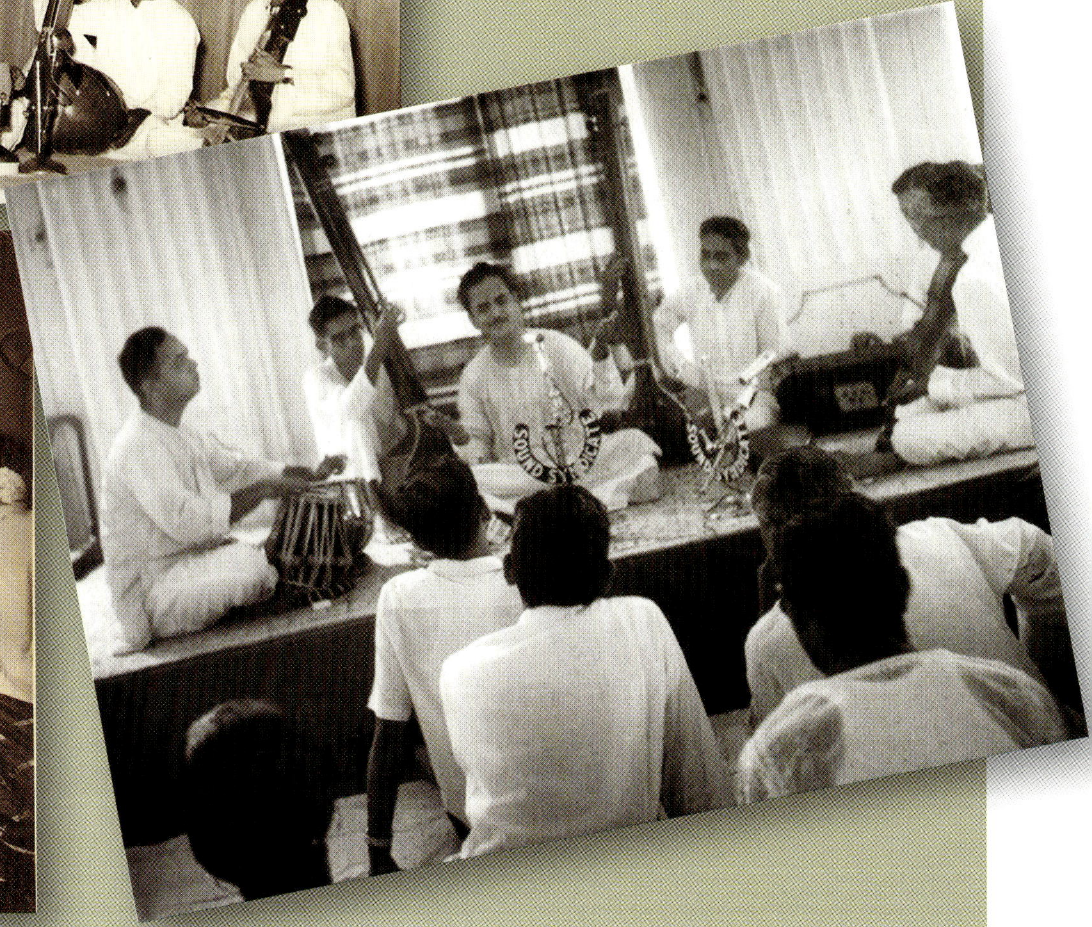

Left: Panditji in concert, Delhi, 1955; Bottom Left: Panditji acting in a drama for the Konkani Association, Delhi, 1956
Below: Live in concert, Hyderabad, 1959, accompanied by Sri Gaurang Kodikal on tablā

Post-Lucknow

Panditji was known as a young artiste to be reckoned with by the time he had left Lucknow. His schedule started to fill up with requests for mehfil-s around the country, and his concerts were very well received by audiences. He travelled to Mangalore, Cochin, Chennai, Kolkata, and around Maharashtra giving a series of performances. He enjoyed a youthful freedom to travel the country to perform, to stay at length with different patrons and well-wishers, and to nurture the musical seeds that had been planted in Lucknow in great depth. It was a period of zealous riyāz and performances that had the gusto of a young man in his twenties, ripe from years of tālīm.

He applied his musical training in different contexts when the opportunities arose. He scored music for theatre and film projects, and on several occasions acted in plays himself. Acting was a second passion of Panditji's – during his summer holidays in Mumbai, he would often act in productions in amateur Konkani and Marathi theatre groups. He had even been offered roles in films, which he declined because of his music studies. His love for theatre continued as he composed music for various plays. He also began a fruitful collaboration with Pandit Ravi Shankar. The young and popular sitār player had invited Panditji to work with him on the Discovery of India Ballet, a musical and dance production detailing the history of India from the Ramayana to Indian Independence in 1947. Panditji worked with the voices of the chorus, sang, and occasionally performed special roles himself.

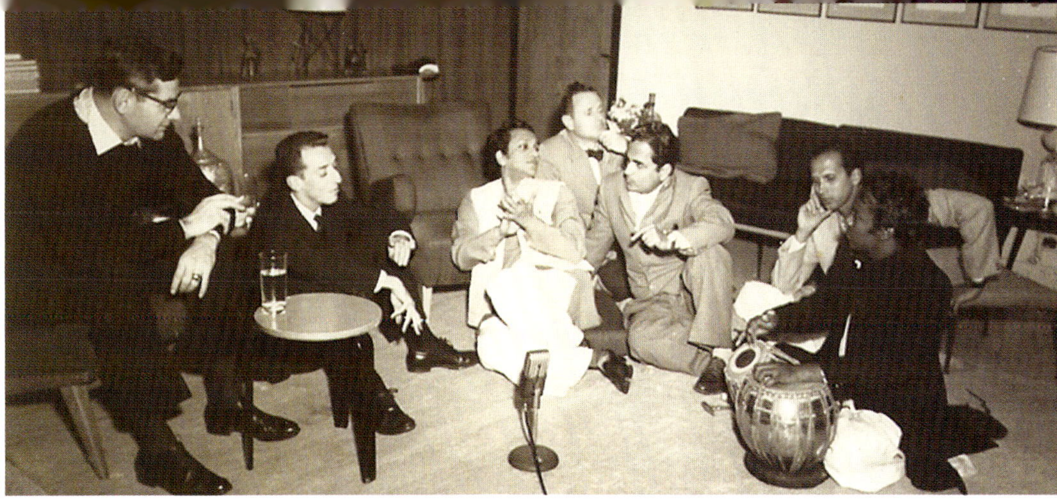

Panditji with Pandit Ravi Shankar and other musicians, Delhi, 1955.

"I would make the sound of the shehnai and other instruments through my voice. When we performed before Nehru, even Lord and Lady Mountbatten said to Ravi Shankar, 'I find only Indian instruments there. During the entry of the character Ghorā Saheb music was played on a trombone. How is that possible?' He replied to them, 'No we have a living trombone with us!' and then he introduced me. 'Can you do it for us?' they asked. I demonstrated for them and they were very impressed!" The show was highly acclaimed and toured Mumbai, Delhi and Kolkata.

During the tour in Kolkata, Panditji had his second opportunity to perform as a soloist in front of Faiyaz Khan Saheb. A major music conference was taking place and on the schedule was a back-to-back programme by Pandit Ravi Shankar and Ustad Vilayat Khan. A day earlier, the organiser of the programme had realised that having two consecutive sitār recitals may not be appealing, and sought to have a buffer concert. He remembered hearing the voice of Tansen in the Discovery of India ballet, and told his secretary to find that singer and give him a 45-minute slot between the sitār-ists. The voice in question was, of course, Panditji, and he accepted the offer.

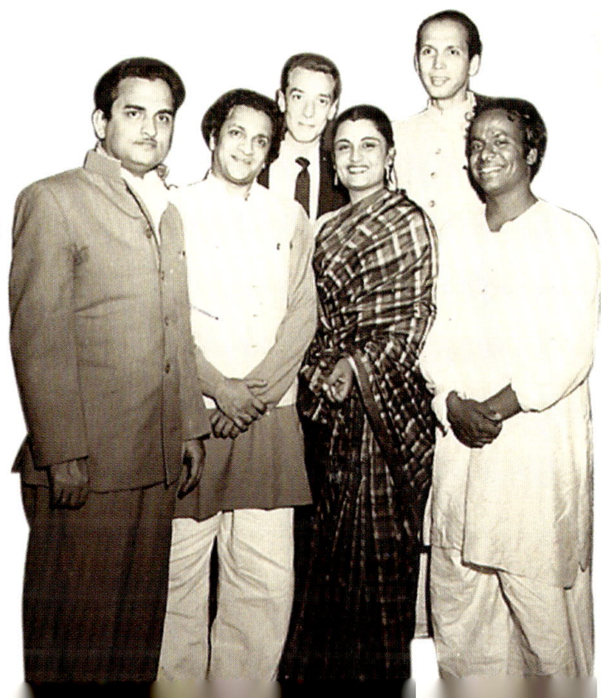

Left to right: Panditji, Pandit Ravi Shankar, Joel Rossen, Sundari Sridharan, Sri Harihar Rao, Sri Chaturlal

Many of the leading artistes of the time were present at the conference. Ustad Faiyaz Khan, Ustad Mushtaq Hussain Khan, Ustad Bismillah Khan, and Ustad Bade Ghulam Ali Khan were all seated in the front, as they had just finished hearing Pandit Ravi Shankar's concert.

"The instant my name was announced – Dinkar Kaikini – which had no 'Khan' in it, and when I appeared on the stage looking frail (I must have weighed only 70 pounds at the time), people started leaving the hall. Khan Saheb was sitting in the front, encouraging me by saying, 'Beṭa, tum gāo.' He insisted that the other musicians stay. 'Arre Ghulam Ali, baiṭho baiṭho. Sri Krishna ka śāgird hai. Bahut achchā gāta hai, suno.' I was inspired, because the great musicians of those days, including Khan Saheb were listening to me. I started with a nom-tom ālāp of Bhairav-Bahār. My concert started at 11:30 am, so I compromised with Bhairav and Bahār, which was unusual. At any conference in Kolkata they would keep loudspeakers outside. My singing was amplified outdoors, and since my style was the same as Faiyaz Khan Saheb's, people thought he was singing! Within five minutes the hall was packed."

The nom-tom ālāp itself took 40 minutes, so Panditji completed it and apologised to the audience. He announced that if they would like him to continue, he would be happy to do so, otherwise he didn't want to exceed the time limit. The organiser was enamoured by his performance thus far and insisted that he continue. He continued with Bhairav-Bahār for one and half hours but the crowd was still not satiated. They shouted requests for a ṭhumrī, so Panditji concluded with Khan Saheb's famous Dādrā in Bhairavi, "Banāo Batiyān." The concert was a tremendous success, after which Khan Saheb immediately asked for Panditji to come forward and take his blessings. "Beṭa, tum bahut achcha gate ho!"

While his performance career was soaring, teaching had also become an important part of his profession – many admirers and aficionados of his individualistic style sought his guidance. One of his students was Shashikala Samsi, a highly talented singer who was preparing for her Vishārad exams. Her family had a longtime association with Panditji; her cousin Mohan Kallianpurkar was a close friend of his and head of the Kathak department at Lucknow as well. Her uncle, Prabhakar Chandavarkar, was an ardent fan who organised his concerts in Bangalore, and had even anonymously sponsored some of his education. Her father, who was intensely passionate about music, also had a very high opinion of Panditji. He sent his daughter to him for training in the more advanced rāg-s required for her exams.

Though he was a severely strict, sometimes tear-inducing guru during lessons, a certain unspoken spark was kindled between him and Shashikala after they had known each other for a few years. "There was that feeling - you don't have to talk about it, you just know. You give those vibes to the other person," said Shashikalaji. Panditji recognised in Shashikala the kind of partner he envisioned to have in life: one who would steadily support his career, share his passion for this art, and nurture a balanced family life. Still, their union took place gradually over a sequence of fortuitous events.

"I had a concert in Bangalore and Shashikala and her mother were to go there to see an alliance for her. It so happened that we all went together, and after my concert, they would go to see the boy. In the meantime my father sent me a telegram telling me that I had been called for a job in South Africa. They wanted to interview me, so I needed

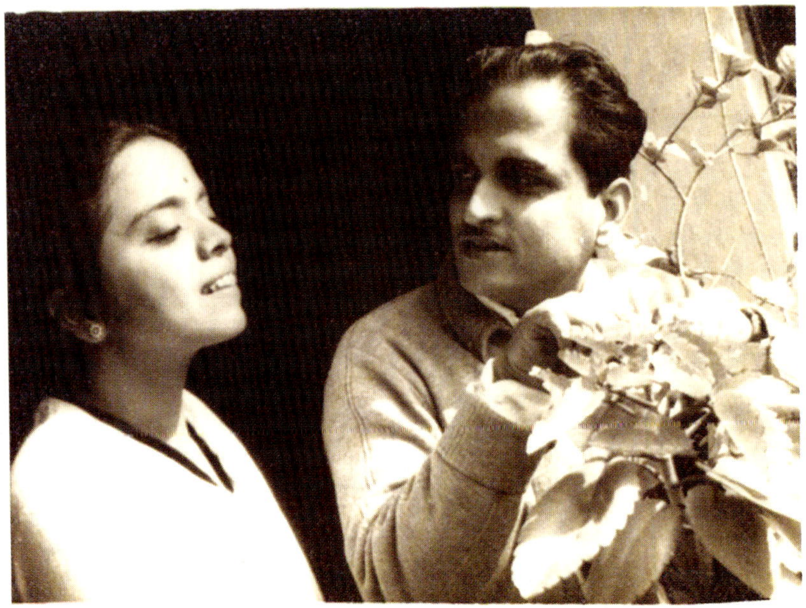

Panditji and his wife, Smt Shashikala Kaikini, Delhi 1958

to go back immediately. I decided to go the next day itself. Shashikala suddenly said that she did not want to see that boy, so that meeting was cancelled. She and her mother suggested that we all go back together."

Suniti, Shashikala's sister, suspected that her sister may have had feelings for Panditji after her sudden decision to leave Bangalore without meeting the prospective alliance, and at the news that he may be leaving for South Africa. She approached her sister, who told her that she would be open to the idea. Suniti then took it upon herself to confront Panditji about his feelings on the alliance. "Suniti came and drove me to some remote place and said, 'There is one thing I would like to discuss with you, if you don't get angry. How do you like Shashikala?' I told her that she was very nice, of a good nature. Then she specified, 'No, as a life partner?' I told her, 'I have not even thought about that at all, and it will be difficult for me to answer this question just now. Because my attitude towards her has always been as a teacher or guide.'"

Panditji then took some time to discuss the prospect with his father. Dattatreya was pleased with the pairing, as he knew the Samsi family and respected them. He was also aware of several women who had shown interest in Panditji earlier, including one young and beautiful Muslim actress. She was a persistent suitor, and Panditji was well aware of the stupor that can result from this kind of attraction. "In that state of mind, you can become totally blind. I might have accepted also, I can't say! But my goal towards music was very high, and I couldn't sacrifice that." After speaking to his father, he called Suniti with his decision, and she proceeded to tell her parents and finalise their engagement.

During the same trip to Bangalore, Panditji made a short side trip to Tirupati. Coincidentally, he was seeking Lord Balaji's blessings for a suitable wife before he possibly left for his new job opportunity in South Africa. "I prayed to Tirupati Balaji that I should get a wife like Shashikala, and it was miraculous," Panditji said.

His prayers were answered, and the marriage was fixed in 1955, to take place in 1957. Because of their engagement, he declined the position he had been offered in South Africa. His father-in-law did not want him to go away for a period of time after they had agreed to get married. Instead, Panditji took a job offer at All India Radio in Delhi as Producer for the Light Music Unit. The newly wed couple would begin their married life in Delhi.

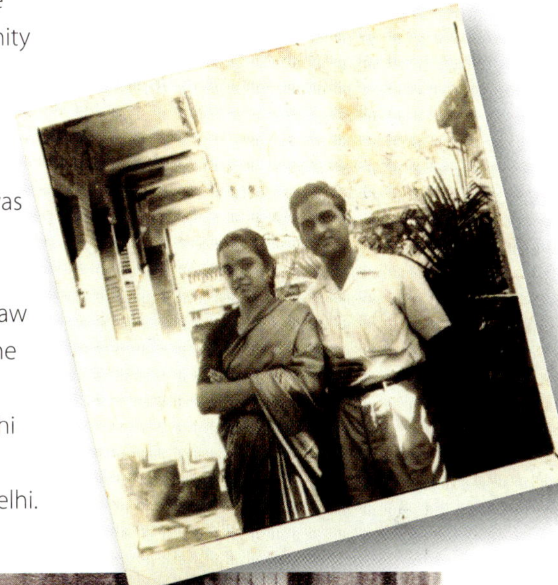

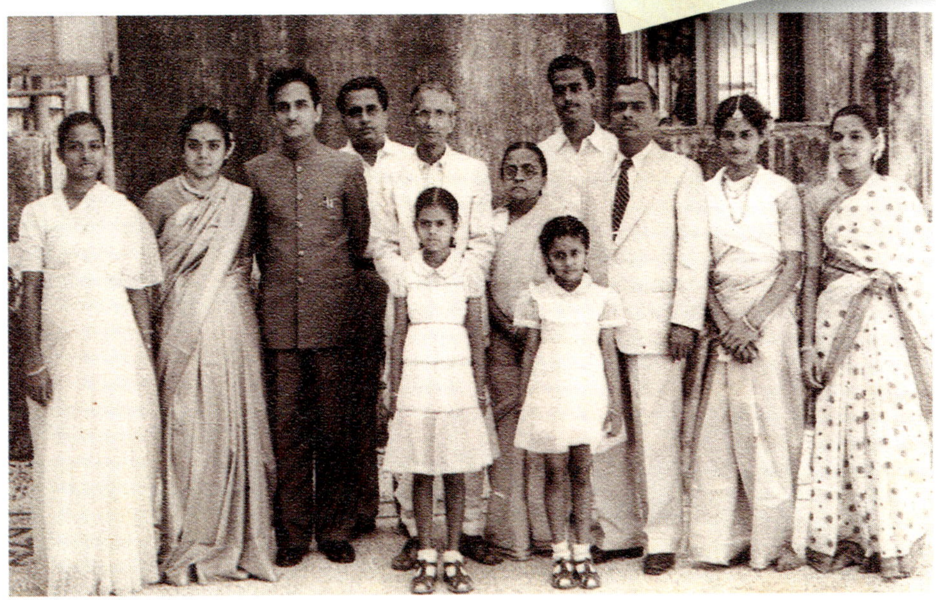

Top Right: Panditji and Shashikalaji outside her home in Mumbai; Above: Kaikini family, December 1956, Mumbai

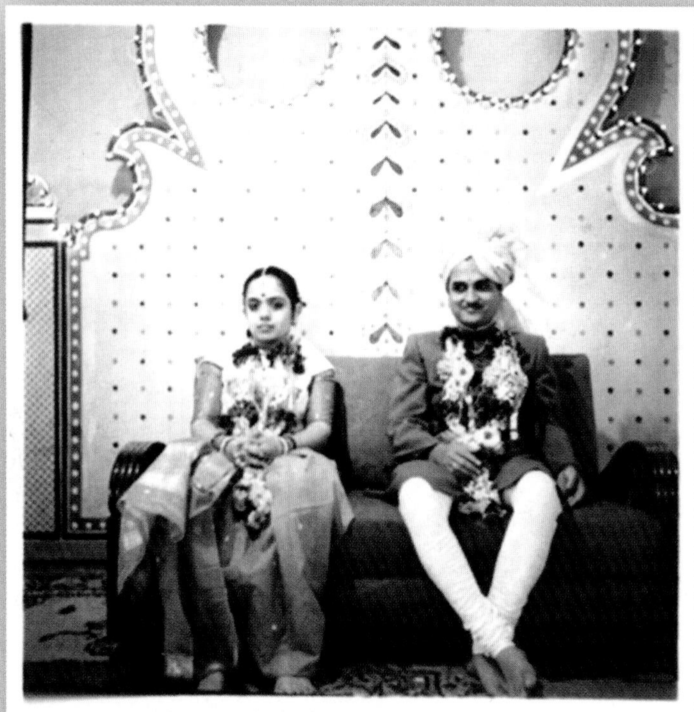

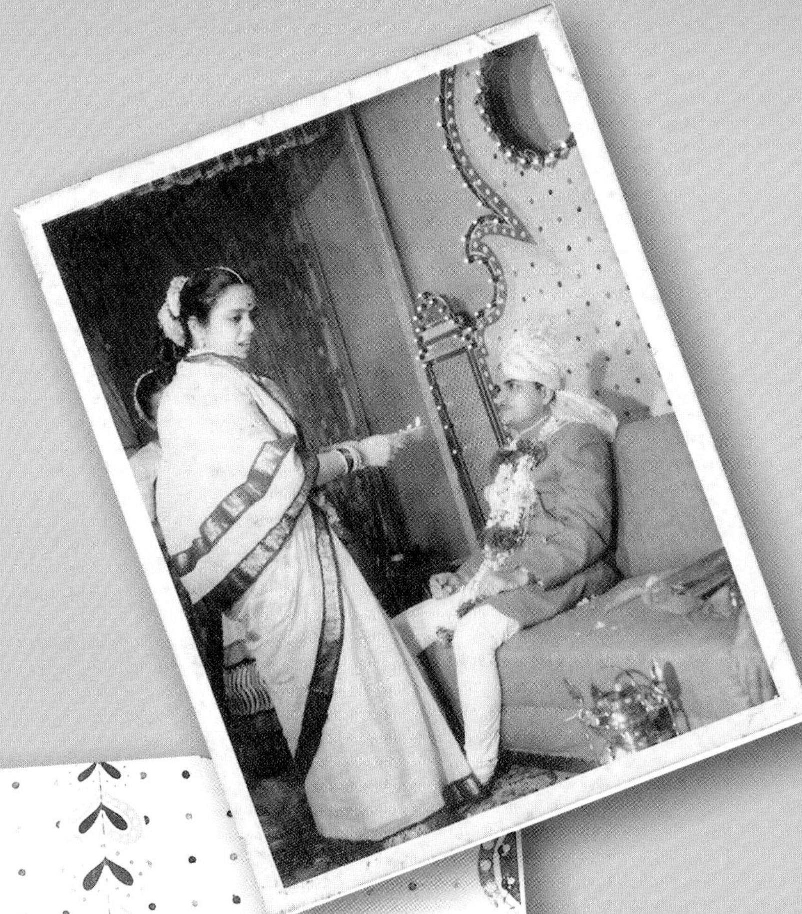

Moments from the wedding of Panditji and Smt Shashikala Kaikini, Mumbai, 1957

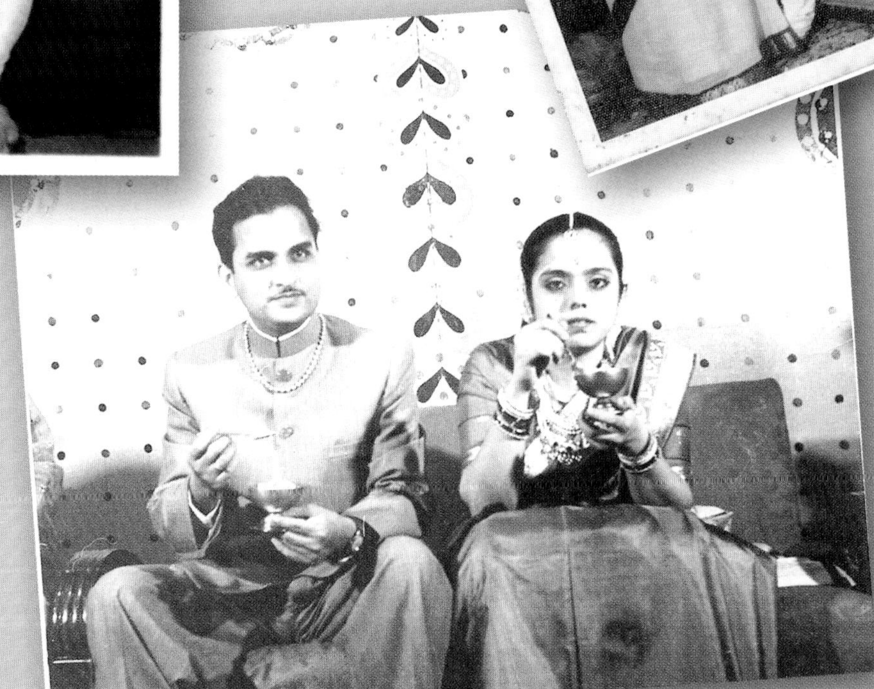

Delhi

"I had a lovely married life in Delhi," Shashikalaji says. "Though there was a financial crunch, I didn't mind that kind of hard life. I was prepared to do any amount of work – housework, outside earnings, my own practising - and I did all of that. His [Panditji's] nature was extremely affectionate, loving. He looked after the children, was interested in cooking – I learned a lot from him. There were certain dishes, especially non-vegetarian, that he taught me to make. He was also extremely particular about the house being neat, the children clean and dressed well before he came in the evening."

In retrospect, Panditji remembered these days and acknowledged the significant role of his wife in his entire life. "In my case, eighty percent of the credit I give to my wife, because she is most concerned about the family, including myself. Whatever help I could have given, I gave. But Shashikala did eighty percent, and she was concerned about each member of the family."

While they were in Delhi, the Kaikini family grew to include their three children: Rajesh, Aditi, and Yogesh. Panditji was a loving and sensitive father to all his children, often smothering them with hugs, kisses and pinches on the cheek.

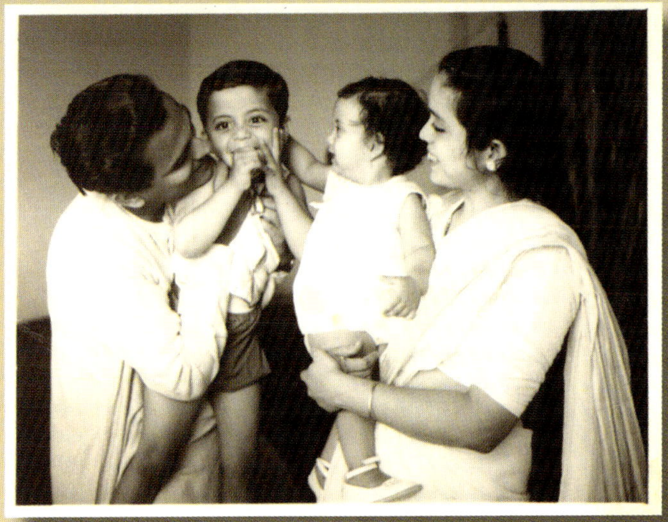

Panditji and Shashikalaji with eldest son, Rajesh, and daughter, Aditi, Delhi, 1962

"He was a very close and attentive father, very cued into what was happening No matter how busy he was he always made time for us... He was very deeply caring, always there when you needed him. He was also very physically affectionate, more so than even my mother," said his daughter, Aditi.

Balance was important to Panditji in everything, including parenting. His eldest son Rajesh recalls how he maintained expectations of discipline while being very loving. "He used to maintain a type of equilibrium. He was a strict parent and expected us to follow a certain discipline. We had to come home at a certain time, keep the house clean, and also help out in household chores. Aside from that he gave us the freedom to do whatever we liked. He told me if I was not interested in music, I could do whatever I wanted in life."

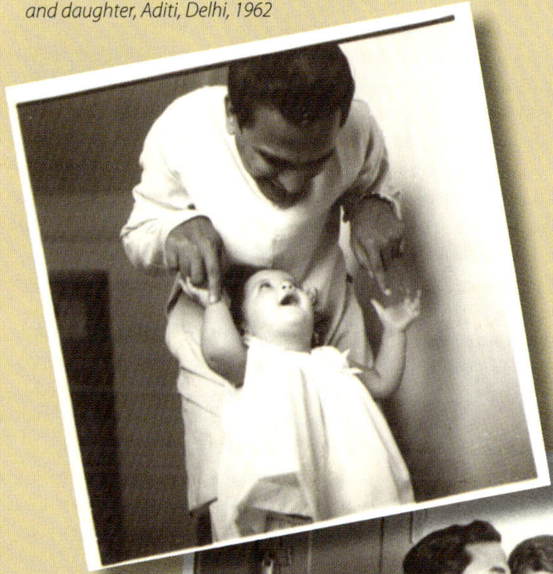

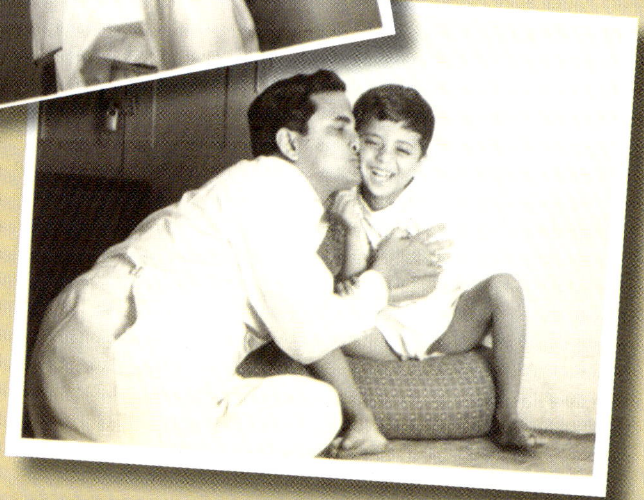

Centre: Panditji with daughter, Aditi, Delhi, 1962
Left: Panditji with son, Rajesh, Delhi, 1965

Having had a childhood rich in sanskār-s of culture, generosity, and humility, Panditji valued these qualities in the upbringing of his children as well. While he insisted that his children pursue their academic studies with diligence, he believed in a holistic approach to education. "My way of thinking about education is not only academic. It is well and good if they have that background and they are groomed, but that is not the only education. Cultural education includes how you behave with others and the way you should think."

This kind of atmosphere was cultivated by quality time that the family had together. "We used to have these spontaneous visits to the nearby parks, which were in plenty then. Amma would pack some food and the four of us would go there on our two-wheeler!" Aditi recalled.

After coming home from work, evenings would be spent listening to the radio, going for walks, or shopping at the vegetable market. "It was all in all a very rich, beautifully simple, and very humble childhood."

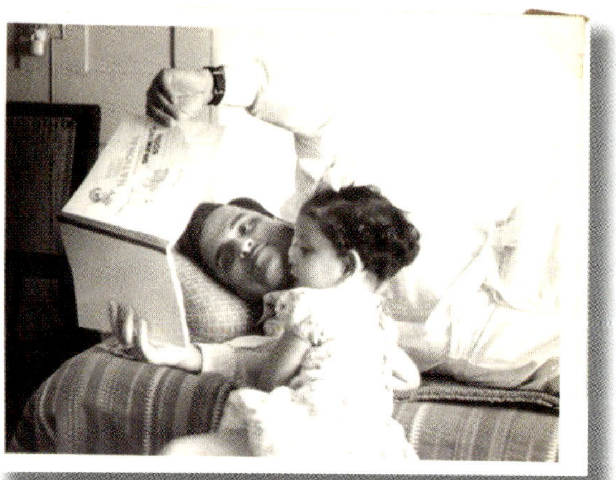

Panditji reading to his daughter, Aditi, Delhi, 1965

His son Yogesh recalls a modest but always tasteful and aesthetic childhood. "We lived an extremely simple life. But I've never seen him worrying about finances. Whenever he got a little more money he would take us out for dinner and spend it. He didn't bother about saving much, trying to create wealth. It was a totally philosophical approach in everything, with probably the finest artistic taste I have ever come across, in every aspect of life. In music, in his attire, in food, cooking - even if it was simple it had to be artistic."

As his family life was getting busier, so too was his career. He was hired initially as a Producer for the light music unit at All India Radio (AIR). "I used to compose almost two to three songs per week, and all the artistes would come and visit me. I would compose the song, teach it to them, and then record it. For nearly 16-17 years, I must have

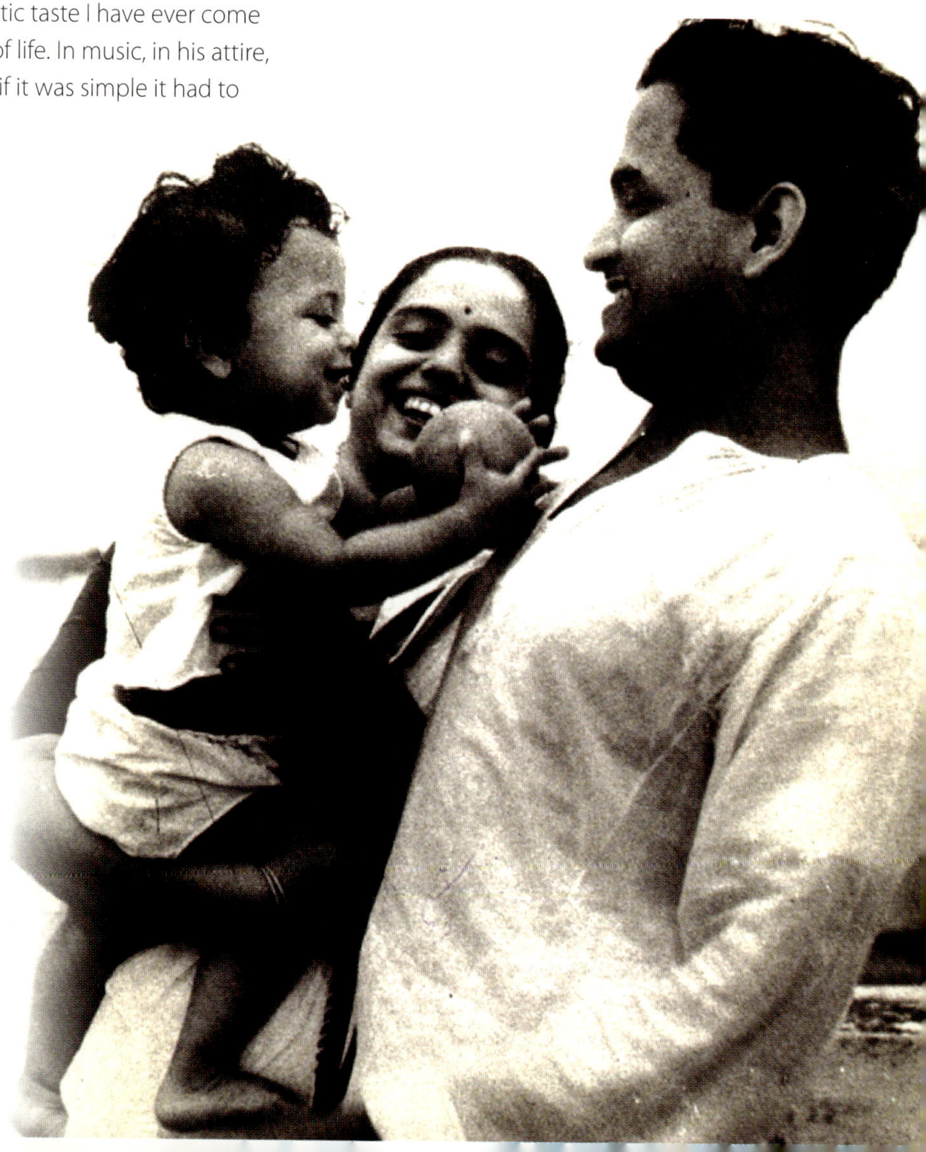

Panditji, Shashikalaji, and son, Rajesh, Delhi, 1959

composed 1500-2000 songs, all light classical." Several years later, Panditji was promoted to Assistant Director for the Directorate, Ministry of Information and Broadcasting, where he was in charge of all musical broadcasts, light and classical.

One pioneering highlight of Panditji's experience at AIR was the art of composing for choruses – a concept he had explored during his work on the Discovery of India ballet. His fame as an innovator with this format increased after an UNCTAD (United Nations Commerce, Trade and Development) Conference, for which he was asked to prepare a chorus for the inaugural function. When he received the lyrics of the composition (penned by his Guruji), he was assigned to direct a chorus of 60 people from all over India for the performance. At first, he found that the choral sound produced had great volume, but lacked depth – it was one-dimensional. The composition, which was of a serious and classical bent, needed a bit more youth and energy for the function. Panditji experimented with the possibilities.

"I added sargam-s, humming, ākār, harmonization with chords, and vocal rhythms throughout the piece, to give it dynamic and rhythmic range. There were no instruments, only 60 voices, so the rhythm was produced only with the voice." The chorus was transformed from singing a composition in complete unison, to several groups singing it in parts, adding various effects and harmonies, creating a musical arch that had a climax and resolution. "The total effect was so good that the delegates who came from

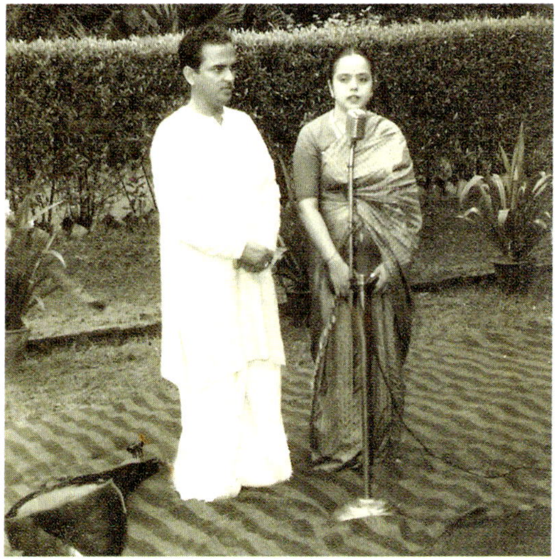

Shashikalaji sings an invocation at the Raj Bhavan, Delhi, 1962

Germany, Russia, Italy, and France liked it very much. Everybody was full of high praise for it. After a month I received an invitation from the Russian embassy, stating that Khrushchev and the Bulgarian President were coming. They requested that they would be very happy if another such chorus was performed!"

What was it about choral music, in the context of Hindustānī Rāgsangīt that was so appealing? For Panditji, the most singular aspect of choral singing was its transformative power, influenced by a contagious quality of singing en masse. In India, the general masses (though not with musically trained voices) sing together regularly during kīrtan (devotional singing). Panditji explained how this evolves into a pleasurable musical experience.

"The Indian concept of choruses is not based on trained voices. In kīrtan, with a devotional atmosphere, one person starts and everybody joins in on a different pitch and svar. On the whole, however, it has some good effect. When about one hundred people sing, they may think that they are singing in tune when each one's sa is totally different. But one voice singing in a different pitch than the leader actually corresponds with some other person who is not in tune. That's how it becomes a harmony of chords. It is like the Western concept, though it is not intentional or trained. When the singing is in rhythm, even if it lacks a certain tunefulness, it becomes a harmony and has mass appeal. You generate a spirit of communion between them, and the main subject there is bhakti. Similarly, when a song of patriotic nature is sung in a choir, there is a similar effect on the masses. There is brotherhood with the medium of music. Gradually, the mind becomes joyful because of rhythm and melody."

Panditji's thoughts were constantly evolving about the different methods of conveying the essence of Hindustānī Rāgsangīt. Whether in light classical or classical broadcasts, or choral pieces, Panditji's trademark stamp of high quality standards, attention to detail, and perfectionism was on everything that he produced at All India Radio.

Despite the demanding hours of his position and the responsibilities as a husband and father, Panditji's own rīyāz and performance career flourished independently and unwaveringly. Because of his tight schedule, he would begin his rīyāz at four in the morning. For his children, his pre-dawn rīyāz sessions are inextricably linked with memories of their childhood in Delhi.

"I don't think I have ever woken up without his rīyāz ringing through the quietness of Sarojini Nagar, where we lived. Every morning he would do his rīyāz and that was our morning alarm," said Aditi.

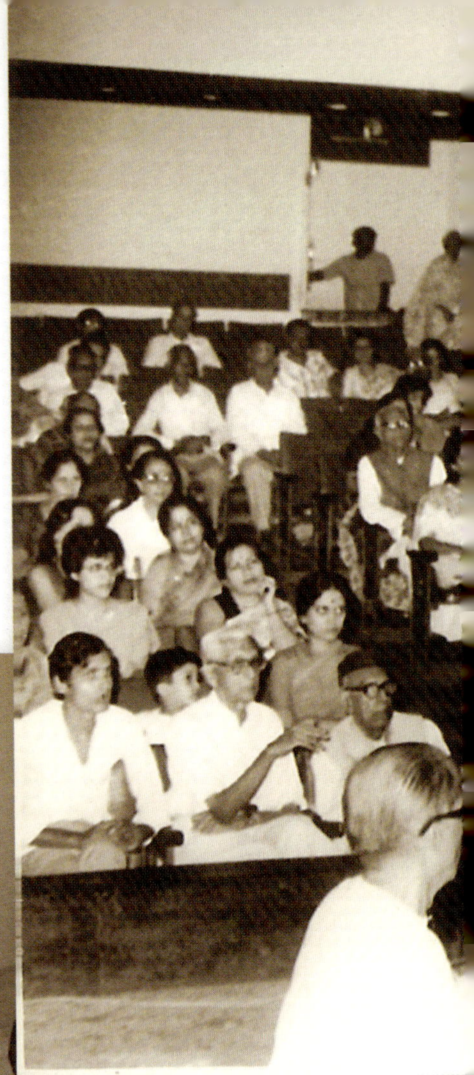

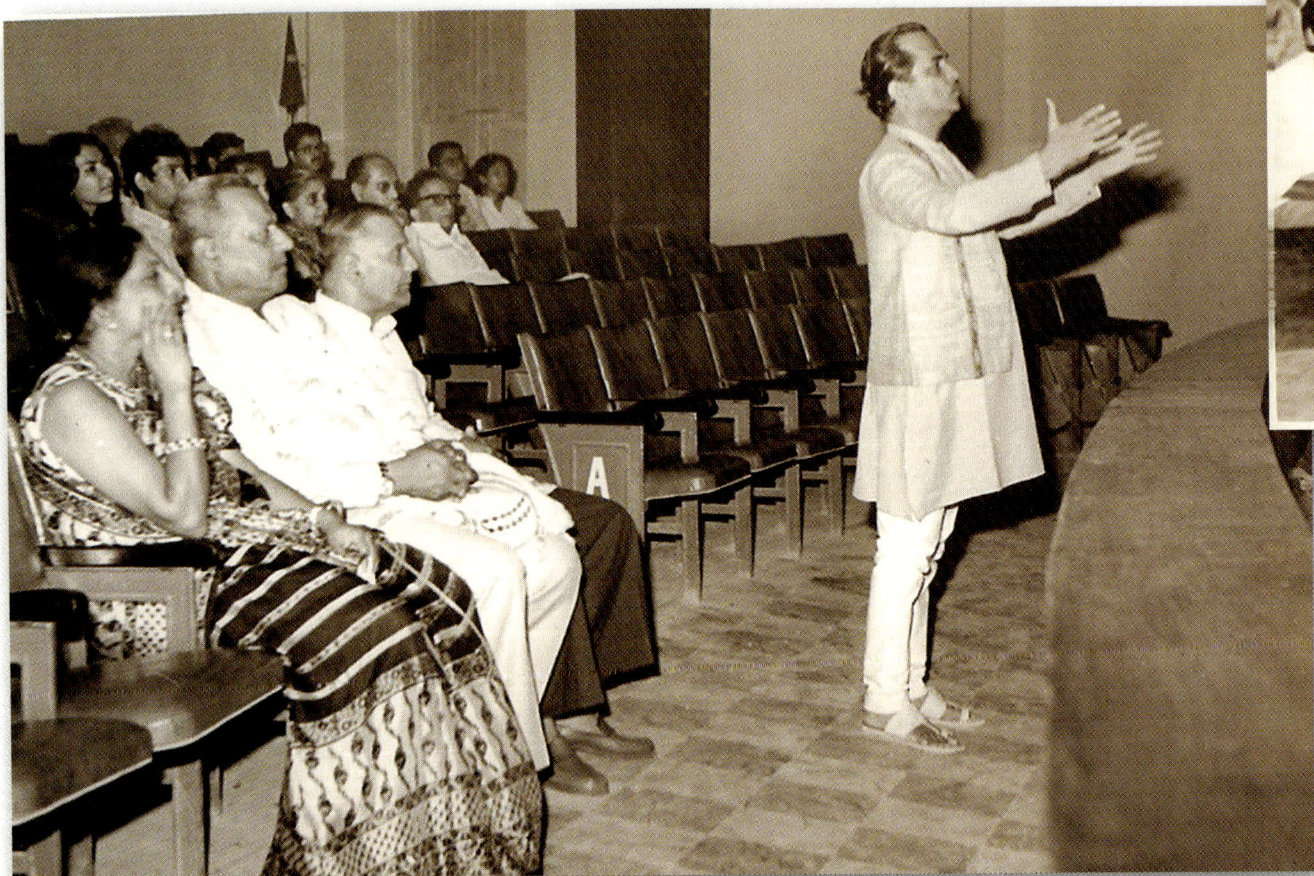

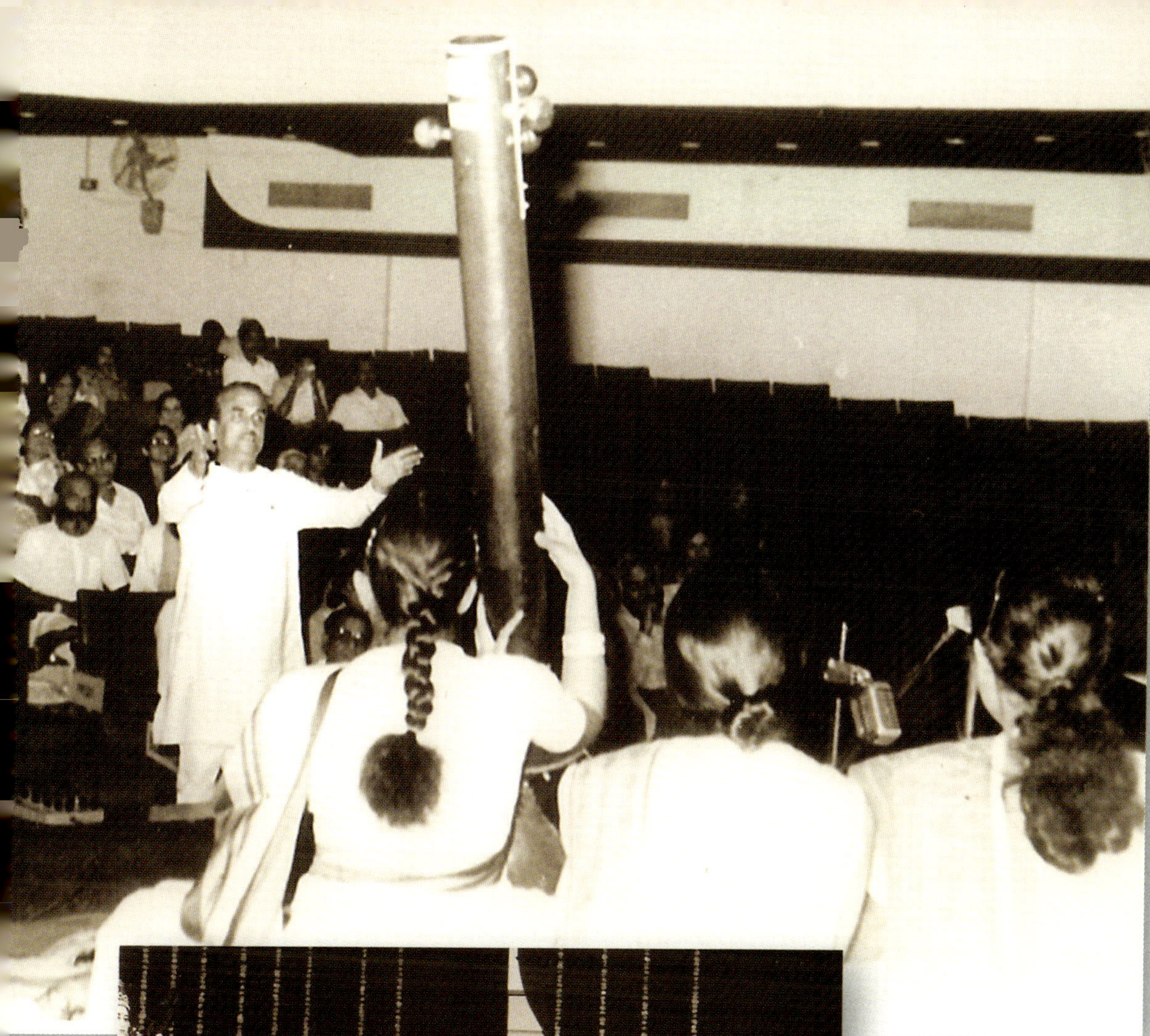

For his youngest child Yogesh, these formative memories established a subconscious idea of the type of authentic sādhanā required of a Hindustānī musician. "I saw him lead a very disciplined life as a rigorous musician. I have those memories, where he used to get up at four and practise. I would still be sleeping on the floor of the room, waiting to wake up for school. It used to be disturbing for me and I used to get irritated many times. But that's how it [music] started going in."

For seventeen years, Panditji lived a fruitful personal and professional life in Delhi, but he was then called back to Mumbai. Anna Saheb had recommended him to be the Principal of the Bharatiya Vidya Bhavan Music and Dance School. As always, his recommendation was given due consideration and taken seriously. The Kaikini family moved back to Mumbai in 1971 where Panditji's career would shift to a role in the educational realm of music.

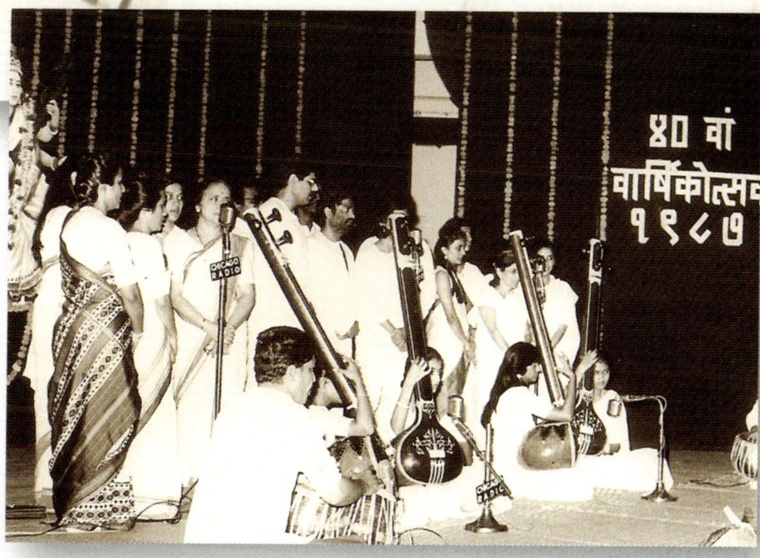

Panditji conducting a chorus rehearsal at Bharatiya Vidya Bhavan, Mumbai, 1987

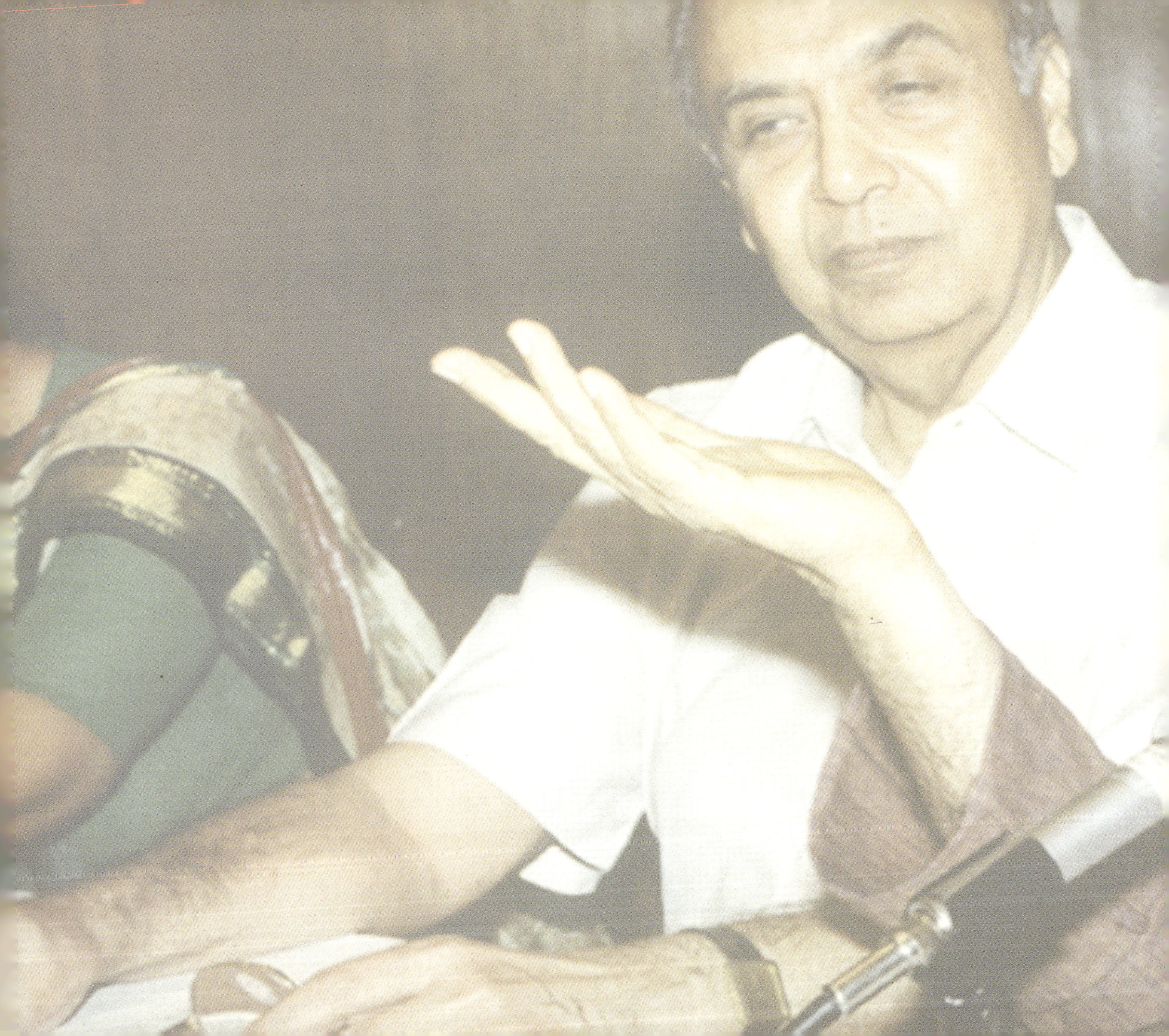

विद्या दान

VIDYĀ DĀN

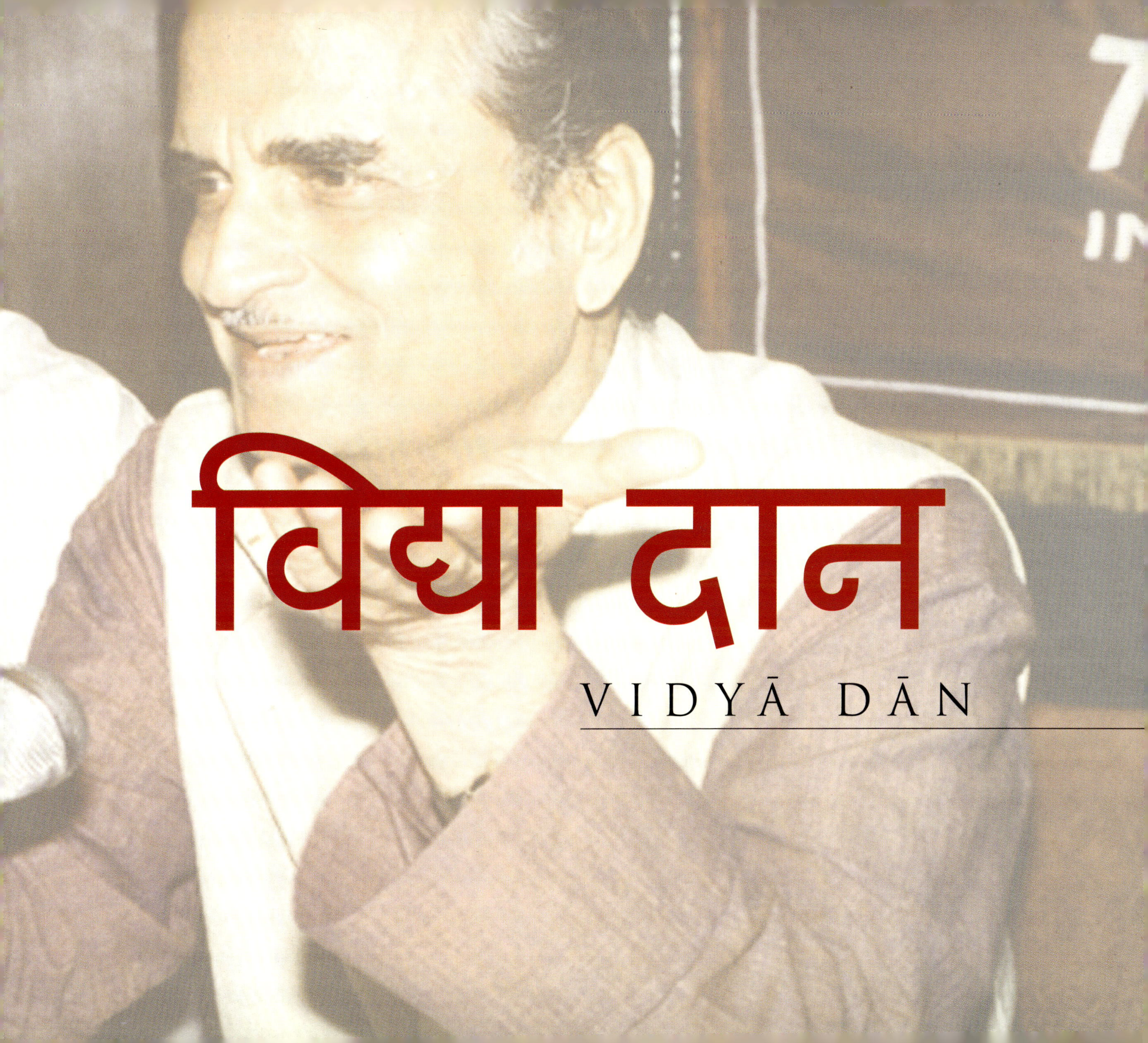

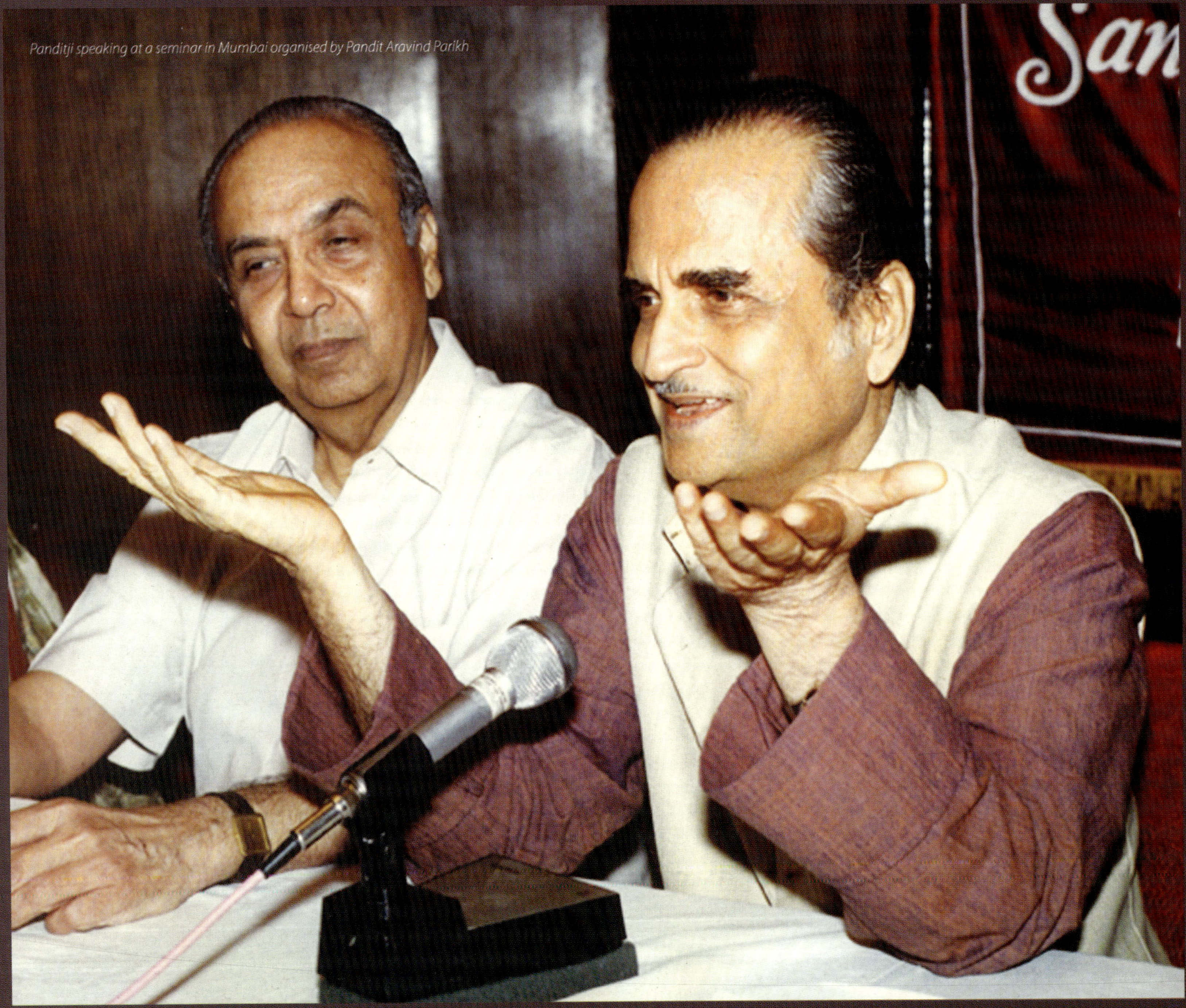

Panditji speaking at a seminar in Mumbai organised by Pandit Aravind Parikh

SĀDHĀNĀ

"When I take somebody as a student, it is my ambition to make that person
a musician. Whether he takes it as a profession or not is a different matter.
To me, being a musician means that a person possess all the qualities that are
required to perform and understand music well.
He can enjoy and be a critical listener; he has cultivated a taste for good,
serious music - that is the musical sanskār of an individual
...I am open-minded and looking to the present day's situation.
You must live in the present, not in the past's glory."

Selecting And Guiding A Śiṣya

Once a student has progressed past the initial stages of exposure to music and received a foundation, she will seek a guru to guide her on the serious path of studying this art.
When interested students approached Panditji, he would first assess where their interest was. "When someone comes to me, I ask, 'What type of music do you like and what do you want to learn?' There are three categories: Rāgsangīt, semi-classical, and light music. I will also ask, 'Whose music did you enjoy that made you feel like singing that particular style or of that calibre?' Then, as far as possible, I guide them to the best guru. Second, I test the voice. For this particular type of music, Rāgsangīt, there must be some gravity in that voice. Then, it is up to the guru to grasp how much musicality the individual has – the combination of talent, gift and voice."

Sanskārā are also critical for the śiṣya. These values, which can be socio-cultural, moral, ethical, or spiritual, are nurtured during childhood and can be influenced and moulded through the guru-śiṣya relationship. "The guru should try to groom the student in a way that comes under sanskār. Teaching is not just rāg, tāl, and composition, but other things also. It requires knowledge of sāhitya, history, geography, to name a few. And the śiṣya should also watch keenly and understand what type of thinking the guru has and try to imbibe that…In this relationship, the underlying idea is devotion, and that devotion is reciprocated between both guru and śiṣya."

Panditji also encouraged the appreciation of other art forms. "It is important to engage with a certain amount of allied arts – painting, dance, instrumental music and percussion, so that your horizon becomes very large. If you stick to one particular thing and focus only on that, like sārangī players and some singers, you sing the same thing over and over and get stuck in that groove. That's why my teaching is sanskār-yukta [based on the principles of sanskār]. Then I leave it to the student: it is up to them to use that knowledge – because that is how I groomed myself."

As a guru, Panditji set forth his goals in creating a worthy śiṣya clearly. Unlike many other musicians of his generation, he did not believe in imposing his own aspirations on the student.

"When I take somebody as a student, it is my ambition to make that person a musician. Whether he takes it as a profession or not is a different matter. To me, being a musician means that a person possesses all the qualities that are required to perform and understand music well. He can enjoy and be a critical listener; he has cultivated a taste for good, serious music – that is the musical sanskār of an individual. Now, some of my students have become top-notch light singers, including Udit Narayan. I've made them musical minded, but they have shifted their profession to the lighter side. Tushar Bhatia, one of my paṭa śiṣya, is an established composer. Even now he sometimes takes help from me. Whatever path they have chosen, I have made them musicians and more importantly, I have groomed without bias. There are certain guru-s who won't allow their śiṣya-s to sing in films. But I am open-minded and looking to the present day's situation. You must live in the present, not in the past's glory."

Sādhanā

Once committed to the path, where does a serious student of music begin? How should the student approach the learning process? As a teacher whose approach was scholarly, Panditji had put extensive thought into understanding how students can effectively learn, practise, and set out to achieve their goals. This chapter explains in detail his systematic approach to meaningful sādhanā.

Sādhanā, a concept that is prevalent in Hindu texts, is often used to describe disciplined and rigorous practice in pursuit of spiritual quests. The sādhanā process is central to both the spiritual and musical context, which many would argue are interrelated.

Panditji defined sādhanā as "the course of action and procedure one takes towards achieving a certain goal." This is the first of three stages of development as a musician and comprises identifying a goal, forming a plan to achieve the goal, and acting upon it. The second stage is sādhya, or realisation of the goal. Sādhya, however, is not the final phase, because reaching the goal does not necessarily equate to mastery of the goal. Thus, the final stage is siddhī, the ability to achieve the goal or effect whenever desired – it is complete control over the goal. "In that state of mind, during siddhi, whatever you utter musically engulfs everybody. "These three phases are important for the disciple to keep in mind as guidelines for self-evaluation and constant reflection. The moment a student stops understanding the purpose of his practice, the effort becomes futile.

"First you have to decide what to achieve, then how to achieve it, and when you do achieve it, you should feel a satisfaction of achievement. This satisfaction is for furthering your own development – it is like tasting a nice sweet. After enjoying it, you may ask, 'How is it made? What are the ingredients? What are the proportions?' Then you will be motivated to start making the sweet on your own, and you will know the value of it."

Naturally, the benefits of sādhanā are proportional to the level of the student's involvement in the learning process. Panditji classifies these levels as: alertness, awareness, and total awareness. Alertness is the immediate ability to grasp and reproduce what is being taught. Awareness is not just a blind imitation, but a complete understanding of what has been grasped, including the larger concept guiding the lesson. Total awareness is the intentional execution of such an idea in any context. Ideally, the student is constantly in a state of total awareness, with command over what is being sung.

To me, sādhanā seemed to be the steadfast commitment to both practising and learning. But as Panditji spoke more, it became clear that sādhanā was not only a physical act but also a state of mind. Focus, involvement, and awareness are all contingent upon a calm, meditative mind. Hindustani Rāgsangīt is characterised by the highly contemplative and captivating mood that it sets, and this is only possible if the artiste performing is engrossed in such a state. Thus, the first step towards sādhanā is the controlling of the mind. "First you have to arrest the mind, because it wanders like a vagabond. Dhyān is total focusing of the mind on nothingness – extreme concentration. When you forget about your own existence, that means you have surrendered completely and there is no ahamkār [ego]. That is non-existence," says Panditji. While students focus most of their time on riyāz, it is important not to forget "mental riyāz," or gaining control over the mind when desired. As Panditji would repeat like a mantrā, "It is the mind that sings, not the voice." In this state of mind, the student is more receptive to the knowledge and the joy of music being passed on by the guru.

"The concept of the vilambit [the slow paced composition] is one of total meditation. What is calmness, and how do you express this musically? Calmness is a prerequisite for the steadiness that exists in the vilambit. The more time there is between each beat, the more concentrated the mind needs to be to sustain the effect. This steadiness is required for the person who is performing and the person who is listening. It is necessary for a performer or else he won't be able to divide the beats equally. To be able to appreciate the music fully, the listener's state of mind must also remain still. That is the peace that the artiste commands - he must cultivate the strength to control his mind and to capture the minds of the audience and create a hypnotic effect."

Panditji receiving the Sangeet Natak Akademi Puraskar in 1996

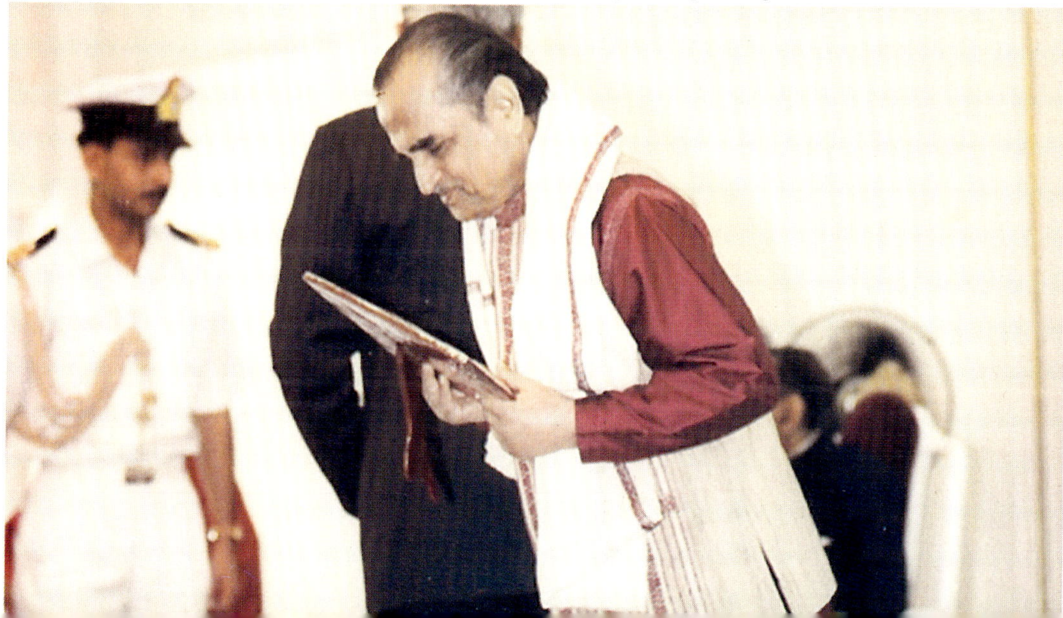

In a lecture to Vedanta students on meditation, Panditji drew the parallel between being a yogī and being a Hindustānī musician. "The whole process of music is nothing but meditation. In that state of mind, we only give musical knowledge. We implement that knowledge through sound, and at that time, the artiste's mind is meditative. The only difference is that the person who meditates with his eyes closed gets personal satisfaction whereas an artiste is able to satisfy all those listening as well."

Of course, it is easy to say that the mind should be still, but most of the time, our minds are busy juggling many unrelated thoughts that surface at any given moment. So, how does one deal with this issue? It is no coincidence that the first lesson of Hindustānī music is also the first lesson of life: "The process of arresting the mind starts from concentrating on the breath." Prān, or life, is another word for breath. "With breath humans create sound – that is why there is life in sound."

First Lessons: Breathing

Focused breathing is the first step towards achieving a quiet mind, after which it is used to maximise vocal technique, sound production, and bring life to music. "Breathing should always occur from the bottom of the stomach (diaphragm), where the lungs have the ability to expand outwardly without being constrained by the ribcage." Thus, upon inhaling, the stomach should expand outward, and on exhaling, it should retract back to its normal position. Panditji emphasises the need to "see" the breath – literally visualise and follow it as it travels through the body. It is necessary to observe and know the body's breathing pattern to be able to gauge the lung capacity.

To develop these breathing patterns, there are several breathing exercises, or kriyā-s, that come from the Yoga tradition. With practice, they expand lung capacity and fortify the vocal cords and sinus passages. Such exercises include: anulom and vilom prānāyām, kapāla bhātī, bhastrikā kriyā, brāmhari kriyā, and ujjai breathing.

Svar Sādhanā

After the mind and breath have been focused, attention should be drawn to mastering the basics: the svar. Svar sādhanā is the in-depth exploration of each frequency, to master the skillful manipulation of the voice to convey numerous emotions.

Given the sophisticated use of microtones in Hindustānī Rāgsangīt, it is critical to develop a ear that can discern the shades of difference between microtones, and to know when to use the appropriate frequency in a given rāg.

Svarsthān - Pitch Accuracy

The first technique to achieve pitch accuracy is what Panditji calls pin-pointed humming. Graphically speaking, humming is a single-point approach to a note, while an open ākār (open "ah" sound) is a plane of sound. That is why the sound produced by humming minimises all other variations in sound quality and focuses solely on pitch. During humming, the mouth must be closed, and the sound should maintain a sharp quality, reflecting off the upper palate of the mouth. With this in mind, the student should hum each svar separately (śuddh or komal), holding each steadily and utilising full breath capacity. The position of each note is known as svarsthān – literally the "place of the note" in the realm of the twelve possible svar-s.

After practising this, the next step is to blend the closed humming sound into an open ākār. On the same breath, the mouth should gradually open while the pitch and quality of sound should be unchanged. This should be practised in the same fashion, on each svar separately, ascending and descending the scale. The primary focus of this exercise is to penetrate the absolute centre of each svar, or svar-bindu, as Panditji called it. "It should not be like handling a crane – constantly adjusting to find the spot." This total oneness with svar should bring pleasure during sādhanā, and propel the student to achieve this on repeated attempts.

Panditji performing in Sri Lanka, January 1980

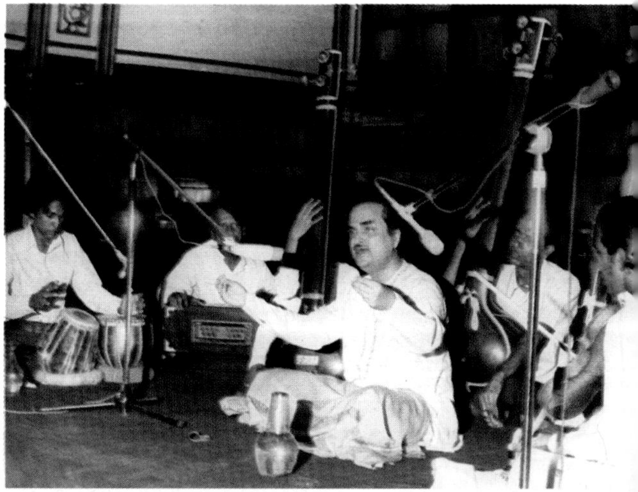

Śrutisthān

Śrutisthān refers to the specific placement of microtones in the context of a rāg. A śruti can only be practised within the frame of the rāg, because the specific placement of each śruti varies from one rāg to another, depending on the rāg bhav and rāg-ang (characteristic phrases). Panditji calls this process of mastering śrutisthān "rāg-ang svar sādhanā." For instance, to internalise the sthān of komal riśabh in the rāg Śrī, the note must be approached through the characteristic rāg-ang phrases and be the centre of development. This would involve taking various note combinations, repeatedly revolving around komal riśabh, in order to establish its exact frequency in relation to the other notes of the rāg. Komal riśabh in rāg Puriyā Dhanāśrī, on the other hand, will have a different shade, and must be practised through the same process to gain mastery over the śrutisthān.

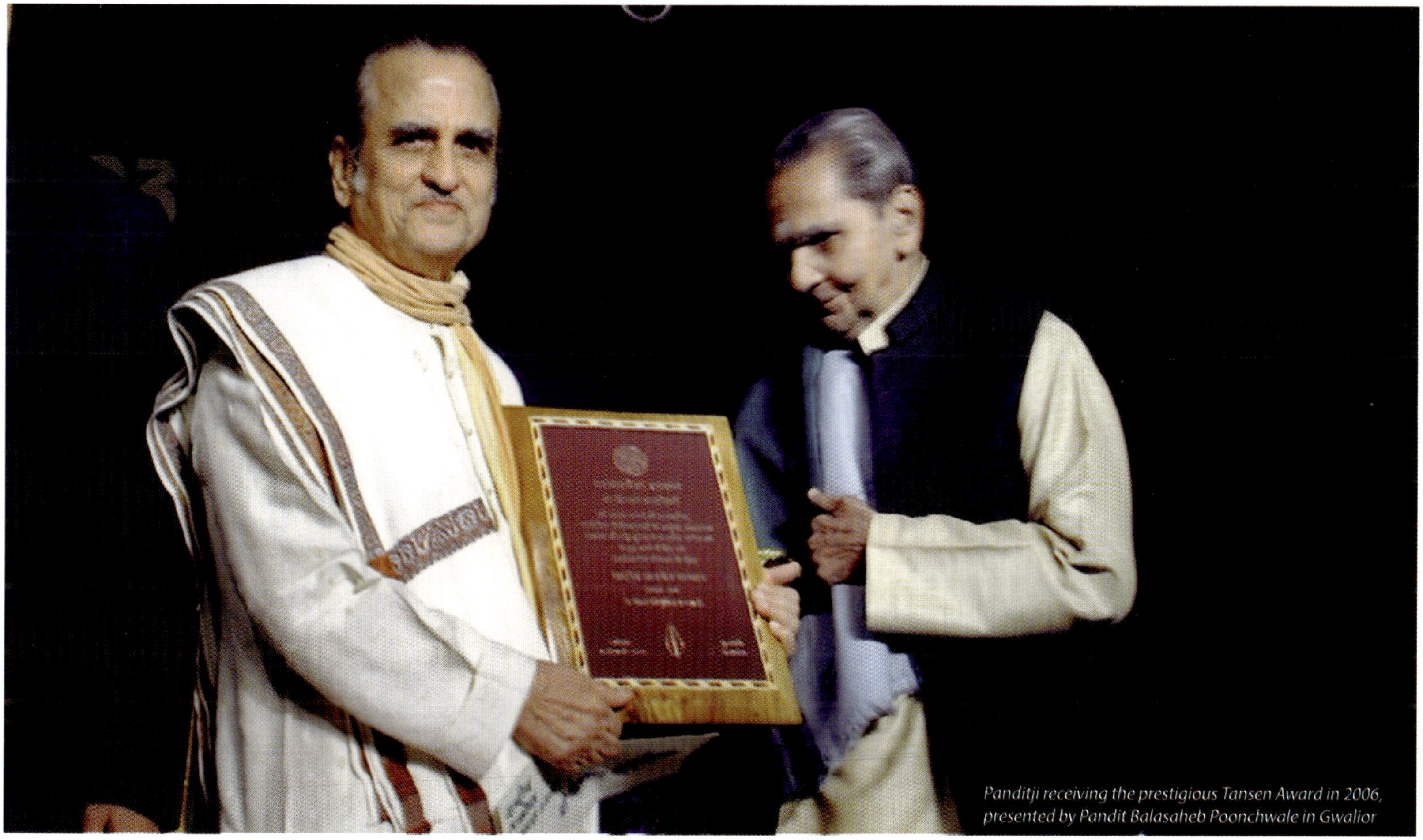

Panditji receiving the prestigious Tansen Award in 2006, presented by Pandit Balasaheb Poonchwale in Gwalior

Svarākriti

While pitch is one focus of svar sādhanā, bhāv, or emotion, is another. How does one give character or feeling to a note? Applying different levels of volume and intensity to a note gives it shape and adds colour and dimensionality. This shape can actually be visualised and then produced with the voice. There are four basic shapes. The first is a crescendo, a gradual increase from soft to loud ("<"). Taking each note on the scale separately, the student should start singing each in ākār at a very soft pitch, gradually but constantly increasing the volume to the maximum and ending as soon as the maximum has been reached. Throughout the crescendo, the pitch, breath, and phonetic (ā or ah sound) should remain steady. This exercise requires a careful understanding of breath capacity, as the speed of increase in volume should be proportional to the total amount of breath available. The student should be able to divide his total breath so that he covers the full range of the crescendo. In the same way, the second shape, a decrescendo (">") should be practised on each note. Once these two have been mastered, they can be combined to form the mridangam shape ("<>"), and the reverse ("><"), all practised in the same manner.
The swelling and diminishing sounds created by these shapes can add a dramatic element when aptly applied during rendition of a rāg or a composition. Isolated practice of the technique at the start of training allows for time to gain control over the breath and the voice, a lifelong process.

Timbre

While doing the above-mentioned exercises, the student must pay attention to timbre, or the quality of the sound produced. Like all of the other exercises, the student must experiment with his voice, identifying the various timbres and the character it can evoke. "If someone plays the violin, and switches to sārangī, you can recognise this - that is the experience of identifying various timbres." Panditji identified two timbres, upper and lower, which produce very contrasting tones. Upper timbre refers to a sharp and crisp sound that is produced by depressing the tongue and contracting the upper palate and the area surrounding the uvula at the back of the mouth. Lower timbre, on the other hand, is a heavier and deeper sound, produced by leaving the uvula un-contracted and throat muscles loose. It is up to the student to discover which timbre is appropriate for which expression. While these are general definitions to explore these sound qualities, each individual's voice and biological make-up is unique, requiring personal experimentation to discover the most suitable method to produce variation in timbre.

Panditji and Late Sri P L Deshpande

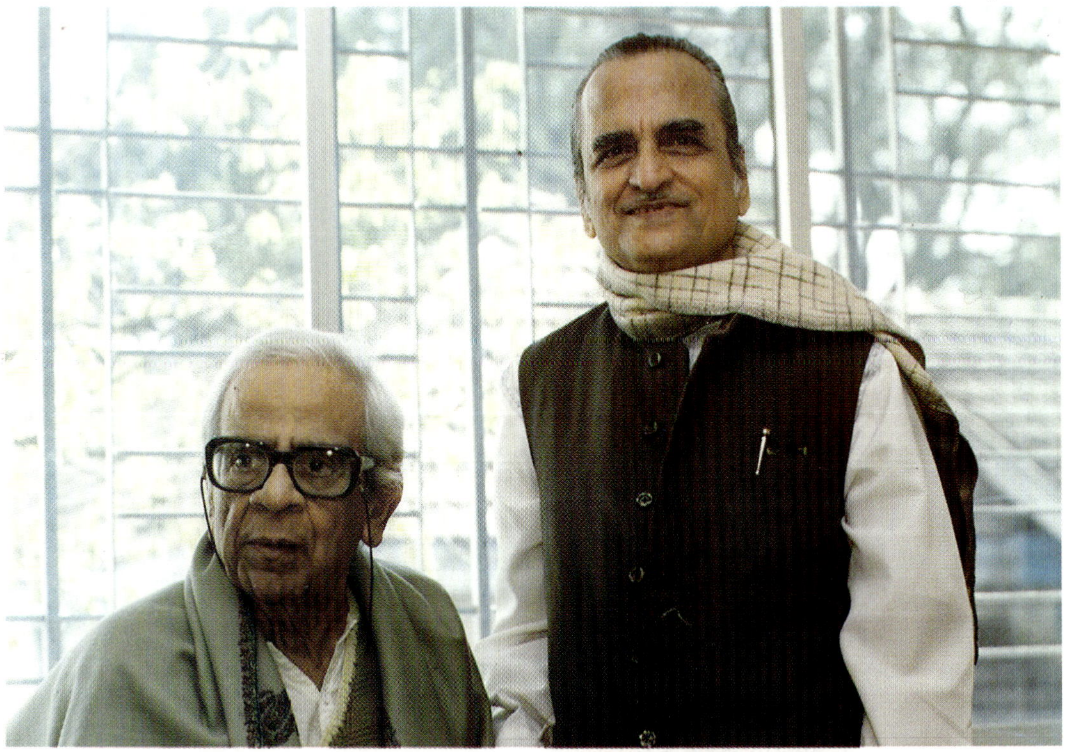

Performance-Targeted Riyāz

For a serious student of Hindustānī Rāgsangīt, keen on pursuing a performing career, it is important to achieve not only quantity, but quality of riyāz that is effective. According to Panditji, this is achieved by isolating the main components of a full rendition, and focusing practice on each for a given period of time.

The ālāp, the gradual unfolding and development of a rāg, often serves as an introduction in a concert. In a riyāz schedule of a month, for instance, a week should be dedicated solely for exploring ālāp in a particular rāg. Attention should be given to perfecting and enjoying each phrase to total satisfaction. It is important not to stray into other aspects, such as the composition, while practising the ālāp. After completing an ālāp rendition, the process should begin again, being careful not to be repetitive or mechanical. "You must enjoy it right from the beginning to the end. It should not be stale, and you shouldn't be unsure. Each phrase should be sung confidently and enjoyed in the process. When you are satisfied, start over and practise the ālāp again."

In the same way, one week should be devoted to mastering the bandiś. First, the composition must be sung many times until it has been internalised. "When you first practise the bandiś, focus on the musical and rhythmic structure." Complete understanding of the composition requires gaining familiarity with the text, the laya, and the rasa. The meaning of each śabd should be clear and the bhāv of the piece should be genuinely felt. Once these concrete elements are in place, the composition is taken to the abstract by giving creative meaning to the composition. Analysing the emotional content of the text can inspire various musical interpretations of a bandiś. As mentioned in the Chapter *Origins*, the word "jāo," which literally means "go," can be expressed with many different connotations. In the context of the composition, all of these should be explored and expressed musically. At no point should the musicality of the rendition be disconnected from the character of the composition.

Tān-s should be the next area of focus. There are several types of tān-s, characterised by the type of pattern formed. Sapāt tān-s are straight ascending and descending scales. Palṭe ki tān-s are a specific pattern repeated throughout the scale (i.e., sa ga re, re ma ga, ga pa ma, etc.) Gamak tān-s are patterns sung with a heavy and fast oscillation placed on each note. Lehak tān-s are patterns sung with less oscillation than gamak, but such that all the notes are connected to each other by a fast gliding motion. Maṭh tān-s refer to a pattern revolving around a specific note, or a few notes, exploiting as many permutations. "Maṭhna," which means to churn, implies the circular movement of the notes in this type of tān. Bol tān-s can fall under any of the previous patterns, but utilise words of the text rather than ākār. Sargam-s are not tān-s but note patterns developed by the same guidelines, in which the notes are each pronounced instead of using open vowel sounds.

Upaj or bol banāo is rhythmic play between the śabd of the composition and the laya. The text is playfully and unpredictably divided within the confines to create anticipation at the resolution.

After these areas have been practised, the conclusion is a final mock concert with accompanists in which all the components come together. It is important to treat this rehearsal as though it were a real performance, to gauge a sense of the total rendition and to identify areas that require improvement.

Planning A Concert

There are several factors to take into consideration when designing a concert programme. First, the performer must consider the audience that will be attending – does the audience consist of seasoned listeners, or less knowledgeable but interested listeners? "At a glance you must be able to grasp the total atmosphere of the audience. You must understand the mindset of who you are performing for, and the mood of the venue." The rāg selected should be suited to the interests of all members of the audience. The performer should also take his or her own physical condition into consideration – what is the state of the voice and health? If there are any unusual conditions or setbacks, the concert should be tailored to meet the comfort level of the artiste.

It is critical that the crescendo of the concert is constantly maintained. The pieces should be selected such that the transition from the first item to the second does not lose momentum – it should contrast the first in rāg, tāl and laya. Overall, the programme should be balanced, not repetitive, and appealing in variety.

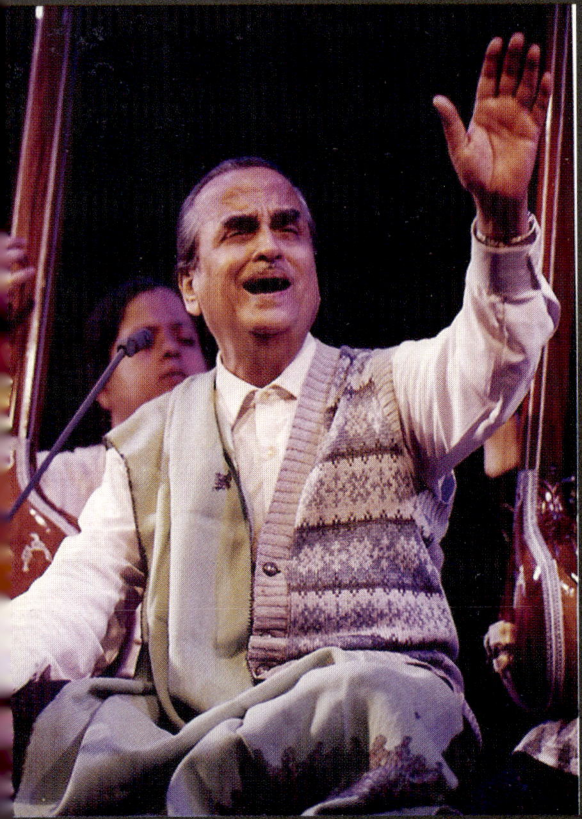

Panditji performing live at Theatre de la Ville, Paris 1997. He had just recovered from a vocal nodule surgery.

Adapting As A Performer

Despite all the preparation a musician may go through for a performance, circumstances can change and one must be flexible and quick to adjust to ensure a successful concert. Panditji recounts the many health problems he faced, and the ways in which he adapted his singing to suit his physical condition.

"I used to model my singing after Faiyaz Khan Saheb to achieve the effect that he used to create. I not only imitated his musical style, but also used to project my voice in the same manner.
I stopped doing this when I got vocal nodules on my vocal chords, and I found that my physique is not suited to that treatment of the voice.
I realised that the desired spirit of his style should come through my own voice, and it required imagination to discover how to do this.

"I had so many setbacks in health that are deadly for a musician, but I wanted to overcome any deficiencies. After my heart attack, my left ventricular system had gone weak; I then had open-heart surgery, followed by pleurisy, and finally paralysis of the left side. Once, my health was so bad that I was hospitalised for three days to treat both my heart and lungs. When I recovered, I came home and gave a performance after just ten days. My doctor came to the concert and after hearing me she said, 'How can you sing for two hours with that vigour? Are you the same person who was admitted into the hospital recently for three days?' I said, 'Yes, but when I sit on the stage, I am not that Dinkar. I am different.' Somehow, I get the inspiration and execute based on my physical state at that time. At one time in my life, my breath capacity was 40-45 seconds. Now I can hardly hold it for ten seconds because it requires lungpower that I don't have. I mould whatever idea I have to fit into that time, and that requires a very high type of imagination. Adapting to these physical limitations is a very essential type of talent for the performer."

Mindset Of A Performer

Once on stage, the artiste experiences the culmination of all of her efforts. This is where Panditji's favourite mantrā and first lesson in music returns: "The mind sings, not the voice." The mind must be arrested the moment a performance begins. This sets the tone and atmosphere for the music to come.

His daughter and śisya, Aditi, has also gleaned many points from Panditji on performance and vocal accompaniment over the years.

"You have no second chances as a performer. Ultimately, no one in the audience is concerned about what you have gone through to put your concert together. It just has to be your best, then and there. Once the tānpurā-s begin, you have to forget your world outside of the music you are about to create," she recalled.

During riyāz one may work extensively on technique and prowess, but in a concert these should not come to the forefront. An artiste

should not abandon the audience and get carried away by all the knowledge that has been amassed in the process. "He used to tell me that if you have an audience, you are responsible for the spectrum of entertainment to soulfulness," said his son Yogesh, who accompanied him on tablā in many concerts and international tours.
"You can't be there to sing for yourself and exhibit your knowledge. It's not an exhibition of knowledge - it's something you need to experience inwards from your soul, from the abstract to the concrete. Take the audience along with you from the concrete to the abstract and bring them back to the concrete. This is something I learned from him in his performances. He used to start with the concrete - with the development of rāg, khayāl, and lyrics, and go into the abstract and inwards. And then the music would become so soulful - he used to take the audience along with him on this journey."

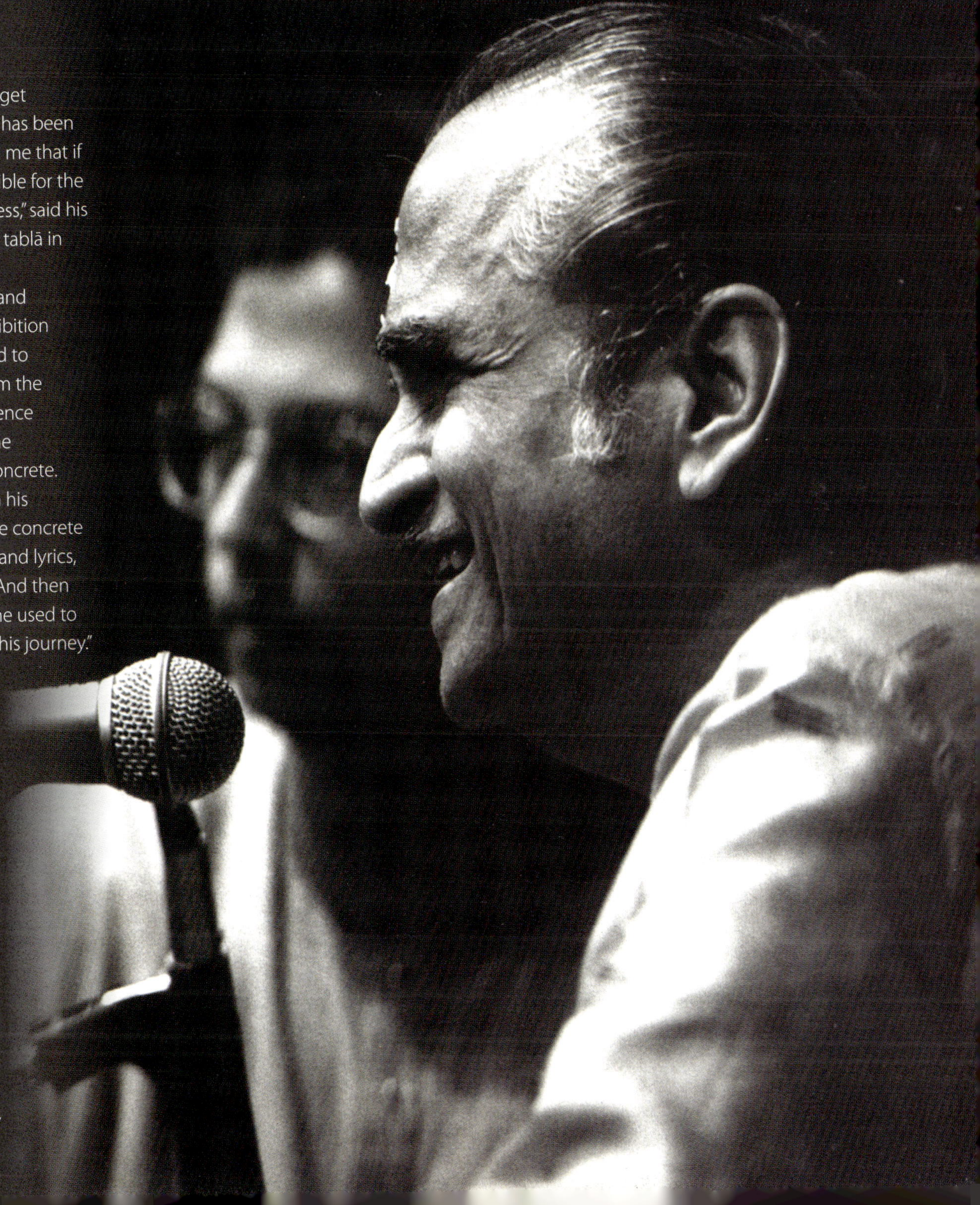

Panditji with his son, Yogesh Samsi, in the background

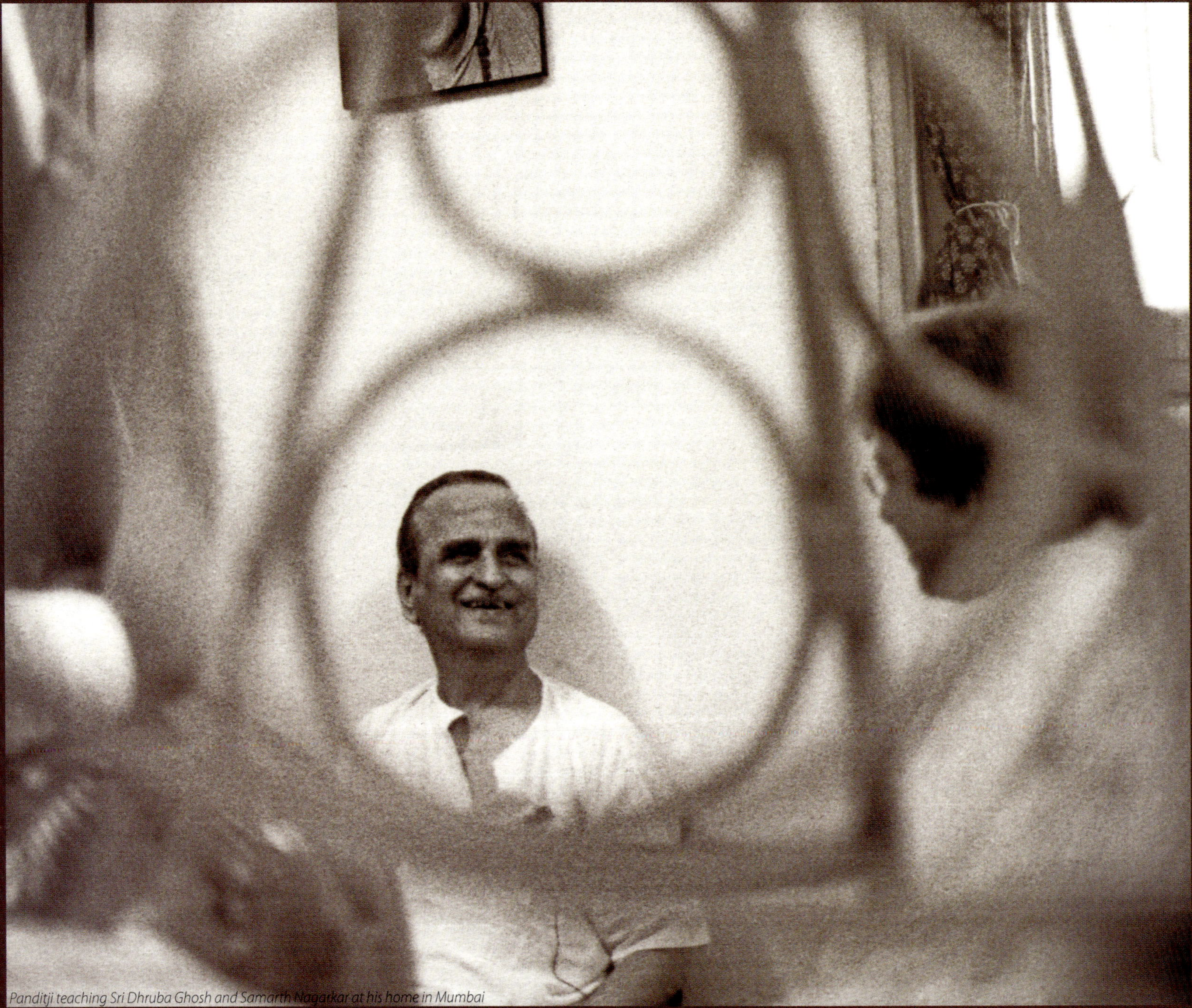

Panditji teaching Sri Dhruba Ghosh and Samarth Nagarkar at his home in Mumbai

ON EDUCATION

"An artiste is born, never made in institutions.
Institutions create many students who appreciate and value that music.
If we don't make such a battalion of appreciators,
who will care for performing artistes?"

For Panditji, moving to Mumbai was not only a return to his hometown, but also a return to the roots he had received at Lucknow. Just as Anna Saheb imparted his knowledge to hundreds of students, Panditji was also eager to get back into teaching to continue the scholastic legacy that his paramparā had established in the field of education.

As Principal of Bharatiya Vidya Bhavan, Panditji was playing the roles of administrator and Guru. Under his tenure, he re-organised the way the institution operated so that it would be more amenable to both students and faculty. He added many new elements to expand the scope of material covered, and the range of people who could benefit. He realised that times had changed significantly from when he was a student. American Pop music and the Beatles dominated the musical airwaves, which required increasing awareness about Hindustānī Rāgsangīt to make it more accessible and achievable for students. To do this, he conducted Lecture-Demonstrations and Seminars for listeners and students. He also instituted teacher-training programmes to improve the quality of instruction, and revised the syllabus to make it more suitable for both student and teacher. He revived the practice of a music circle that featured students and artistes on a fortnightly basis. He made huge strides in improving the institution so that the cause of music could be furthered without compromising on standards – this was always his primary aim.[1]

"Many people used to come to me when I was the Principal of Bharatiya Vidya Bhavan and ask, 'How should we inculcate music in our children?' I used to tell them, 'Do you have a tape recorder? Whose tapes do you have? If you want them to get a taste of classical music, don't ask them to learn anything. Each morning just put on a good cassette, and let the mind and ears get trained. Then at some point, they will like it and want to learn on their own.'" Listening is a critical part of learning Hindustānī music, as it is a "śravan vidyā" – music to be absorbed primarily through listening.

In fact, because of such a strong interest amongst parents to have music classes for young children, and a dearth of suitable Indian music available for this age group, Panditji was inspired to take on this task. He thought about how one could teach

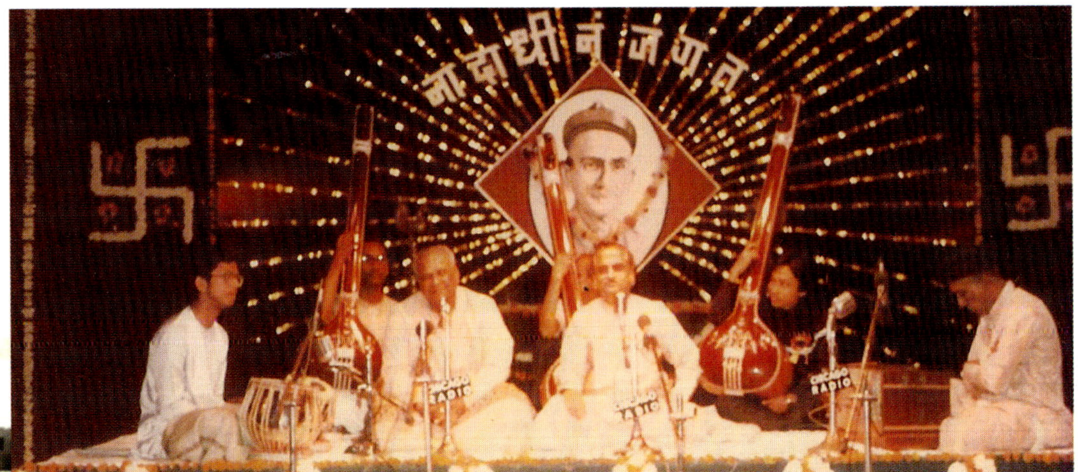

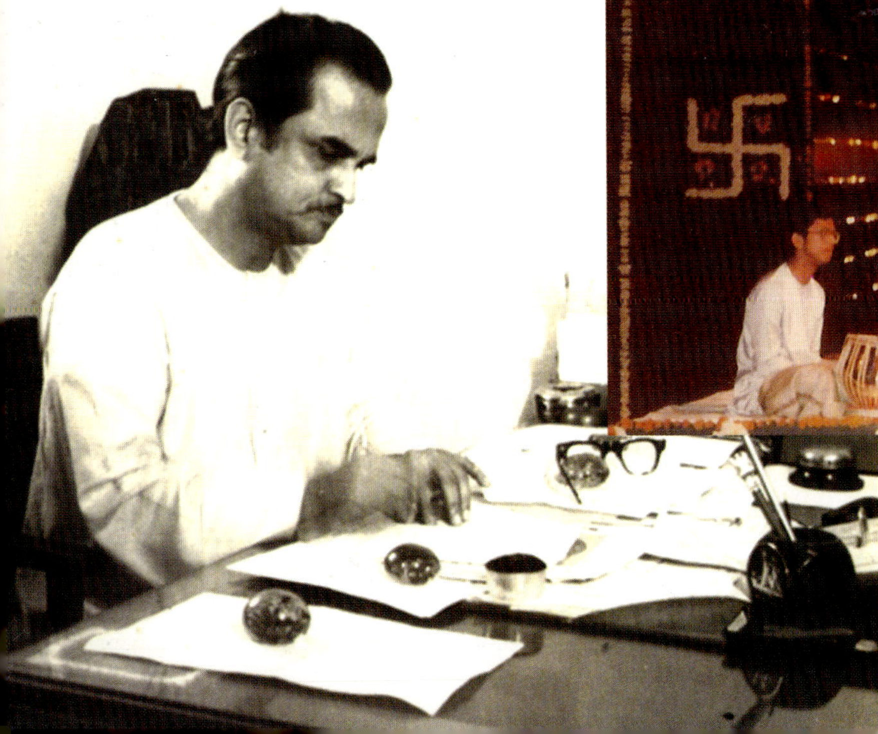

Left: Panditji in his office at the Bharatiya Vidya Bhavan, Mumbai, circa 1971; Above: Panditji and Pandit K.G. Ginde, accompanied by a young Yogesh Samsi on tablā, performing a jugalbandi for the 50th Bhatkhande Sangeet Mahotsav, Mumbai.

[1] *Referenced from "Dinrang," by Sadashiv Bakre. English translation courtesy of Ramesh Gangolli.*

children about music without weighing them down with the heavier concepts of rāg and tāl. At the ages of five and onwards, singing is a simple and joyful expression. It is also an impressionable age at which music with meaningful lyrics and catchy melodies can remain with the child. With these thoughts in mind, Panditji composed a series of children's songs titled "Āo Sab Mil Gāo," consisting of appealing melodies that deal with themes like nature, patriotism, and spirituality in simple, easily understood, and poetic lyrics.

While not explicitly teaching rāg and tāl, these songs were built upon the foundation of Rāgsangīt, instilling sanskārā-s into the subconscious of the young ones. A class was started at Bharatiya Vidya Bhavan and became hugely successful (it continues to this day), and the songs were then recorded in an album for which Panditji went to several schools in Mumbai to select a group of children whom he trained for the recording. His disciple, well-respected composer and sitār player, Tushar Bhatia, accompanied him for this project. "It was a treat to watch him train kids," he recalls. "He used to carry a box of chocolates for them and be like a doting grandpa when they sang!" These songs are still taught in schools across India.

Panditji was always ready to take on education-oriented projects like this one, unlike many other musicians. The government often asked him to search for and select music faculty for schools and universities. Despite the tediousness of this task, he would take it up with full sincerity, always concerned that wherever music was taught, it should be done with high standards.

Role Of Institutions

As the number of music institutions across the world grows, it has prompted the question, "What is the role of these institutes?" Are they responsible for producing quality performing musicians, just as medical schools produce doctors? How can we maintain a consistent standard across the board? For Panditji, it was naïve to have such expectations of music schools.

"It is wrong to expect that all the students from our music institutions will become musicians. It is not the institute's responsibility, nor is that the claim. What they are doing is making music minded, music loving, theoretical thinkers. They create Kānsen not Tansen! The institute's job is to bring awareness and make students lovers of music with the right perspective. In Lucknow, when I was learning, almost 1500 students were studying music. Only about five of us became musicians, performers – that is an individual, God-given quality. An artiste is born, never made in institutions. Institutions create many students who appreciate and value that music. If we don't make such a battalion of appreciators, who will care for performing artistes?"

For Panditji, these institutes should also strive to make the modern day student well informed about this ancient art form. After all, how does a tradition that dates back thousands of years remain relevant to all of our lives? Although the underlying human emotions are timeless, how can we relate to the contexts in which these compositions were born? How can they

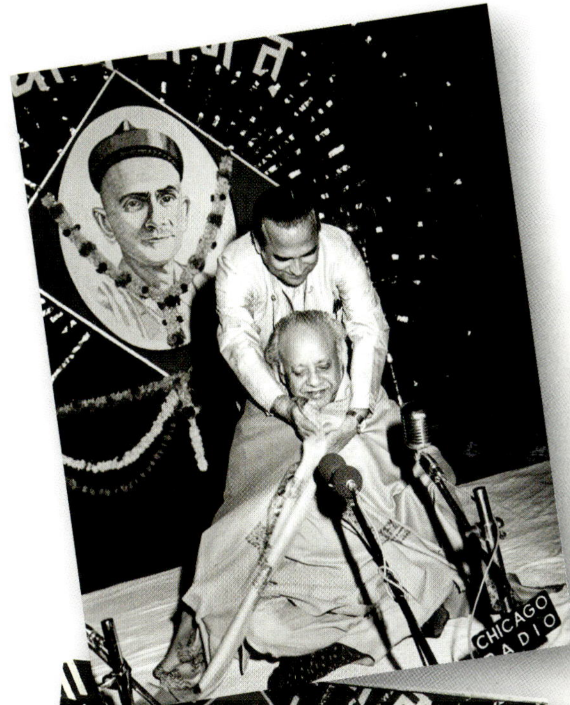

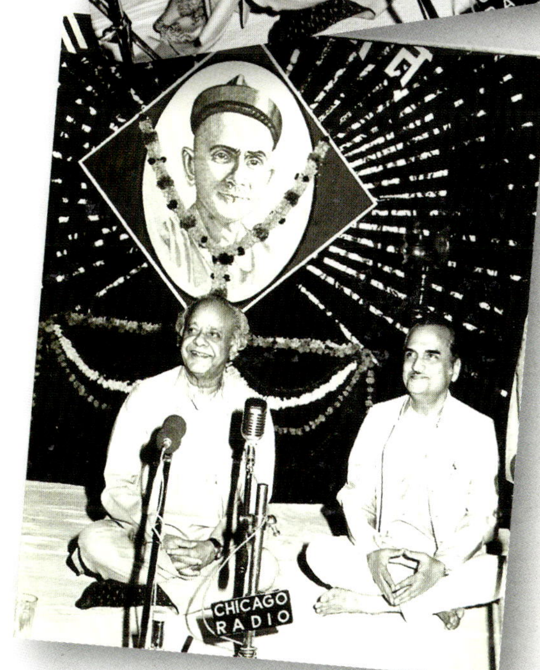

Panditji felicitates Ustad Alla Rakha Khan Saheb at the Bhatkhande Sangeet Mahotsav at the Bharatiya Vidya Bhavan, Mumbai

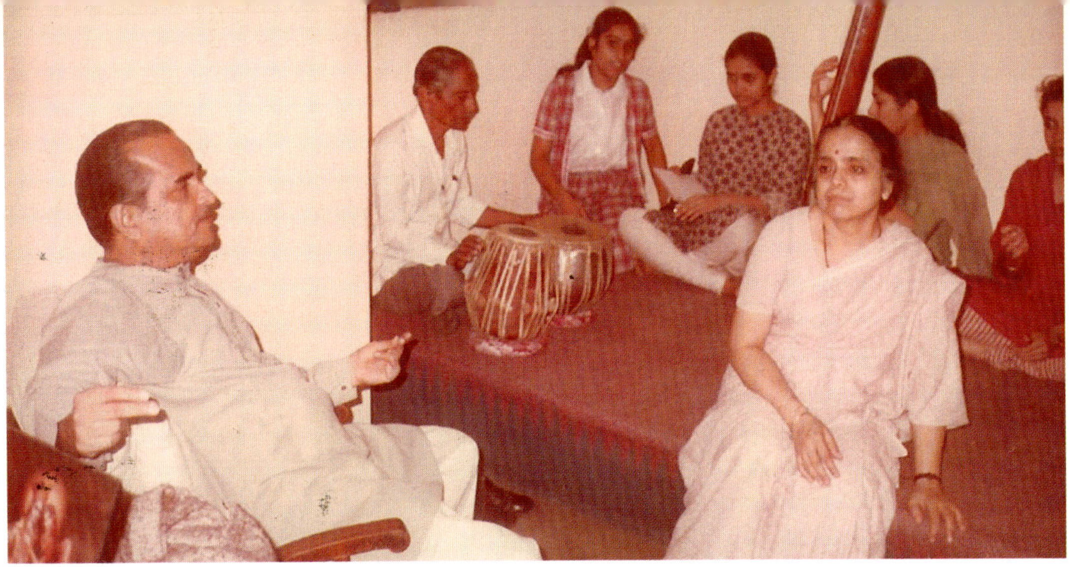

Panditji and Shashikalaji at a chorus rehearsal at the Bharatiya Vidya Bhavan

remain current and sincere? Or does change and reflection compromise the integrity of the tradition? In essence, how do we ensure the sustainability of Hindustānī Rāgsangīt with authenticity?

"Music is always changing, and changes have been taking place for 3000 years. Dhrupad is going into oblivion now, and before that there was Prabandh Gān, but does anybody even know that? Nobody. Changes have taken place and will continue to take place. In this modern era, the people who study music are much more intelligent and educated, so they want reasoning for everything. To suit the present day learners, you need to provide this reasoning while teaching so that they understand. We never used to think of reasoning – we accepted whatever was taught as the final word."

Panditji's students recognised and appreciated this openness in his teaching. "We were always taught to question and not accept things as his word, or of the teachers that came before him, which was fantastic as I have always questioned everything that I did not immediately understand. His knowledge was vast, and he always had a practical demonstrative way of answering queries," said Simeen Oshidar, who was an advanced student of Panditji and is an acclaimed visual artist in Mumbai.

Panditji himself was honest about the facets of Hindustānī Rāgsangīt that needed revisiting rather than blind continuation. "Nowadays, if you want to popularise our music, you must look at whatever drawbacks may exist and remove these. For instance, there are a number of compositions for which nobody knows the meaning. These should be explained so the student knows who has composed it and what it means."

He remembered teaching a group of his students at Bharatiya Vidya Bhavan a traditional composition in Multānī, which describes a young girl who has dropped her nose ring into a well. "In those days, young girls used to go to the well to fetch water. At that time, that young bride's nose ring fell down. All passers-by came to look since a costly item had fallen in! A crowd had gathered – some people were feeling sorry for her and wondering how they could take it out and give it to her. In modern thinking people will ask, 'Why are so many people crowding around? It's not as though somebody's life is at stake.' In those days, that composer was enamoured by

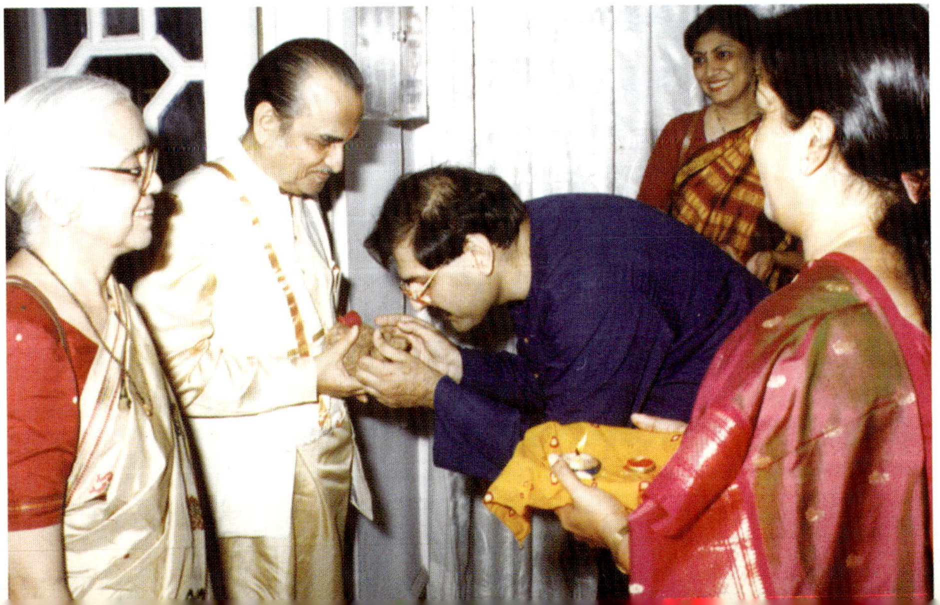

Tushar Bhatia and Meera Chikhalikar take the blessings of Panditji at his 60th birthday celebrations

this situation. The language used has regional character, but now it is outdated. For me, the lyrics are also very nice, and when I sing that I depict sringār and karunā ras. If I don't understand it, the bhāv won't be there. I will just blurt out the sāhitya in tāl and tune. What is missing is the emotion, so that is bound to change."

This level of understanding and accessibility is not just for the student – it is equally important for listeners as well. "That is why in my latest compositions I have tried to put more khaḍi bolī – spoken Hindi. When I sing, people understand the text. Whatever I'm saying should reach and reach with perspective – that should be your attitude. I'm singing for the audience, otherwise I can sit at home and sing for hours together. When you sing for others that means you must cater to them. They should understand whatever you want to say - then the mehfil is successful."

Being A Guru

In his early years as a Guru, Panditji was notorious for a severe strictness and short temper. Right from his Delhi days, he had very high expectations of his students and would not alter these at any cost. His seniormost students, his wife and Premlata Puri, learned from him during this time. Despite the demanding lessons, neither was deterred from pursuing careers in music. Shashikalaji has become a reputed performer and guru, and Premlata Puri is a distinguished musicologist and former Director of the Centre for Cultural Resources and Training.

His ironclad approach was not arbitrary or temperamental. It was guided by his philosophy on teaching, which he had devised after years of experience as a student and teacher.

Panditji in conversation with Smt Arati Ankalikar-Tikekar at his home in Mumbai

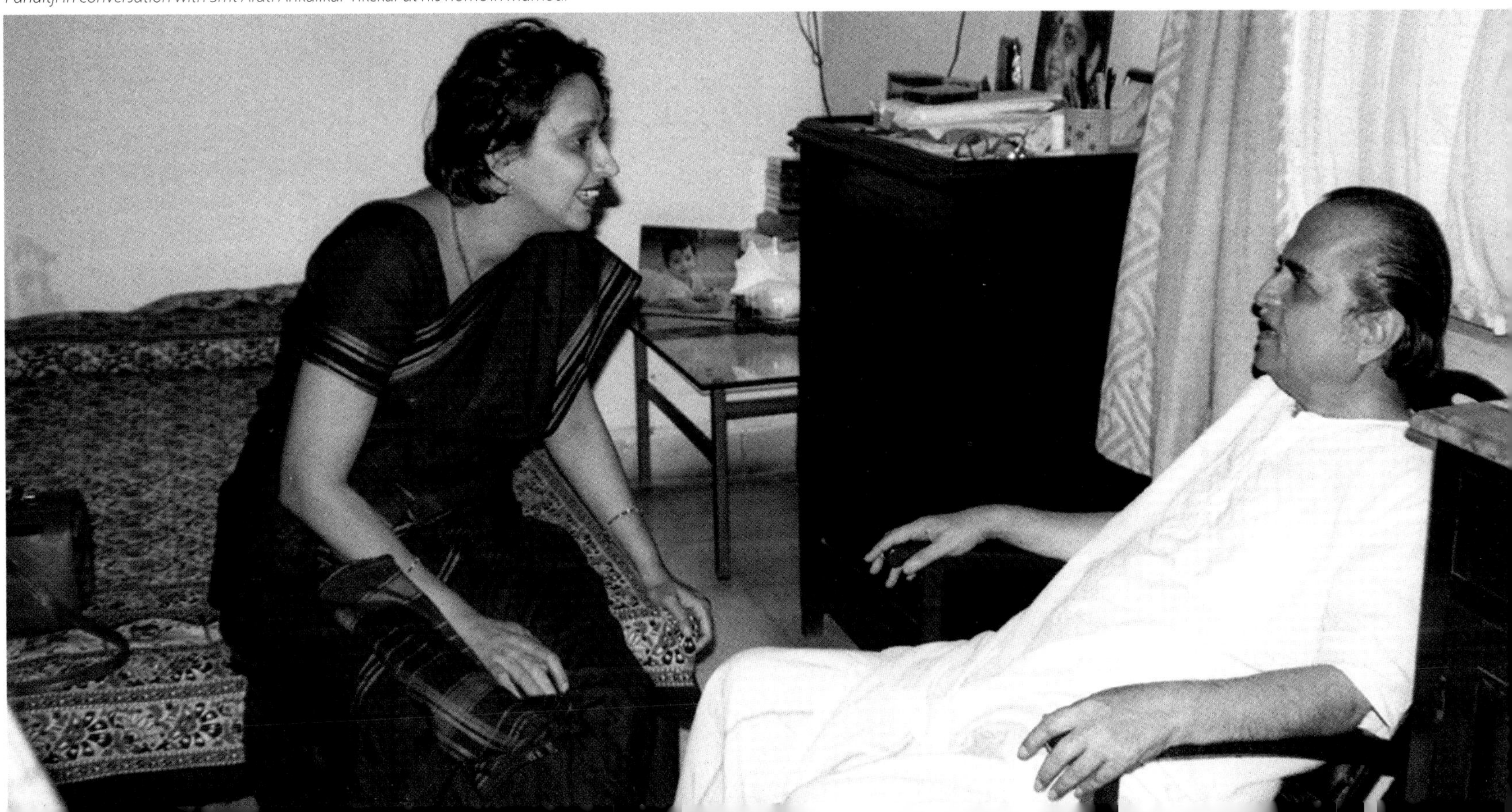

"Each person is at a different mental level, so you cannot apply the same technique to everybody. You have to understand the psychology of the student. To do this, you have to study that student's nature." This was at the basis of all of Panditji's guru-śiṣya interactions. He would assess students based on aptitude, disposition, the way their minds worked best, their intentions for learning, and then decide on an approach to teaching.

He believed that to teach in the most genuine and thorough fashion, all vocal students should not only learn rāg, tāl, and bandiś, but also the techniques of the abstract human instrument: the voice. He identified various areas of vocal production, such as breathing, timbre and dynamics. He strongly believed in making students aware of these areas to give them a complete vocal music education. "These concepts must be taught, then left to them [students] to discover while practising. If you sincerely want to share the art of music, then all these things are required. Because that is what heightens their awareness and sharpens their alertness. When they indulge in it themselves, awareness of these areas helps them and becomes their inner guru."

The teacher must therefore be in command of these techniques before instructing anyone. "If you want to teach, you must experiment yourself, teaching comes after that. In performance,if a person is just imitating the gharānā style, then it is merely happening without knowing these mechanisms. He is deficient in these areas and can't become a good teacher."

The popular vocalist, Smt Arati Ankalikar-Tikekar, was under the tutelage of Panditji for a period of time later in her training and received much guidance in the area of vocal technique. "He taught me a lot about my voice, which was very integral - how to use my voice to its best capacity. Though he used to say it is not the voice but the mind that sings, it is still the medium that we use. Naturally, technically you have to be perfect in the voice, and then only the mind can sing. He really taught me about all the shapes of sound and how to use them properly, and how to use your voice without disturbing the nād of the svar. That is a different dimension to creativity that Annu [Panditji] had given. People do it unknowingly most of the time, (modulation, or fading in and out), but he used to do it very intentionally, so it gave his singing a different dimension. I always feel that expression in your music can only come from the different shapes of sound. This is a great contribution of his. All these things made his music so rich and different," she said.

Though Panditji's detailed approach to teaching the elements of vocal music was more conducive in one-on-one lessons, he also managed to cover all of these in the group classes that he taught

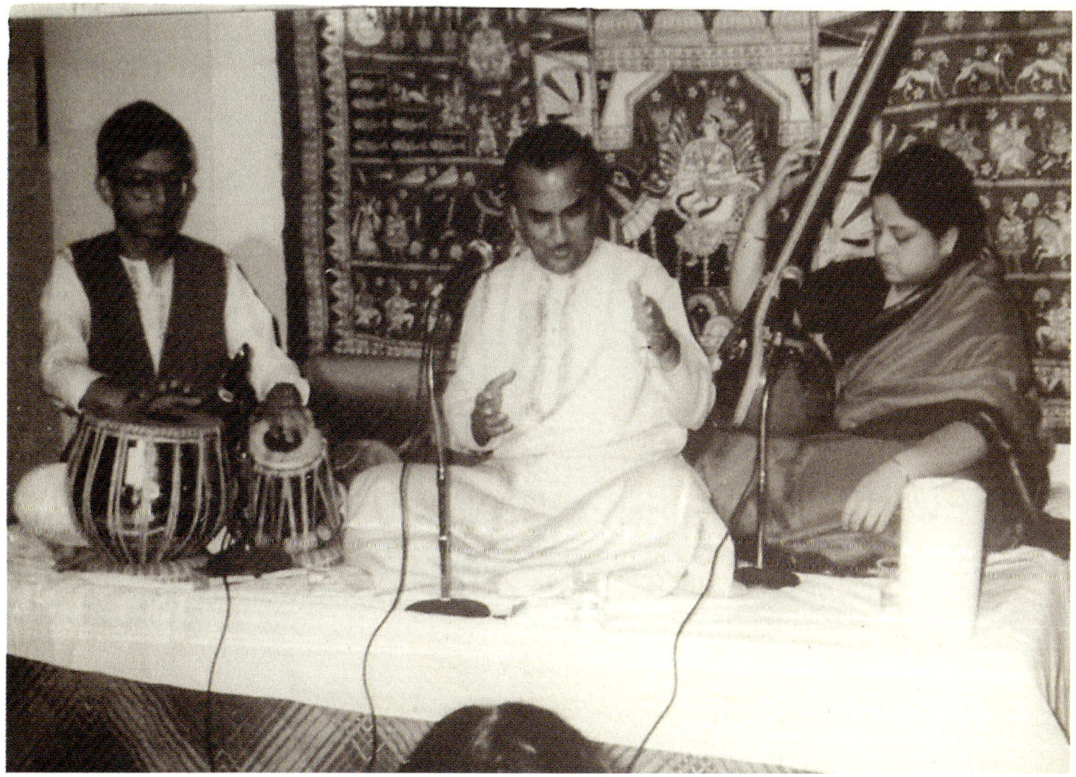

Panditji in concert at Huntsville, Alabama, 1986. He is accompanied by his son, Yogesh on tablā, and daughter, Aditi, on tānpurā and vocal support.

at Bharatiya Vidya Bhavan, where he instructed fourth and fifth year Sangīt Viśārad students. Among these students was his daughter, Smt Aditi Upadhya, an accomplished vocalist and guru. While she too learned from him during one of his strictest phases of teaching, often bearing the brunt of his anger, she is one of the few disciples who has received the quintessence of his vidyā. "The best part about his tālīm was that it was never simplified. He gave us what he sang in concerts. Nothing was ever modified or given extra time. He sang and expected us to give back immediately. And this kept us on our toes all the time. He believed that this is a śravan vidyā, and unless you build really high standards in listening you would not know how the music should sound," she said. This approach was applied to the entire group – whether the student was an aspiring performer or a housewife interested in music. Even if it was more challenging for some than others, he believed that each would be pushed to gain a better understanding within the limits of his or her ability. All his students may not have wanted to be vocalists, but they would leave with a more nuanced appreciation of the art. To him, this was equally important to cultivate. And all of his students were inspired by his total involvement to achieve this while teaching them.

Panditji imparting the nuances of Hindustānī Rāgsangīt to a student visiting from Czechoslovakia.

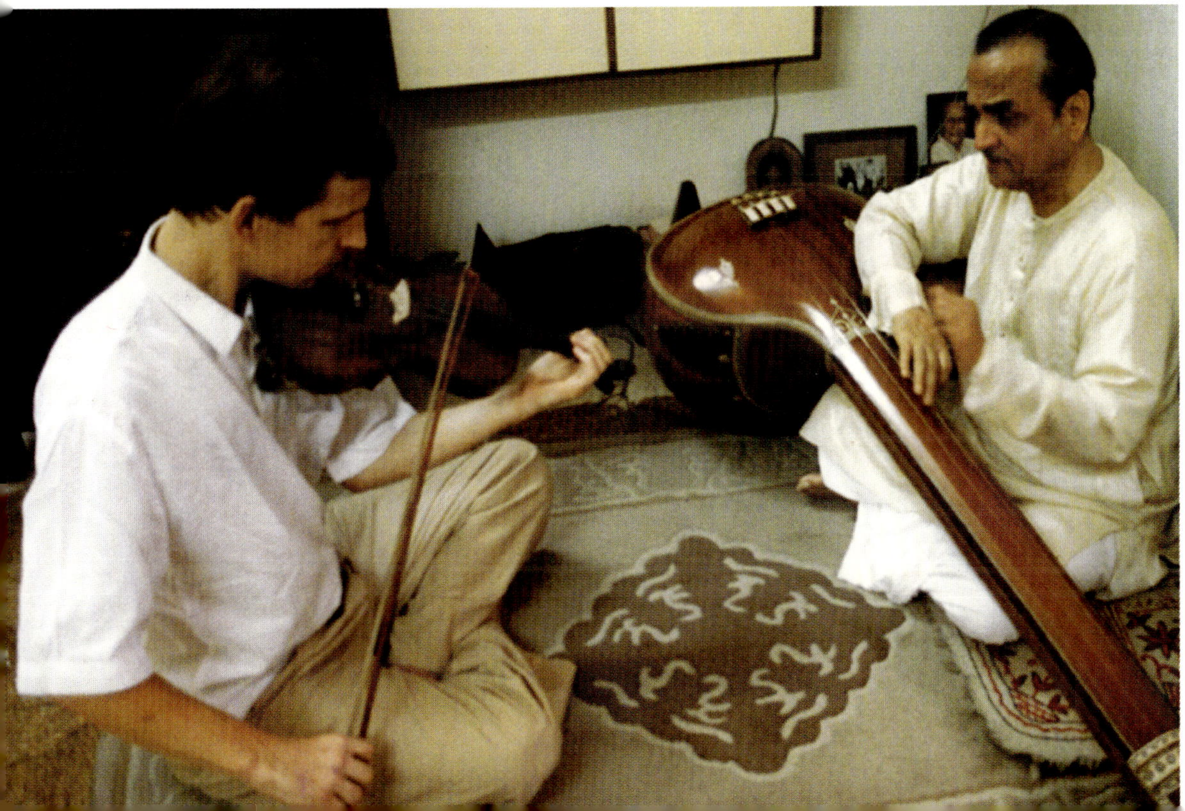

"'Sir,' as we used to call him, was a serious minded teacher," recalls Dr. Anand Nande, a senior disciple of Panditji and a distinguished gastrointestinal and laparoscopic surgeon practising in Mumbai. "Since the beginning he stressed the importance of recognising the svarās that we were singing. He would sing an ālāp or a tān and ask us to recognise the pattern and the notes correctly. And it had to be done immediately or there was hell to pay and a tongue-lashing to be received! This meant that during the class we had to develop tremendous concentration. I remember one instance when he scolded me for repeating his tān without conscious understanding of the notes. 'Don't sing like a parrot. Your mind should be like that of a hawk ready to swoop down at a second's notice,' he said. The end result of all this was that I developed the faculty of being able to concentrate the mind on the task at hand at will to the exclusion of everything else. This faculty is now useful to me every day. Whenever I am doing a complicated operation, I am able to blank my mind of all extraneous things and concentrate on the job at hand."

The intensity of Panditji's lessons and the high standards he expected of his students were clear from the outset. "His lessons were so interesting and examples spilled out of him from some deep unending source. He held me captivated in his lessons as he did during his performances," said his disciple Simeen.

"He kept us wanting more at the end of every class. He would really shake us through the class, and then leave us on a high at the end of it. That inspired me to go work on the matter and come back the next day. I learnt a lot about teaching from him - how to teach, how much to push, when to push, when to let go and when to let the student go on. The way he used to walk that path was unbelievable," said Aditi, who is an active guru herself.

This sense of balance and proportion was a common thread in anything Panditji touched – in his approach to teaching, his musical aesthetic, and even in his personal demeanour. "I first met Sir (as we called him) when I was ten. My feet just about touched the floor as I sat in one of the chairs at the Bhavan's office and sang my bhajan as my entrance test! I remember him, behind the desk, impeccably dressed - everything about him was precise and nothing was extraneous, not in his dress or appearance. Later on I noticed it in his music. How he knew when it was just enough, not a note more not a note less. Just the correct amount of expression required to get the message across. Nothing was loud or flashy or vulgar. Everything was conveyed with the minimum amount of fuss. He was the expression of minimalism. The truth or reality is simple, never complicated, but the difficulty is knowing how and what to whittle away, leaving but the bare bones of what you mean to convey," Simeen observed.

Panditji's students outside of Bharatiya Vidya Bhavan also covered a wide range, from professional musicians to connoisseurs who wanted to delve deeper into his scholastic analysis of Rāgsangīt. Kishore Mariwala, a Mumbai based industrialist, had been following the career of Pandit Dinkar Kaikini since they were both youngsters and Panditji was a young budding performer. He gathered the courage to seek Panditji's guidance later in his life, and the guru- śiṣya relationship that ensued was not just of formal practical training, but also extensive discussions of theory and appreciation of the finer aspects of Rāgsangīt.

"Having started to learn very late in life (around the age of 40 or 45 years), my progress was slow. Yet, he never lost his patience and kept his cool. He appreciated my genuine interest and also my habit of asking about the theory of music whenever I had any questions. I reached a stage where I could sing reasonably well, when I repeated what he taught in our sessions. Sometimes, he would come and say, 'Today I will not sing - you sing what ever comes to your mind.' That is the time I would freeze! He would burst out laughing and say 'I was hoping some day I will put you on stage but alas my wishes will not be fulfilled it seems!' Ultimately our sessions became essentially discussions where he demonstrated what he explained. One of the most important

Panditji performing in Hyderabad, 1988, accompanied by his son Yogesh on tablā

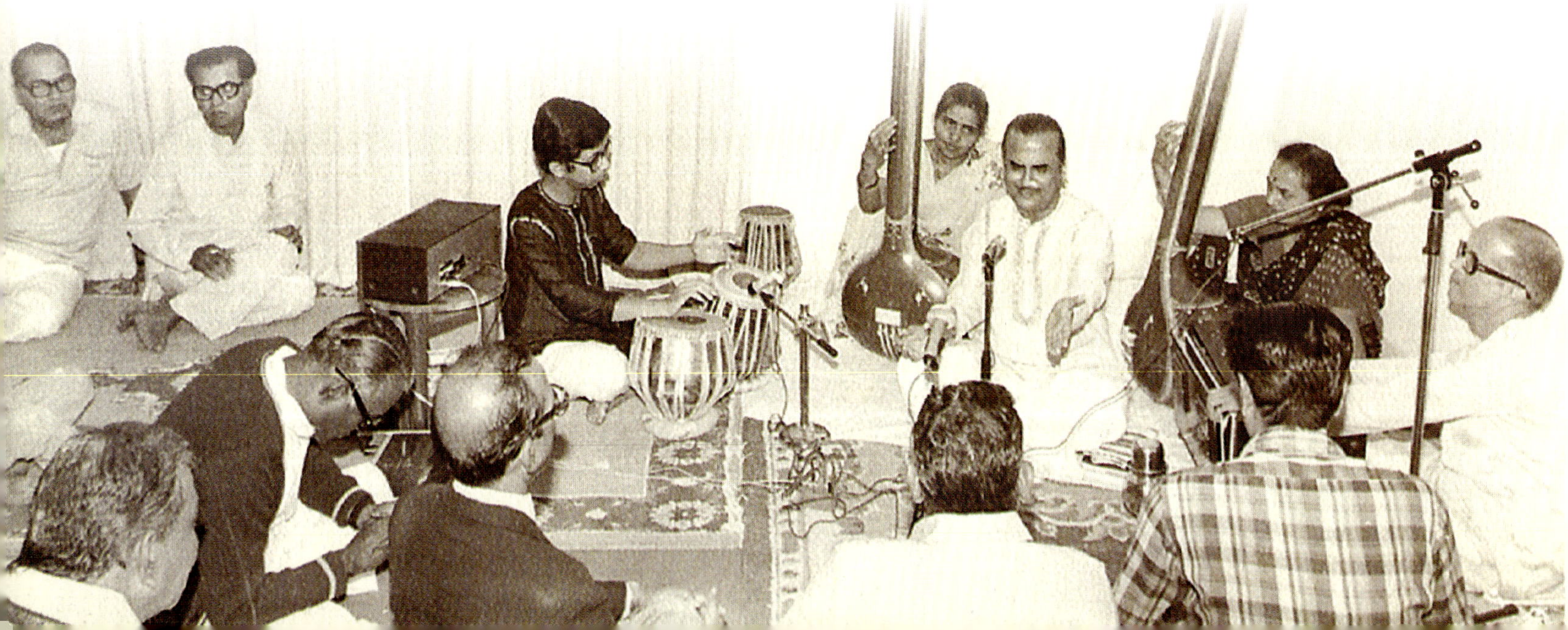

things he told me was not to criticise any style, or the calibre of the musician. He always said – 'Look for what is good in it - look for uniqueness in each piece or each musician - you will enjoy it if you are open.'"

Noted vocalist Sri Madhup Mudgal, who received select training from Panditji, was drawn to his unusual combination of scholasticism and performance mastery. "He had a very high standard of teaching, and the way he taught rāg was very precise - bahut sūkṣma. The way he would differentiate between rāg-s was very clear and very easy to understand. He was one of the very few persons who could explain theory while teaching the practical side," he said.

Smt Arati Ankalikar-Tikekar recalls her inspirational lessons of rāg Bhairav with Panditji. "Once he was teaching me Bhairav for two and a half hours, and I felt that he was literally Bhairav. He taught me about being one with music, rāg rūp and rag svarūp. His unfolding of each rag was very subtle, with a lot of discipline but also a lot of scope for creativity and spontaneity. I can never forget his sayings, such as 'the mind sings not the voice,' or 'music is ātmaranjan not manoranjan.' Every student should know that - these sentences are the whole focus of every musician."

Another disciple of his, Sri Indudhar Nirody, is a highly regarded vocalist based in Mysore. He took in-depth lessons from Pandit S.C.R. Bhat and Panditji, and often accompanied him during concerts. For him as well, Panditji's teaching style was a uniquely carved system. "It was not a routine type of teaching found normally. He would give us an idea and make us think about it, and facilitate us in the developing of the same… Another special aspect of his teaching was giving emphasis on how to perform…his teaching used to give us the stimulus of a concert performance. Not only did he teach us music, but he also talked about psychology, philosophy, and other aspects."

His singular approach to teaching made his lessons with many of the students he taught unforgettable. "He followed an extremely unconventional method of teaching. He strived to bring his student to his own level of creativity. He converted his student into a thinking musician and not a blind imitator of his guru's art form. He had rationale and justification of every phrase that he taught, and yet the total picture of that exposition went way beyond mere logic, technique, and science," said Tushar Bhatia.

As a composer, Tushar also benefited from observing Panditji during his innovative musical experiments. "He imparted a full vision of the magnitude of the form and, to me, even an insight into other structures like the Western Classical symphony, choral compositions, Indian folk music, ślokā-s, bhajan-s, instrumentation, and aesthetics of lyrics. I find his words coming back to me again and again during the process of stagecraft, rehearsals with chorus, training singers and musicians, writing and orchestrating my own compositions, sound balancing and mixing. These lessons were learned by observing him during our choral reherasals and performances of each of his masterpieces."

"He inspired and encouraged me to compose dhrupad, dhamār, khayāl, ṭhumrī, and tarānā. He would patiently hear my compositions and sometimes suggest a review from another perspective. When I sang my first bandiś to him, he did not praise it but asked me to repeat the composition to Amma [Smt Shashikala Kaikini] with his eyes beaming proudly and satisfaction written all over his face. He suggested a phrase be taken off-beat. I was quick to realise that it lent a new dimension to the composition. Acknowledgments were rare to come by but when they did, they meant a whole world!" he remembered.

Sri Dhruba Ghosh, the well-respected sārangī player and current Principal of Bharatiya Vidya Bhavan, was also under the tutelage of Panditji since 1995 and appreciated his specialised approach to teaching the student that allowed a lot of room for self-discovery. "He was an insightful person with great precision available to him to take a laser view of the inner workings of the student's mind and then either teach him how to fly, or else teach him by dropping him from the high cliffs and seeing how the student would flap his wings and then learn to fly on his own. Or else, he would take the student to heights not scaled before and then leave him there to see for himself the panoramic view of the rāgā superstructure," he described.

Panditji's youngest son, Yogesh, though a tablā player, also received guidance from his father in a more unconventional manner. From the age of one and half years, he displayed an extraordinary gift for tablā. Recognising this, Panditji directed him to the appropriate guru-s and nurtured his talent, never with an agenda of making him a musician. As Yogesh grew to his teens and was deep into his tālīm with Ustad Alla Rakha Khan,

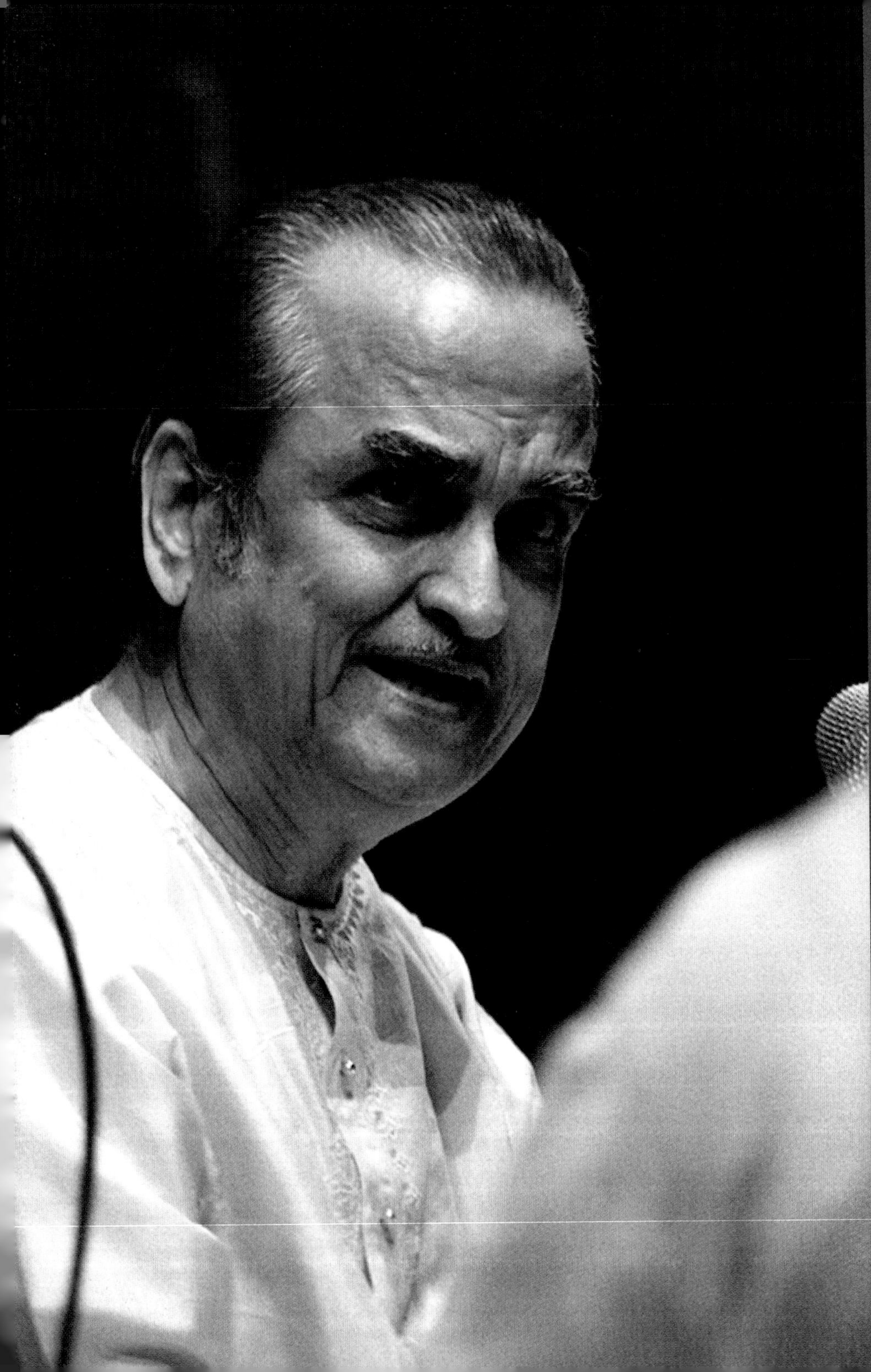

Panditji started to ask him to accompany him at home for his evening riyāz. "When he used to sit for his practice sessions after dinner in the night, I used to enjoy it. I would look forward to it. I was just in school, about 13. I remember the things that I learned from him regarding tablā were about a detailed and most sensitive approach to accompaniment. The most important thing about accompaniment is patience. While accompanying vocal music you need a lot of patience, and if you don't have it, you cannot keep vilambit laya where it should be - it will keep shifting. Most tablā players suffer from that problem. Internally, they have so much to show, they have practised so much, they have so much to express, so those kicks are coming from inside. But to hold on to that and be patient is very difficult in the beginning. Patience makes your laya solid, and patience makes you listen to the other person. When you become a good listener, you start observing and learning more things that enhance your tālīm. And that's what I learned from him at a very young age - when to play, when not to play. I learned and experienced all these nuances of vocal accompaniment by playing with him at home. Sometimes he would give me ideas or even recite something, to give me an idea of how it should be. Which piece should be played, at which speed it should be paced, how busy it should be, how relaxed it should be, things like that. And that was the solid foundation for what I am today. That's why in all the three branches of accompaniment, vocal, instrumental and dance,

Left and Right: Moments of intensity while in concert in Mumbai, April 1999

artistes want me to accompany them. Because, in all these three aspects of accompaniment, you need to know where you have to be patient. This process happened naturally, without me knowing that it was happening."

For Panditji, teaching, giving, and sharing were integral parts of a complete musician. He often used the phrase "uttar dāitva," giving back, to emphasise the responsibility of a musician. This is embedded in the concept of paramparā – a lineage from guru to śiṣya in which the next generation is entrusted with the vidyā and sanskār-s to ensure continuation of the art. "When the śiṣya's attitude and thinking process becomes that of the guru's, then he carries on the tradition. There is a saying: an ideal guru should be one who is very happy if his śiṣya surpasses him. When Anna Saheb heard one of my concerts he said, 'You have sung this rāg very well, as I would have sung it, but I never taught you that rāg. How did you do that?' To which I replied, 'You didn't teach it to me, but you have given me that nazar [vision or perception] to explore it on my own."

It is evident that Panditji too continued to practise the concept of "uttar dāitva" during all of his years of being a guru, by planting seeds of thought in the minds of many musicians who have had the courage to exercise their own nazar as a result.

"Panditji was a father, friend, companion on the journey, critic, inspirer and above all a teacher who strongly encouraged me to gamble with artistic creativity," said Dhruba Ghosh.

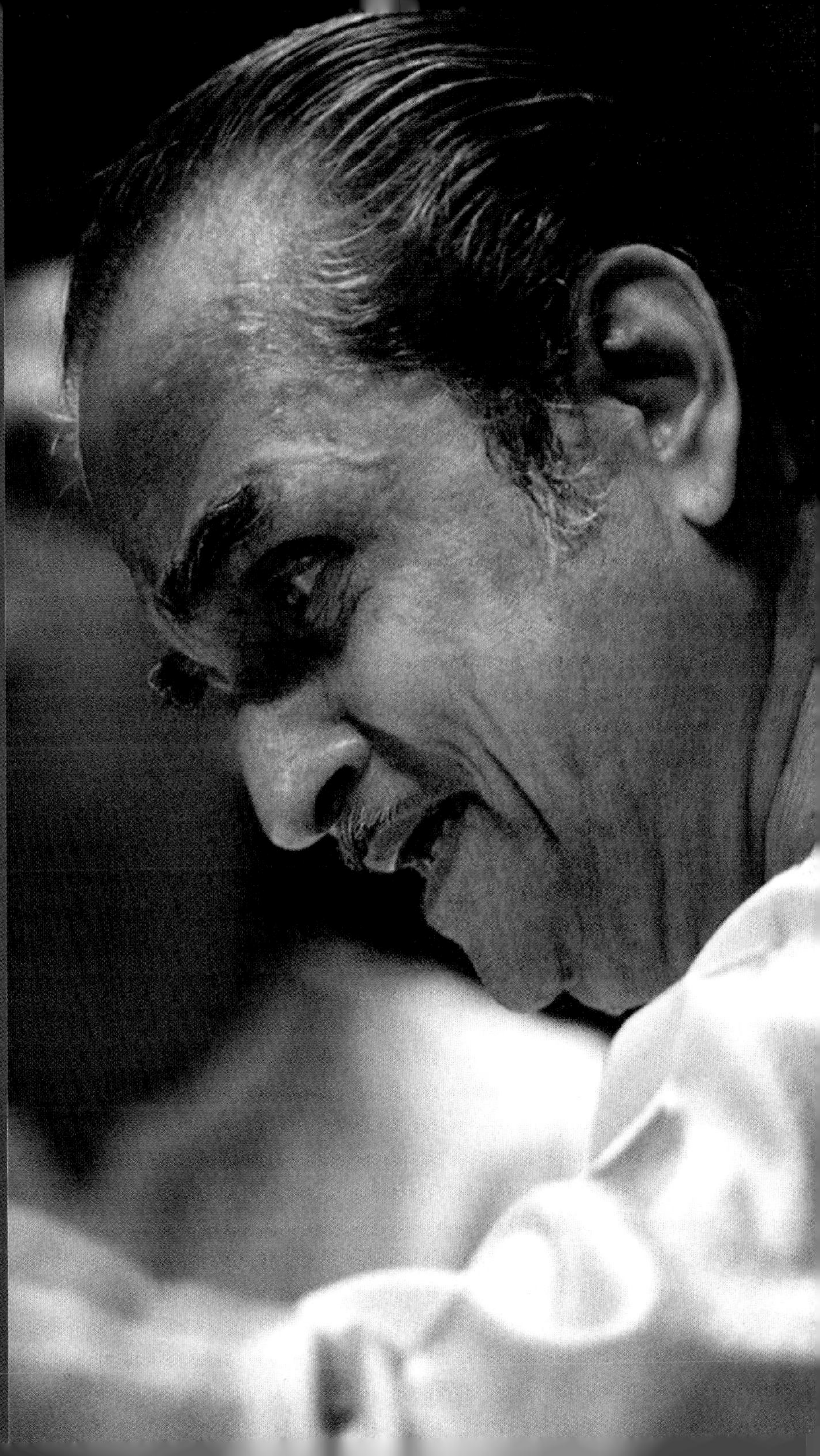

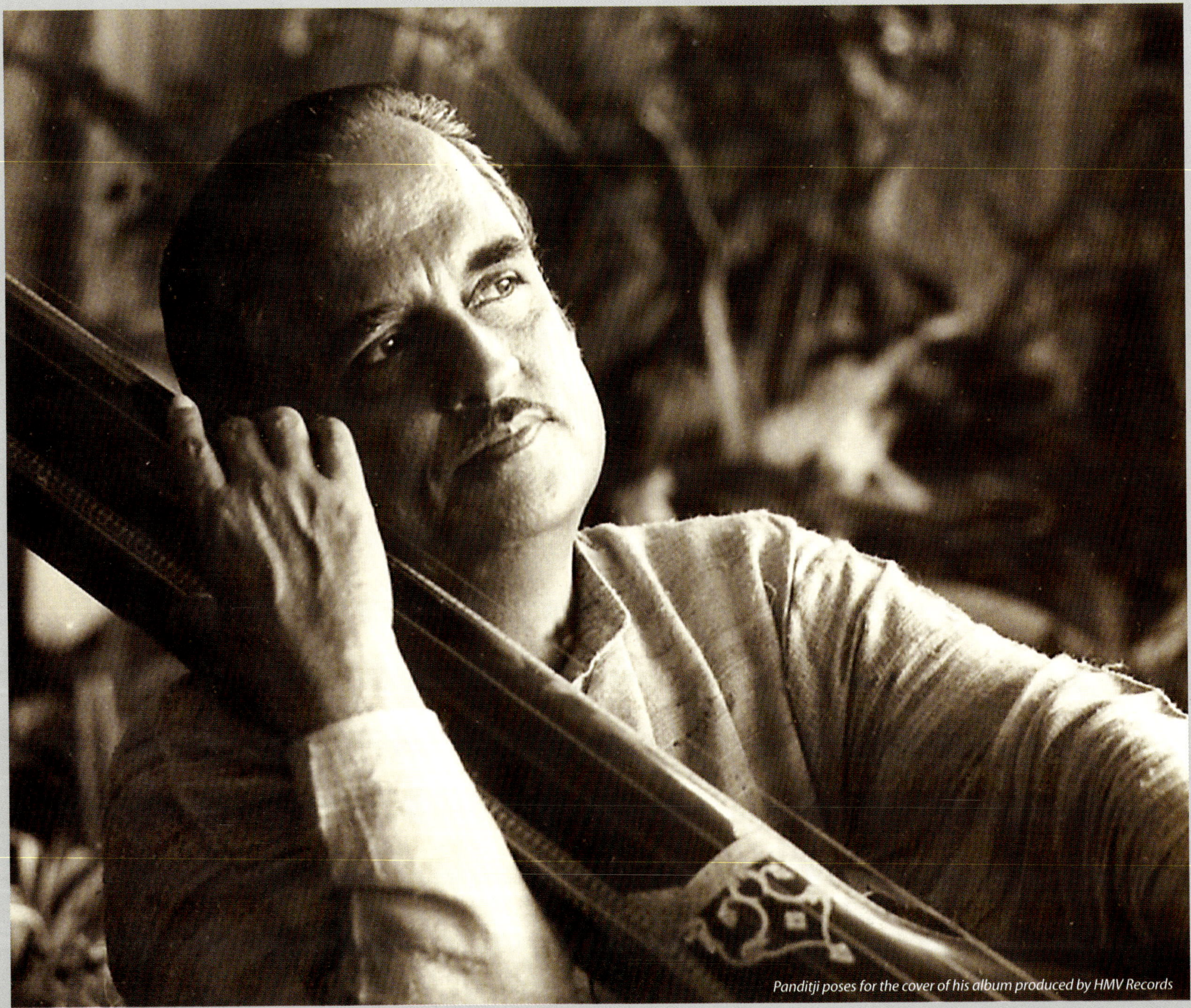

Panditji poses for the cover of his album produced by HMV Records

EPILOGUE

On January 23, 2010, Pandit Dinkar Kaikini passed away of cardiac arrest, sitting in the very same chair in which he answered so many of my questions for this book. The same chair in which he composed many of his inspired bandiś-es. The same chair in which he was often lost in cintan, deep thought and reflection on musical ideas.

It was a very peaceful death. After having iḍlis for breakfast and chatting with his grandchildren, he sat down in his chair, had his daily pān, and began reading the newspaper. Moments later, he left us, his soul re-entering the very same cosmos in which he believed all musical energy flourished.

It is especially hard to believe he is gone when his presence is felt in so many places. One evening I am swept away in his rendition of Sāvni Bihāg, another night in his majestic Darbāri. Listening to his music, singing his compositions, and trying to apply his theories in day-to-day practice, make me realise that his presence will remain all my life, as it will remain with the many people whom he has touched.

This book is about a highly evolved soul whose lifetime was undividedly devoted to Hindustānī Rāgsangīt - as a sādhak, as its exponent, as a guru, and in whatever capacity he was needed to render his sevā towards music. True sevā is done without any expectation of returns. In a performing art, there are very few who actually practise this approach in their lifestyle, doing sevā for kalā. At a public condolence meeting held for Panditji, in which several revered musicians and scholars spoke, Pandit Shivkumar Sharma said, "To say no to visibility and be happy with that state, that is living that philosophy. He didn't chase fame or visibility. A truly philosophical musician is beyond all of this - nothing affects them… Dinkarji was one of them."[1]

Once, during our conversations, I had brought up a similar topic that had been on my mind. The modern world bombards us with so many conflicting messages: extensive publicity and fast rising success, versus less publicity and a steady and gradual immersion into the field; financial gain versus pursuit of art for art's sake. What should be the lifestyle of a modern musician? To this he told me, "Artistes totally engrossed in their art rarely think about lifestyle, the outer side of it. Both performance-oriented and knowledge-seeking musicians seek gyān [knowledge] and anubhav [experience] to realise what they do and do not possess, and all through their lives they essentially remain as students." It was a simple answer that went beyond my questions, revealing their irrelevance. Panditji's life was one of tremendous gyān and anubhav– the knowledge he imparted had such impact because it came from a place of experienced truth, and this is not something that can be gained through any shortcuts. When a person pursues music with dedication, involvement and focus, there is no room for any other questions to creep into the mind. The mind is in a state of blissful cintan, which keeps a musician evolving and the rest follows as it is meant to.

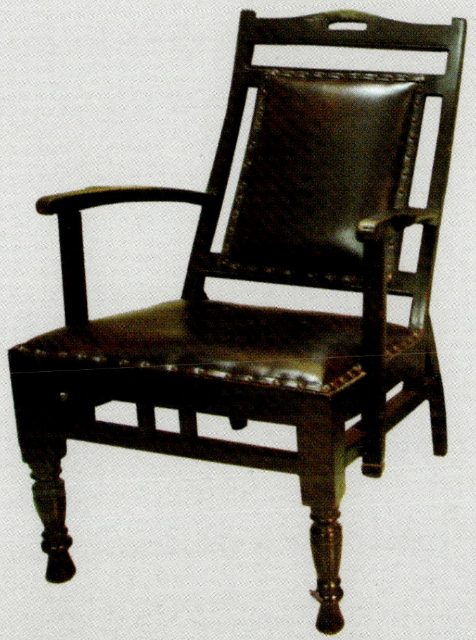

This was how Panditji lived his life until the very end, ruminating on possibilities and always seeing new ones. Pandit Suresh Talwalkar described Panditji in Marathi as a "cintan-śīl manuṣya," a thinking individual. His way of looking at music changed because of cintan. One of Panditji's oft-repeated sayings to students was, "Ab cintan karo." While almost all guru-s will encourage their students to do vigorous riyāz, there are few who will also tell them to take time to think, honestly and questioningly, about what they have learned and how it can be put into practice. A guru who tells his śiṣya to do so has confidence in his vidyā, and faith in the robustness of his or her style of music.

[1] *Translation of condolence meeting speeches given by Pandit Shivkumar Sharma, Pandit Suresh Talwalkar, and Sri Ashok Ranade, courtesy of Smt Aditi Upadhya*

This too was a conclusion Panditji drew from his own anubhav, not something that was explicitly stated to him by his guru-s. Analysis and approach was never explicated – it was Panditji's nature that inclined him to take the knowledge he had received and scrutinise it, understand the thought process that went behind it, and finally, make it his own. This was evident in his rendition, which was a highly individualistic approach to the vidyā he had amassed from Anna Saheb and the gāyakī of his idol, Faiyaz Khan. An amalgamated approach like this, which comes together as a completely new style, is a product of immense cintan. As the noted music critic and scholar Ashok Ranade said, "He questioned every aspect of the Agra Gharānā and changed it aesthetically to suit him – the throw of the voice, the pronunciations, the way you play with laya. It's very easy to say that you should do this and that to evolve, but to do it is very difficult. Here is a man who did it. He did it because he wanted to, and this kind of selfishness was what went to his advantage. He questioned himself, and he evolved himself."

Panditji did not exempt his own attitudes and behaviours from this ideology of critical thinking. With great frankness, he told me of what happens to some, himself included, as a result of accumulating such a vast resource of gyān.

"Some people who are very learned have an ego because of their knowledge. That is a stage that I also went through. But when you reflect a bit, you realise that there is always so much still to learn in your subject and other subjects as well. Gradually you start imbibing that knowledge and you know that you are nowhere, and the ego vanishes."

But his thoughts on the concept of ego for a musician do not end here. "Occasionally, there is a specific need for ego, but only in homoeopathic doses – to cure yourself and others. Having an ego also means that you must have strong faith in whatever knowledge you have. If something is said to challenge it, you have to rightfully contradict and defend it. If you don't have that level of conviction in your knowledge, then you don't have faith. You might wonder: 'I studied this particular way – is it correct or not? Many people who don't have this knowledge are popular and thriving – maybe I should follow their footsteps instead?' When these doubts arise, you must use your ego in the right way to cure yourself and remain loyal to your gyān."

I was intrigued by the way he could view ego and gyān in two such different ways. It showed his humility and respect towards this art, without undermining his immense conviction in the knowledge that paved the path for creativity.

"Knowledge should never be a burden," he told me once. Knowledge is the foundation – the solid bedrock that is laid. But how will you tread on it? That was the liberating experience of moving freely, at your own will, on that path. It is not meant to confine, but to open up the personal musical experience.

"On the stage, knowledge should never be shown. If you show too much of vidvatā in your performance, then it is not pleasant to listen to. If the art form is there, then a certain amount of your knowledge can be kept aside. When you see beauty in something, do you look at the knowledge? No, you only see beauty. If a piece of art is presented and it is enjoyable, then that is the final verdict."

This was at the core of Panditji's performances. As Pandit Suresh Talwalkar said, "In his [Panditji's] rendition, you would always see rāg-bhāv, accuracy of svar, thought process, and the way he would systematically arrange his ideas. And yet, he used to go beyond all this grammar to reach that place of ātmānand."

This experience is exactly what Panditji intended for his music to induce – ātmaranjan. Pleasure or bliss for the soul. And what quality of music gives the soul this kind of gratification? Beauty. "Art is beauty which penetrates within you and reaches the soul," he had told me.

Panditji and Shashikalaji on the occasion of their Golden Wedding Anniversary, 2007

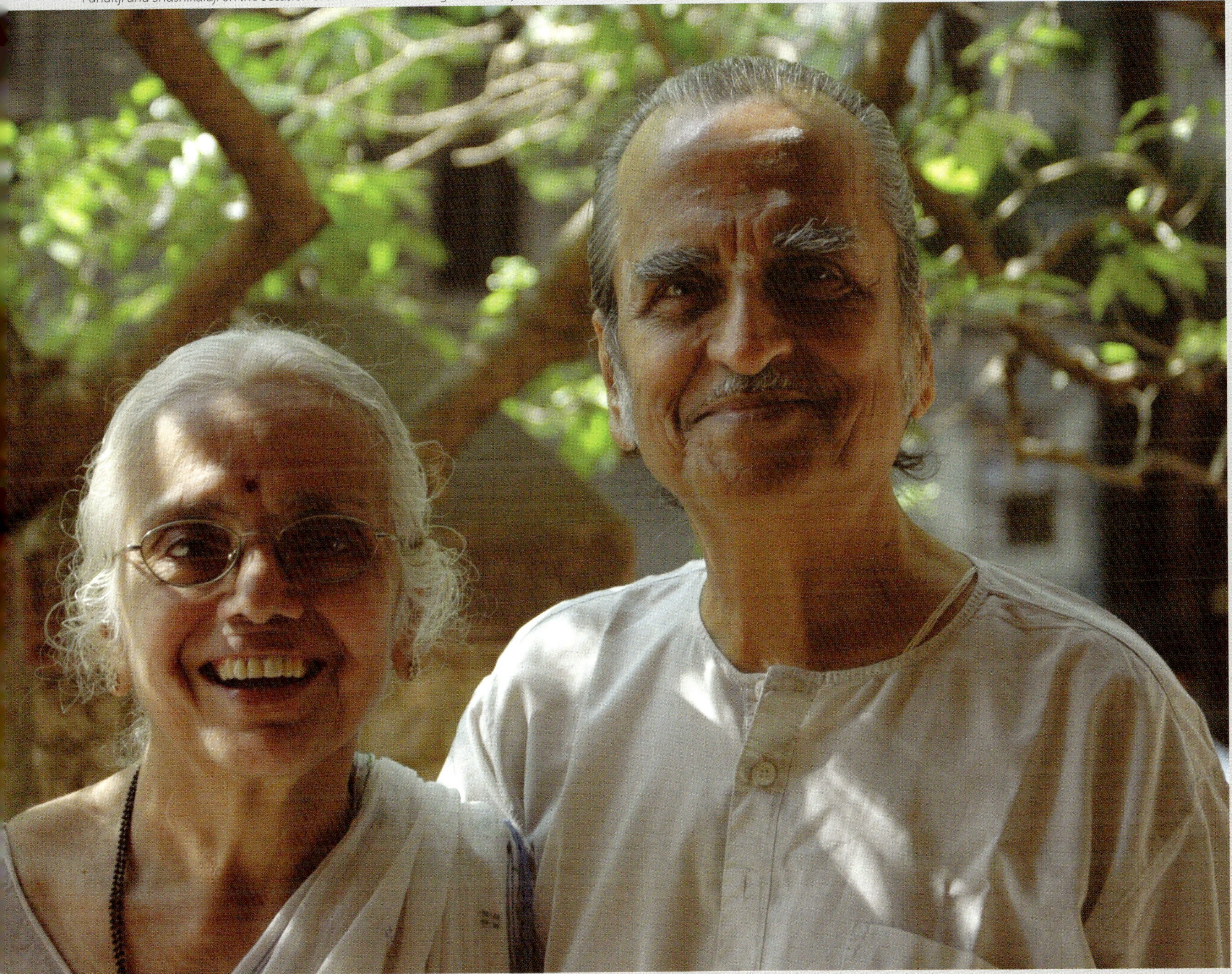

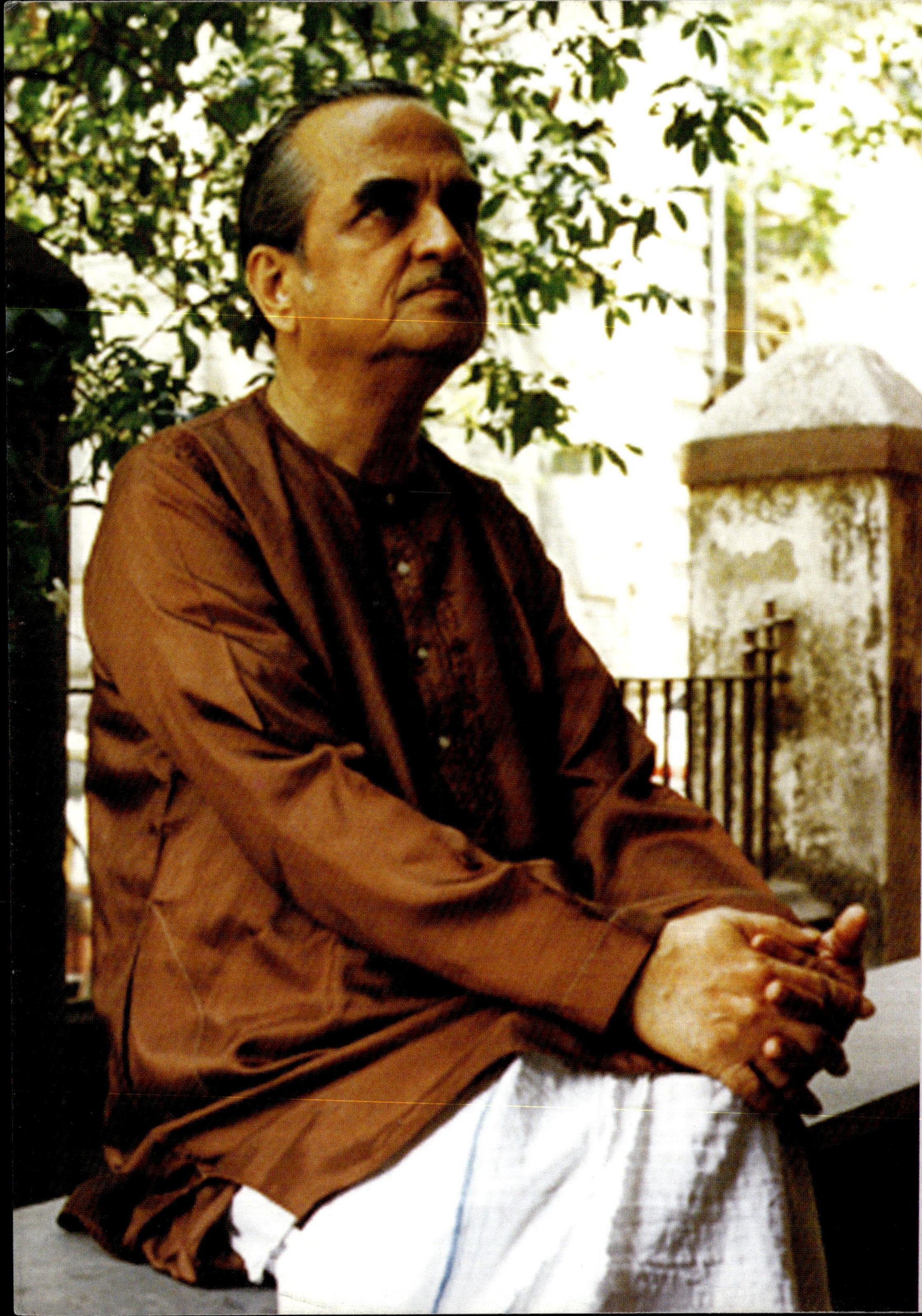

Aesthetics over imagination. This was the final dictum for the end product. During tālīm we acquire the tools and skills for the craft, but when we are actually creating the object, our attention should not focus solely on the skills we have developed. It should be on ensuring the beauty of the object – always stepping back to make sure it has not deviated from this ideal.

For Panditji, this was evident in all aspects of his life. He found beauty in places one would not normally look, and sought to bring beauty to anything he created. Whether it was the delicacy with which he would cook his favourite mutton rogan jośʹ, or the elegant and precise way he would cut and serve a fruit platter with an array of carefully self-selected fruits, Panditji took immense pleasure in the aesthetics of life. And this permeated his every utterance as a musician. "His way of looking at life was so simple," said Pandit Suresh Talwalkar. "Sangīt was his life, and his life was kalā. That was Kaikiniji."

We are left with the experiences and thoughts he has shared, the live recordings and hundreds of compositions that live on, the example he led as a musician, and foremost, as a human being. And yet, in following his example, we cannot merely imitate him. Just as he did not strictly conform to his predecessors, we too must grasp the spirit of his ideology and have the courage, faith, and insatiable desire to find our own voices. Doing so will be capturing the true essence of Pandit Dinkar Kaikini.

Left and Right: In a contemplative mood outside his home in Mumbai

"For last year's words belong
to last year's language
And next year's words await
another voice."

T.S. Eliot

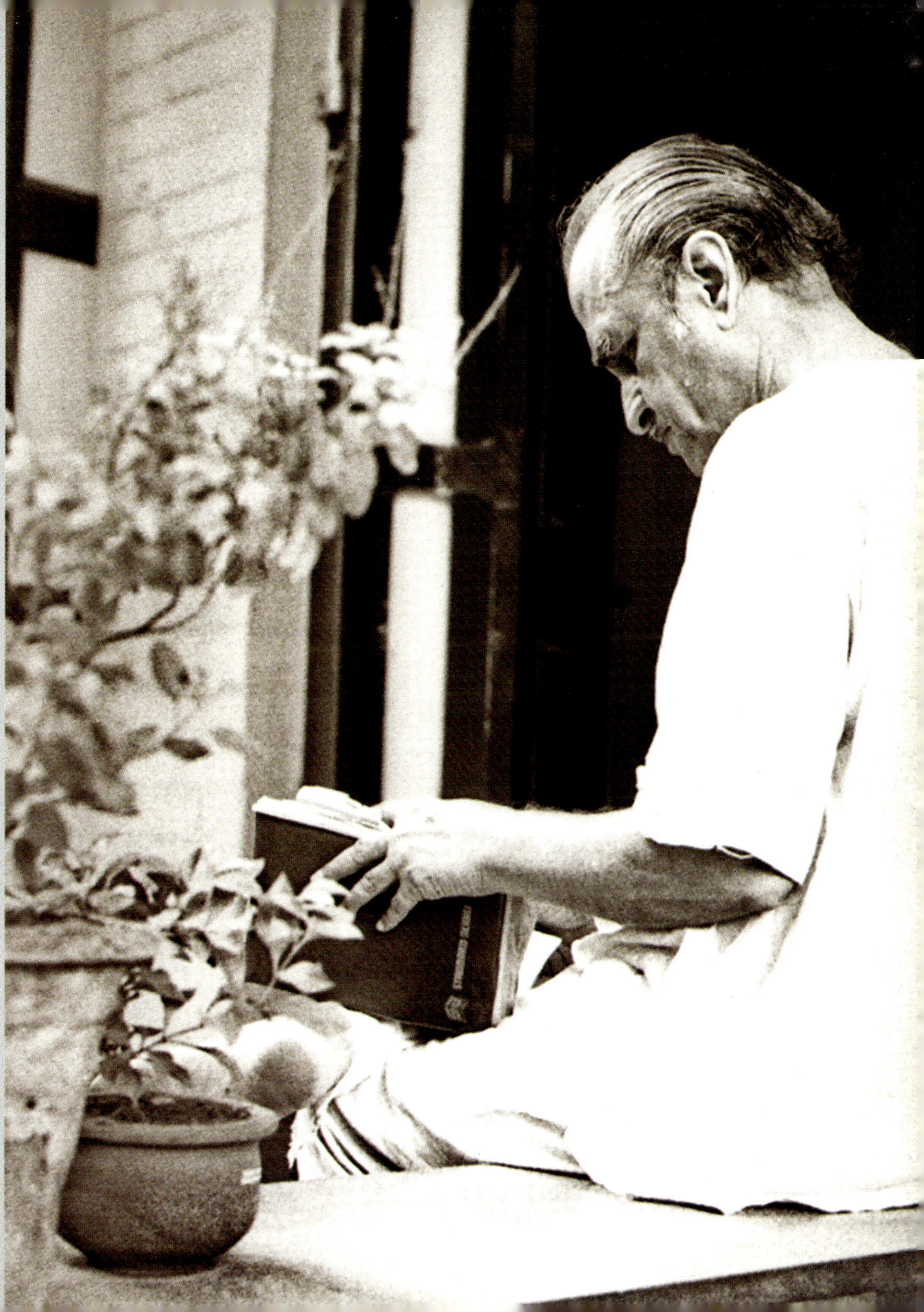

ACKNOWLEDGEMENTS

This book would not have been possible without the help and generosity of many supportive friends and family. I am blessed to have you all. A big-hearted thanks to:

All those who made time for my interviews and shared their memories of Panditji with me.

Ranjita Bhagwan, for the many hours devoted to scanning all of Panditji's handwritten work.

Kodi Saravanan, for his impeccable eye and careful review of the final product.

Ramesh Gangolli, for his inputs on the manuscript, for sharing drafts of his translation of the Marathi biography, "Dinarang" with me, and for his skillful translation of the Foreword by Pandit Suresh Talwalkar.

Rajani Kapse, for sharing so many treasured moments through her beautiful photographs, which have brought this book to life.

Pandit Suresh Talwalkar - it is a privilege to commence this book with his insightful Foreword.

Ramdas Bhatkal, for his open-minded consideration of my manuscript, and to Jayanthi Mahalingam of Popular Prakashan for her patience and tremendous cooperation in publishing this book.

The entire Kaikini family, for the warmth and openness with which they have treated me. They have shared any information I needed for this book, and I am grateful for the trust they have shown in me.

My late grandfather, Sri S.K. Rangarajan, who wanted to see this book completed more than anyone I know. His painstaking editing of my initial drafts and his feedback stayed with me throughout and guided me to improving this book until its final version.

Ammamma, Shashikala Kaikini, for sitting so patiently with me on numerous occasions to answer any number of questions on all topics, and for the motherly care she showed me during my many visits to her home. Also to Kavita Samsi, for her ever-ready help sending photographs and any other details needed from Mumbai.

Sundar, the philosopher who made me question the foundations of music and find the answers to these. His feedback from conception to completion and his persistent goading are greatly appreciated.

Hari, who was a limitless sounding board for ideas and improvements and helped a lost traveller find her way back on the path. His detailed editing of later drafts made this book evolve greatly from where it started.

Ravi Y Adivarekar, who so generously, unassumingly, and patiently designed a highly aesthetic book about a highly aesthetic man.

My parents, Ramaa and Sampath Purushothaman, for unconditional love, support, and strength. To my father, who edited every single draft with patience and efficacy.

My guru, Smt Aditi Upadhya, for having the faith to entrust me with the responsibility of conveying the thoughts of her father and guru. And for her unwavering commitment to seeing that this book becomes a reality.

Finally, to Panditji, for living music

PHOTO CREDITS

Kavi Arya (92)

Nikhil Bhatia (91)

Rajani Kapse (6, 17, 40, 75, 76, 81, 86, 87, 93)

Priya Purushothaman (71)

Sita Saran Singh (56, 59, 60)

Niyati Upadhya (89)

All other photographs belong to the Kaikini Family Archives

प्रस्तावना

मनापासून ज्यांचे गुणवर्णन करावं, ज्यांच्याविषयी आदरानी बोलावं, ज्यांच्या कार्यातून स्फूर्ती घ्यावी आणि ज्यांचे ऋण मान्य करावं अशा संगीत जगातील 'गुणीजनांपैकी' एक ऋषितुल्य व्यक्तित्व म्हणजे पं. दिनकर कायकिणि! म्हणूनच त्यांच्यावरील पुस्तकाला प्रस्तावना लिहिताना मला आनंद होत आहे.

भारतीय संगीतातील शास्त्र आणि कला या दोहोंच सखोल चिंतन आणि समतोल साधलेला हा तपस्वी! गायनातील सर्वच घराण्यांच्या सौंदर्यमूल्यांवर त्यांची श्रद्धा आणि निष्ठा होती. कोणत्याही एकाच घराण्याचा 'अतिपक्ष' घेण्याचा अविवेकीपणा त्यांनी कधी केला नाही. कै. अण्णासाहेब रातांजनकर यांच्याकडून त्यांनी भरपूर तालीम आणि विद्या प्राप्त केली. आणि दैवयोगानी रातांजनकरांचे रचना कौशल्यही कायकिणिजींना प्राप्त झालं.

मुळात असंख्य पारंपारिक आणि दर्जेदार बंदिशींचा संस्कार, पं. कायकिणिजींचा राग-तालाचा व्यासंग, उत्तरेतील अनेक वर्षाच्या वास्तव्यामुळे बंदिशीला लागणाऱ्या साहित्य अंगाचा उत्तम परिचय आणि या सर्वात नवनिर्मितीसाठी लागणाऱ्या आंतरिक उर्मीचं इश्वरी वरदान अशा सुवर्णयोगातून त्यांच्याकडून अनेकानेक, उत्तमोत्तम दर्जेदार बंदिशांची निर्मिती झाली. त्यांच्या बंदिशीतून उत्तम रागांग, उत्तम लय-ताल विचार आणि उत्तम भाषा साहित्याचा जो परिचय आपल्याला मिळतो तो याच कारणांनी.

चिंतनशील स्वभावामुळे कायकिणिजींचा सर्व संगीत व्यवहाराकडे बघण्याचा दृष्टिकोन हा खूप विशाल, बहुढंगी व बहुआयामी होता. रागाच्या बंदिशी असोत, ठुमरी असो, भक्तिसंगीत असो सर्व प्रकारातील कलात्मक उंची अतिशय उच्च दर्जाची असे. नुसतीच विद्येची पारंगतता, शास्त्राची क्लिष्टता किंवा तंत्राचा दिखाऊपणा अशा तुकड्या-तुकड्यात त्यांचा कलाविचार कधी साकळला नाही. विद्या-शास्त्र-तंत्र याचा योग्य अंगीकार करून त्याही पुढील कला विचाराची उंची आणि त्याचा उत्तम दर्जा हा कळस कायकिणिजींनी सहजपणे गाठला व सांभाळला. कायकिणि म्हणजे उत्तम दर्जा हे जणू समीकरणच झालं आहे. परंपरेतील सर्व मूल्य आणि तत्त्व पाळून संगीतातील नवकल्पनांची पहाट ते पाहू शकले या त्यांच्या गुणविशेषाला मनोमन सलाम/अभिवादन करावेसे वाटते.

पुन्हा कायकिणिजींची परिपक्वता अशी की उत्तम बंदिशी करूनही बंदिशीच्या प्रेमात ते अडकून राहिले नाहीत. तर बंदिशीतील मूर्त आशयाला त्यांनी विस्तारातील अमूर्ततेपर्यंत नेण्याचं कर्तव्य ओळखलही आणि ते समर्थपणे पारही पाडलं. बंदिश हे संगीताचं 'मूर्त' स्वरूप आणि गायकी हे 'अमूर्त' तत्व हे सत्य अंगीकृत करूनच त्यांचा सर्व कलाव्यवहार झाला. त्यांच्या सादरीकरणातून रागविचार, स्वरसुक्ष्मता, विचारांतील प्रगल्भता, मांडणीतील शिस्त व नियोजन सर्व गुण प्रत्ययास येत असत आणि अशा परिपूर्ण सादरीकरणातही मनाच्या एकतानेतून रागरंजनात रममाण होत, सर्व भावविश्वाच्या पलिकडील एक 'आत्मिक' समाधानही ते देत असत.

उत्तम अध्यात्मिक विचारांनी परिप्लूत कायकिणिजी कलासाधनतेतील अनेक सूक्ष्म गोष्टींचे अतिशय उत्तम विवेचन करत असत. कलासाधनेतील अनेक समस्यांचे त्यांनी केलेले सहजसुंदर निराकरण मी कधीच विसरू शकणार नाही.

या बाबतचे त्यांचे विचार ऐकणे हा माझा अत्यंत आवडीचा विषय असे. त्यांचे विचार मला स्वतःला बोधकारक तर ठरलेच शिवाय माझ्या कलासाधनेलाही ते मार्गदर्शक ठरेल.

संगीत म्हणजे काय? संगीताकडे कसे पहावे? संगीत का करावे? त्यांनी काय साधते? त्यांचा जीवनावर होणारा परिणाम काय? या आणि अशा अनेक प्रश्नांवरील त्यांची उत्तरे इतकी मार्मिक व समर्पक असत की त्याचे जणू सर्वांनी पालन करावे आणि कृतकृत्य व्हावे.

या त्यांच्या अनमोल विचारधारेचा परिचय या पुस्तकातून वाचकांना करून देताना लेखकानीही फार मोठ पुण्य कर्म केलं आहे असंच म्हणावं लागेल!

धन्यवाद !
पं. सुरेश तळवलकर

International Alphabet for Sanskrit Transliteration

अ	a	क	ka
आ	ā	ख	kha
इ	i	ग	ga
ई	ī	घ	gha
उ	u	च	ca
ऊ	ū	छ	cha
ऋ	ṛ	ज	ja
ए	e	झ	jha
ऐ	ai	ट	ṭa
ओ	o	ठ	ṭha
औ	au	ड	ḍa
		ढ	ḍha
		ण	ṇa
		त	ta
		थ	tha
		द	da
		ध	dha
		न	na
		प	pa
		फ	pha
		ब	ba
		भ	bha
		म	ma
		य	ya
		र	ra
		ल	la
		व	va
		श	śa
		ष	ṣa
		स	sa
		ह	ha